CURAÇAO

Caracas

TRINIDAD

VENEZUELA

Mérida

Georgetown

Paramaribo

Medellín

Ciudad Bolívar

BR.
GUIANA

SURI-
NAM

Cayenne

FR. GUIANA

Ibagué

Bogotá

COLOMBIA

Orinoco

Quito

ECUADOR

Guayaquil

Barcelos

Negro

Óbidos

Manaus

Amazon

Belém

Fortaleza

Iquitos

Purus

Madeira

Tapajós

Natal

Recife

PERU

BRAZIL

Tocantins

Maceió

MATO GROSSO

Francisco

São

Salvador

Lima

Cusco

Arequipa

BOLIVIA

Mato Grosso

Brasília

Goiânia

La Paz

Sucre

Iquique

Potosí

PARAGUAY

Belo Horizonte

Campinas

São Paulo

Rio de Janeiro

Antofagasta

Salta

Asunción

Paraguay

Curitiba

Santos

San Miguel de
Tucumán

Paraná

CHILE

Salado

Uruguay

Pôrto
Alegre

Córdoba

Santa Fe

Valparaíso

Mendoza

Rosario

Pelotas

Santiago

Buenos Aires

La Plata

URUGUAY

Montevideo

Talca

Concepción

ARGENTINA

Bahía Blanca

Pacific
Ocean

Atlantic
Ocean

I. CHILOÉ

PATAGONIA

Strait of
Magellan

FALKLAND IS.

TIERRA DEL
FUEGO

Cape Horn

Miles

0   200   400   600

Atlantic

Ocean

Nationalism in Latin America

Nationalism

IN

LATIN AMERICA

*

Diversity and Unity

*

by GERHARD MASUR

The Macmillan Company, NEW YORK

Collier-Macmillan Limited, LONDON

SECOND PRINTING 1967

The Macmillan Company, New York

Collier-Macmillan Canada, Ltd., Toronto, Ontario

Library of Congress catalog card number: 66–12974

PRINTED IN THE UNITED STATES OF AMERICA

To my students

Contents

PREFACE ix

I *Introduction* 1

II *The Independence Movement* 22

III *The Road to Nationhood* 32

IV *Latin America and World Economy* 62

V *The Mexican Revolution* 73

VI *The Andean Countries: Indian Renaissance* 93

VII *The Bolivian National Revolution* 106

VIII *The National Revolution in Brazil* 123

IX *Enigmatic Argentina* 152

X *The Cuban Revolution* 198

XI *Conclusion* 226

NOTES 252

INDEX 271

Preface

IN THE FALL of 1962 I participated in a conference initiated by the International Society for the History of Ideas and held in Mexico City. The subject chosen for discussion was "Ideas and Social Change in the Western Hemisphere." In considering this theme it became ever more clear to me that the ideology which has most deeply penetrated Latin American political and social thought in the twentieth century has been nationalism, and, further, that nationalism has acted as a catalyst for many of the social adjustments which have taken place throughout the continent.

I first encountered nationalism in Latin America when the frenzied nationalism of the Third Reich compelled me to seek refuge in the Western Hemisphere. My interest in Simón Bolívar led me to study the origins of nationalism in the seventeen republics. It was not long before I realized that nationalism changes complexion and function in Latin America fully as much as it does in other parts of our perturbed and convulsed world.

This book is an attempt to trace the evolution of nationalism in Latin America from its first appearance to the present day. It is offered in all humility as an essay that must remain fragmentary, not only because so vast a portion of the world is difficult to comprehend, but also because the writer must end his study at some necessarily uncompleted stage. Subsequent events which might change his appraisal can only be assessed when they in turn become a part of the past. This is a dilemma which confronts most observers of the contemporary scene, producing a feeling of frustration and inadequacy in the commentator.

A great deal has been contributed to this essay through the efforts of anthropologists, social scientists, economists, and others interested in the fate of Latin America. I am, however, still of the opinion that the historical approach to the problem of nationalism holds greater promise of a fuller understanding.

I have kept text references to a minimum and have omitted a bibliography, which, though desirable, would easily run to a full volume.

I am indebted to my wife, Helen Gaylord Masur, for editing the manuscript of this book and for sharing in the labor of preparing it for the printer.

GERHARD MASUR

Freie Universität Berlin
November, 1965

CHAPTER I

Introduction

THE STUDY OF NATIONALISM, whether general or specific, presents a paradox. Although it is admittedly a manifest and salient feature of the contemporary political scene, there is, nevertheless, little agreement as to its fundamental characteristics. Innumerable questions erupt, which have disparate and often irreconcilable answers. Just what is nationalism? How may it be defined or even described? Is it a constructive or a destructive force? Is it a transitory phenomenon or has it now taken up permanent residence on this planet?

The origins of nationalism are unmistakably European, but other parts of the world have been attracted to one or more of its facets. In the conflicts which dominate our times, it is found as a common denominator in every continent, regardless of political affiliations. The countries which call themselves "western" show it as much as do those which adhere to the communist faith. Unaligned nations use it as a shield against participation in conflicts which they consider alien to their proper development. Its universal reach cannot, however, obscure the fact that nationalism is a complex phenomenon; its meaning and social functions are subject to constant change depending on where it appears.

As a result, nationalism continues to be a challenging problem for the analyst in search of restrictive definitions. A large amount of literature has already been devoted to the task. The European origins have been extensively studied. Hans Kohn states that nationalism ". . . is not older than the second half of the eighteenth century,"[1] and most historians would agree with him, since nationalism and the idea of popular sovereignty, first conceived during the French Revolution, are inseparable.

Carlton J. Hayes defines nationalism as a blend of patriotism (obviously a much older emotion) and the doctrine of popular sovereignty, a blend which resulted in the assumption that man's ultimate loyalty belongs to the national state in which he lives and in which he wishes to live.[2] Following the French Revolution, nationalism became one of the guiding principles of European politics, and the nation-state became the goal toward which the European people moved with ever increasing speed. In the nineteenth century it had two dominating aspects: one external, freedom from foreign control; the other internal, freedom from despotic rule. Many of the conflicts of the century were given over to the attainment of these ends, as proved by the independence of Belgium, the unification of Italy and of Germany, and the emergence of independent Slavic nations in the Balkans. By the same token, the concept of the nation-state in its twofold aspect was also used as a yardstick for the measurement of progress or reaction in the political world; those countries which would not or could not adhere to it stood condemned as retrogressive in the eyes of political observers. Russia and the Hapsburg and Ottoman empires were foremost among those so condemned.

In view of the triumphant sweep of the idea of nationalism, political scientists and historians attempted to crystallize the underlying concepts of the new ideology, and their efforts, quite naturally, advanced the idea to other countries and continents. Certain affirmations were made: A people was a group of individuals who had various characteristics in common; these included language, territory, religion, tradition, customs and habits, and historical memories.[3] Many times it was stated that a nation lives in a "state of its own," which German writers liked to call the mind or soul of a people (*Volksgeist*). Nationality was also described as one of the characteristics of a people having a drive toward political, economic, or cultural autonomy. Other writers, like Ernest Renan, stressed the possession of a rich heritage of memories, a heritage of glory and grief, which was shared in common. "*L'existence d'une nation c'est un plébiscite de tous les jours.*"[4] Renan's contemporary, John Stuart Mill, observed that the historicopolitical element might be of decisive influence. "The strongest cause of the feeling of nationality," he wrote in 1861, ". . . is identity of political antecedents; the possession of a national history, and a consequent community of recollections; collective pride and humiliation, pleasure and regret, connected with the same incident in the past."[5]

But eventually all of these definitions encounter difficulties, and the exception becomes the rule. What was the elusive element termed the "national character"? And how could it be explained? Otto Bauer, an Austrian social democrat, tried to answer the riddle by interpreting "national character" as the product of one and the same effective force which has worked on all the members of a given community; thus national character becomes the result of a "community of fate." Still others asserted that a nation was a cultural community held together by a scale of values which made the individual members accept certain objects and reject others; thus nationhood becomes essentially a "state of mind," or a spiritual community, as Friedrich Meinecke has put it.[6] But again, the explanation seems to renounce the more tangible foundations on which national life has been built.

Nor did the First World War clarify the situation. Fought in an atmosphere of overheated nationalism, its conclusion left nations and nationalities opposing each other with conflicting claims. Finally, the appearance of a totalitarian nationalism based on racial purity and superiority brought any progress toward conceptual clarity to a temporary halt. Yet it was precisely the arrant nonsense of the German and Italian ideas which set social scientists on the path again. A study group of the Royal

Institute of International Affairs scrutinized the phenomenon of nationalism and came forth with a detailed report. Although the chairman, H. E. Carr, states therein that "the nation is not a definable and clearly recognizable entity,"[7] he continues in the same paragraph to list such elements as speech, attachment to one's native land, and a sense of kinship beyond the family as integral elements in the feeling of nationalism. He further adds that the modern nation is a historical group. Other members of the same group noted the importance of elites in shaping the national will and the national consciousness.[8]

Recently Karl W. Deutsch has made a gallant attempt to come to grips with the dilemma by searching for qualitative as well as quantitative criteria in defining nationalism. He lays down certain rules which every student of the subject will find useful, such as that each concept of nationalism should be operational, or functional. The concepts should be fruitful, should be applicable to the behavior of individuals and groups alike, and should account for rational as well as irrational attitudes and acts of the nation and the nation's members.[9]

As the most useful concept in distinguishing the nation from other groups, Professor Deutsch suggests the principle of communication. A people, he states, is a large group linked by complementary habits and facilities of communication. Membership in a people consists essentially in wide complementarity of social communication.[10] Such a definition seems acceptable, though its precision seems to have been purchased at the price of profundity. We venture to ask for the origin and impetus of social communication, and we find ourselves thrown back to such concepts as language, religion, history, tradition.

Nevertheless, the long discussion about the nature of nationalism has not been unproductive, and certain conclusions may be drawn. Quite obviously, nations, nationalities, and nationalism resist any attempt to define them by singling out any one element, such as race, geographical situation, religion, politics, or language. They are the result of a combination and interaction of different aspects of social life, where any individual element may be omitted and replaced by another. It is not essential that all the elements of nationhood be present in each instance. "Nationalities come into existence only when certain objective bonds limit a social group. A nationality generally has several of these attributes; very few have all of them."[11]

The boggle over definitions should not, however, discourage further study of the problem. The social scientist's difficulty in framing a concise definition may work to the advantage of the historian, whose duties are more descriptive. Since the days of Ranke, the historian has known that he must behold human behavior rather than dissect it.[12] He can, therefore, use all the categories which have been advanced in the discussion of nationalism, well aware that they will rarely appear as elements of chemical purity. He will look for the unique combination which may explain the case in hand, since each element which has cropped up may represent not one factor but variables. "Geographical conditions" vary from country to country and from continent to continent; "language" and "religious beliefs" are not necessarily components of differentiation. "Historical memories" differ from group to group not only in their content, but in their dynamic aspects, *i.e.*, in the way a nation depends on them for its identification in the historical process. In other words, clarity of definition will not suffice, if we are to ferret out the significance of nationalism in operation. Our need is for detailed studies of the various societies in our contemporary world where we find nationalism at work.

The present volume is devoted to a study of nationalism in Latin America. Although the importance of nationalistic motivation is readily admitted by students of Latin American politics, economics, literature, and art, few attempts have been made to trace its development or to distinguish Latin American nationalism from nationalism in Europe, Asia, and Africa. Given the enormous expanse and complexity of the Latin American world and the embryonic state of the research on nationalism, it is impossible to present a full or in any way complete study of the situation. However, it may be of value to investigate some of the salient problems. The experiment stands in no need of apology; scholarship succeeds by trial and error and is bound to be superseded all along the way.[13]

It has long been recognized that the name "Latin America" is neither exact nor accurate. Very likely, it came into use in contradistinction to the term "Anglo-American," meaning the United States and Canada, and since no better one has come up, it still holds its place. It has geographical connotations—all the lands from south of the Rio Grande to Cape Horn—but it also has cultural connotations implying a close association with Rome and the Mediterranean. The people of Latin America are both conscious and proud of their affiliation with the Latin world across the seas, and few would care to change the designation.

Of course there are many Latin Americas—Argentina, Chile, Uruguay, Paraguay, Brazil, Venezuela, Colombia, Ecuador, Peru, Panama, Bolivia, Costa Rica, San Salvador, Guatemala, Honduras, Nicaragua, Mexico, and Cuba—and each is in one or more ways unique. It is this diversity coupled with their geographical proximity that obliges us to seek some common ground of interest or necessity. Other questions arise to confuse the issue: Should we exclude Haiti, or Martinique, or Jamaica from our survey because they were not colonized by Spain or Portugal?

The commonly accepted meaning of the term "Latin America" is those independent republics which emerged from the Iberian colonial empires in the New World—in other words, the succession states of Spain and Portugal. Logically, then, the period of the Latin American independence movement would indicate the point of departure for a study of nationalism in this part of the western hemisphere. Before 1810, there were no nations, and there could not have been anything called nationalism before this date. Yet the emergent republics and empires of Latin America cannot be understood without a backward glance at their precolonial and colonial status. The Latin American past has cast a long and somber shadow across the Latin American present.

When Spain and Portugal entered the age of their New World discoveries they found themselves face to face with the only civilizations which had developed in complete independence from the general matrix of mankind.[14] The Orient was part of the inhabited world; there already existed links, however tenuous, between the Asiatic and the European civilizations.[15] Only in the western world had higher civilizations evolved in complete isolation from the rest of the world. The most notable of these were the Mayan, the Aztec, the Chibcha, and the Inca cultures. These were the societies that the Spaniards invaded unaware of the universal significance of their undertaking. Thus a New World was called into existence, quite accidentally baptized with the name America, and here the Spaniards, and to a lesser degree the Portuguese, projected their vision and their greed, their imperial aspirations and their missionary zeal. This was 1492, and the story needs no retelling, but any study concerned with the growth of nationalities in Latin America must emphasize certain events that shed light on the tortuous road to political and cultural identity which the various countries were obliged to travel.

The grandeur of the Iberic enterprise was unique and can never fail to engage the imagination of those who care to read about it. Beginning with Columbus, the discoverers who set their prows toward the west made use of the superior maritime knowledge which was of such signal benefit to mariners in the Mediterranean area. Following the discoverers, individuals and small groups crossed the ocean and began the exploration of the continent. In little more than a half century they had occupied the larger portion of the southern New World and conquered a population which surpassed them by millions. These *adelantados* and conquistadores rarely reaped the benefits of their labors; they were the emissaries of the crowns of Spain and Portugal and took possession of the new and fabulous lands in the names of their rulers. At the beginning there was a great deal of "free enterprise" in this fearless conquest of an alien world, a great deal of anarchy and bloodshed, but once the dirty work was done, the state took over. The officials of the crown arrived, bent on establishing the royal prerogatives, humiliating the proud, subduing the rebellious and rewarding the faithful. Very few of the first generation of the conquistadores died in the enjoyment of their king's grace or the peace of their beds. These early days were a configuration of the future of Latin America. The bloodshed, the rivalry, and the anarchy subsided, but the traces of these sanguinary events were forever etched on the countenance of the colonial realm.

Spain's genius for empire was the result of its long struggle against Islam and the Moorish rule, a period which goes under the name of *la reconquista*. In seven centuries of fighting the Spaniards had developed the "martial virtues of physical endurance, personal heroism and steel-like temper."[16] Their dislike of foreigners was congenital. Spain epitomized the male virtues; honor was essential, submission a disgrace; retaliation for any slight to personal or national pride was swift and merciless. Such was the mold in which Cortés, Pizarro, Benalcázar, Jiménez de Quesada, were cast, and the image of heroic virtue they created has never languished.

There was, however, another human model that shaped the vision of national grandeur in Spain. For Catholic Iberia, the saint of the holy church of Rome was as important as the knight. The crusading spirit which had maintained the fight against Islam was equally relentless in the battles across the Atlantic and gave to the conquest of the New World the hard and fanatical character of a delayed Middle Age. It might be termed the last crusade. Conquest and conversion went hand in hand, and colonial rule was to be based on both.[17] The crowns of Spain and Portugal secured from the Holy See the right of the *patronato real*, the royal patronage over the affairs of the church. Thus the Spanish kingdom became a state-church or a church-state, depending for its function on the unity of *fe, rey, y ley* (faith, king, and law).[18] This unity was transferred to the transatlantic world, albeit with certain moderations that tended to mellow the iron rule of the Spanish Inquisition.

A third element must be mentioned if we wish to comprehend the colonial society that came into existence in Latin America. It is a more elusive element and concerns what Max Weber would have called the *Wirtschaftgesinnung* (economic mentality) of the conquering nation. Spain is said to have been motivated by God, glory, and gold in her great enterprise. The desire for quick and fabulous rewards in return for sufferings and sacrifices is notable in the annals of the conquest and in the colonial period that followed. Even at the beginning of the sixteenth century, Spaniards had a reputation for avoiding economic enterprises that involved hard and constant work. The Italian humanist Francesco Guicciardini remarked in 1513, "All Spaniards look down on trade, which they regard as degrading, and they put on airs as hidalgos and prefer to be soldiers or highwaymen than to engage in trade or in any other such occupation . . . Spaniards are fond of show, wear fine cloth and ride a stylish horse."[19] This characteristic Spanish aversion to commercial activities extended also to agricultural labor. Both commerce and agriculture had for centuries been in the hands of infidels, the Moors and the Jews, and were consequently looked upon with scorn. In the national scale of values, the religious and the military offices occupied the highest rank. Quite naturally, the same values were applied in the lands which were conquered. The treasures of which they had dreamed, the gold, the silver, and the precious stones, accompanied them on their return voyage to the homeland, but they failed to satisfy the rapacious greed of the adventurers; moreover, their plunder was decimated by the crown's claim for one-fifth of all the gold and silver that might be discovered. America's greatest wealth was land, but land without the labor to work it was of little benefit to the Spaniards. In an attempt to solve this problem, Spain introduced a number of socio-economic institutions in the colonies, the most important of which were the *repartimiento* and the *encomienda*.[20] By means of these channels the Europeans were able to take lawful advantage of the native population, forcing it to do the work which they were loath to do themselves. Columbus had already advocated the advantages of such a system. Native labor, he said, would be far more efficient than the work of "any kind of slaves." His conclusion was not borne out, however, and Spain was obliged to recruit additional labor from Africa.

The *repartimiento* implied the distribution of natives among the Spanish "patrons"; the *encomienda* system, introduced in 1503, granted the Indians officially the status of free persons. They were required to work, but for wages; they were organized into communities, and their land was declared inalienable; they were to be taught the message of the Catholic faith. These were the declared intentions of the system, but in practice it assumed quite different features. *Repartimiento* and *encomienda* brought a form of feudal serfdom to Latin America which forced the natives to work on the plantations and in the mines for the exclusive benefit of their European masters. The significance of these institutions is still a subject of heated debate, but certain conclusions may be drawn. The economy that came into being early in the sixteenth century was an economy of extraction; it depended on the rich resources of forests, fields, and mines. It committed Latin America to a continuance of this type of economy long after colonial rule had disappeared. It favored the large-scale enterprise at the expense of the small, and laid the foundations for the latifundium, the concentration of landed wealth in the hands of the few. It encouraged the plantation type of economy as against the farm type which prevailed among the settlers of New England.[21]

It must be admitted that Spain was in no condition to send a massive farm population to America. Colonization of the enormous spaces opened up by the conquistadores was in great need of Indian labor and later imported Negro labor. As a result serfdom, and soon slavery, became the basis for much of the life of the colonies. The Latin American Indian was spared the fate of his North American brother, but at a price. He was not driven from his land, nor was he threatened with extermination, but he forfeited his freedom and was preserved as an instrument of production for the feudal overlords, who considered him only as a beast of burden. The Negro slaves whose importation began in the sixteenth century enjoyed no legal status except as a commodity. When the *encomienda* was finally abolished the Indian had become accustomed to a life without hope or initiative. He became the easy victim of peonage and debt slavery, which perpetuated his condition of servitude.

We can only conjecture whether the Indian had a better lot in precolonial times, but it is certain that his circumstances did not improve under Spanish rule. The agriculture of the homeland during this period of Spanish history depended on superannuated methods, and there was little it could teach the Indian. Nevertheless, the Spaniards maintained that the natives were lazy and essentially unteachable, and their attitude has carried over into the postcolonial era.

Finally, there was an aspect of social organization which the people of the colonial period were prone to ignore. Every society is a form of cultural community, but there could be little cultural communication between the Spanish victors and the vanquished natives, between lords and serfs, between freemen and slaves. The Indians preserved many of their ancient customs, in their manner of dress, in the choice and preparation of their food, in the pursuance of their sexual habits, and even sometimes in their speech. The amazing endurance of African lore among the Negro slaves has often been noted. The culture of the colonial period was, therefore, not homogeneous but consisted of superimposed layers, a phenomenon that sociologists describe as *Überlagerung*. Gradually the different layers began to act on each other. Spanish culture did indeed permeate all strata of Latin American social structure, but there was also an interaction of the old and the new through which language, religion, music, and the arts were transformed.[22] This combination of three different civilizations, the European, the Indian, and the African, was one of the most important phenomena of the Latin American world. Out of it grew a new type of culture, and the process of nationalism in Latin America is closely tied to this cultural development.

The colonial society which evolved from these involuted civilizations was castelike in character, with strict hierarchical distinctions. The European occupied the top position; next came the American of European descent; then the mestizo, who was considered a freeman, though of lowly status; finally, in descending scale, the Indian, the mulatto, the Negro, and the zambo, who was of mixed Negro and Indian blood. The racial prejudices which the Spaniards had harbored in Europe against the Jews and the Moors throughout the years was maintained in the New World against the native population. It was decreed that purity of blood (*limpieza de sangre*) was mandatory for a title of nobility. In spite of this, miscegenation was widely practiced, resulting in a mixture of the races. The Portuguese were considerably more lenient than the Spaniards in regard to interracial combinations, but racial barriers were beginning to crumble even in the Spanish empire by the close of the colonial period (1810).

The Roman Catholic Church was in part responsible for this commingling of Spanish and native blood. The priests and monks were the first to defend the status of the Indian; they insisted that he should be treated as a reasonable human being (*gente de razón*), and from the earliest days they had endeavored to bring him into the fold. Las Casas is the most notable example of this missionary zeal, but he was by no means the only one. Indoctrination rested on education, and in colonial times education was exclusively in the hands of the clergy, whether regular or secular. Spanish and Portuguese were the languages used in this process and hence became the languages of the New World. Schools and universities were founded throughout Latin America; the oldest universities in the Western hemisphere are those of Mexico and Lima. The great effort to educate the native was not everywhere successful; entire Indian tribes proved recalcitrant, clinging to an idiom which they have preserved to modern times. Old customs and ancient religious rites endured, sometimes openly, sometimes in secret. Yet withal, the foundations for new national structures began to take shape.

The church of Rome gave the Latin American world a religious homogeneity, and Roman Catholicism is still the religion of the overwhelming majority of its people. This circumstance, however, had its drawbacks. The Inquisition, which was both a political and an ecclesiastical institution, not only supervised the intellectual commerce between the colonies and Europe, but also maintained a close supervision over immigration, rejecting all heretical elements, whether Protestant or Jewish, that attempted to penetrate the Iberic possessions. Although isolated cases may have escaped the vigilance of the authorities, the colonies on the whole were well shielded from the crosscurrents of European life. One is inclined to think that this protective attitude influenced Latin America's feeling toward immigration in general. Even today a certain amount of xenophobia appears to be a characteristic of many Latin American countries. In the United States, on the other hand, one could find as early as 1790 "a strange mixture of blood" not encountered in any other country.[23] Although European immigration later played a significant role in such countries as Brazil, Argentina, Uruguay, and Chile, the idea of the melting pot has never appealed to the people of Latin America.

John Stuart Mill asserted, the reader may recall, that one of the strongest causes for nationality is identity of political and historical antecedents. Mill's observation is borne out by the developments in Latin America. Spain and Portugal were absolute monarchies with a well-developed apparatus of bureaucratic administrations. The colonial governments were created in their own image; Spain followed this policy even more closely than Portugal. The Spanish empire was divided into administrative subdivisions, viceroyalties, *audiencias* (law courts), and *capitanías generales,* which bore the names of regions in the mother country—New Spain, New Castile, New

Granada—and occasionally names that had sprung up in the New World—La Plata, Venezuela. These divisions, many of them larger than Spain, were ruled by officials sent out from Spain. Their tenure was usually of short duration, rarely exceeding five years in the higher positions—a clear indication of Spain's distrust of her own emissaries. Yet the administration brought a minimum of law and order; the habits of bureaucratic government by writ and legal decision took root. A code of laws, the famous Leyes de las Indias, was assembled which had to be respected even if it was not always adhered to. A group of men trained in paperwork and legal discipline carried on the humdrum of the daily routine. More of this colonial tradition persists today than the casual visitor might suspect.[24]

Eventually the people who lived in New Spain, in New Castile, or in the La Plata region came to know each other. They developed a feeling of kinship and belonging that formed the cornerstone for the future nationalities. In other words, regionalism preceded nationalism.

One other feature of the Spanish heritage must be mentioned. It concerns the economic policy of the mother country toward her colonies. In the beginning this was one of strict mercantilism, which endeavored to channel the flow of raw material and revenues unhampered and unencumbered between Spain and her empire. Taxes were collected from white men and Indians alike. Commerce was restricted to trade between Spanish and American ports and was hamstrung by the two-fleet system; ships plied between Europe and America once a year, touching on Central America and South America respectively. The empire was supposed to be a closely knit economic unit, self-sufficient in its production with the exception of those goods that the mother country would supply. Yet it is well known that the economic realities gave the lie to this theory, that Spain, impoverished through long wars and price revolutions, was in no condition to fulfill the economic demands of the Latin American colonies, and that other nations tried to break her monopoly by conquest or by smuggling.[25] Spain also restricted its colonies in the agrarian and industrial production of many items, including wine, silk and olive oil, in order to discourage competition with the mother country. And Spain saw to it that commerce between the different sections of her empire was limited to a bare minimum, thus forestalling the development of a network of common economic interests. After the termination of the Hapsburg rule in Spain, a more enlightened type of mercantilism was introduced. Intendants took the place of the former officials, and commerce was in many instances entrusted to companies who held a monopoly on certain routes. Yet essentially the mercantilistic viewpoint prevailed. Though the economy at the end of the eighteenth century was booming, the colonists felt that all the benefits were reaped by the mother country.

Finally, a word must be said about the trend toward urbanization, so characteristic of the Spanish empire. Latin American civilization today shows a startling growth of urban life, and few are aware that it, too, dates back to colonial times. The Spaniards had not been content to set up trading posts along the coastline; instead, they had from the beginning insisted on founding cities after the model of Spain. Before Cortés entered the Aztec empire, he founded the "noble city of Veracruz" and had himself appointed *alcalde* (mayor). All through the conquest we can observe a similar trend. In some instances Spain used previous Indian settlements, as in Mexico City, Bogotá, Quito, and Cuzco. In other cases new cities sprang up: Santiago de Chile, Buenos Aires, and Caracas. The organization of urban communities is thus an essential feature of Spanish rule and followed the Spanish pattern; there were *alcaldes* with numerous assistants; there were city councils, and there were even in a few instances open town meetings, the famous *cabildos abiertos* which played a large part in the independence movement.[26] It may be said that the urban communities formed from the outset a counterweight to the feudal tendencies of the landed aristocracy. However, there was no self-government in Latin America as there was in the Anglo-Saxon colonies in the north.

This brings up a point of great importance. Spain had transplanted many of her institutions across the Atlantic, but the form of national representation that had developed in Castile and Aragon, the Cortes, have no counterpoint in the New World. Actually, Charles V expressly forbade the establishment of any form of representation in the colonies.[27] The colonists had no voice in the conduct of their affairs, save that of complaint and petition to the royal authorities in Europe. Here again is one of the differences between the colonies of the North and those of Latin America. The settlers of Massachusetts, Connecticut, and Virginia voiced their grievances in assemblies which were part of the legal structure of British colonial rule. As Britishers, they felt themselves heirs of the long struggle between crown and parliament during the seventeenth century. The Latin Americans, even those of European descent, would not have found it so natural to identify themselves with the basic principles of Spanish history.

The decline of Spain's might during the eighteenth century did not visibly affect the empire. The European powers, France, England, and Holland, had tried to break into the Iberian colonies in America, but had made no substantial inroads. In the eighteenth century the jealousy of the great powers protected the empire more than did its own strength. However, the barriers that kept European trade out of Latin America were considerably weaker now. Intellectual intercourse likewise had more chance of penetrating the closely guarded walls of the Inquisition. This was, after all, the century of the Enlightenment, and glimpses and reflections of the all-encompassing European movements reached the Iberic possessions overseas.

By 1750 the ideas of the Enlightenment had conquered all of Europe from Russia to Spain and Portugal. This was the period that d'Alembert called "the century of philosophy *par excellence*." The Enlightenment prided itself on having recognized the true system of the world, and according to its belief in the unlimited power of reason, it proceeded to discuss everything from the secular sciences to the very foundations of religious revelation, from music to morals, from taste to matters of trade, from the laws of princes to those of the people, from the laws of nature to the arbitrary laws of nations.[28] The Enlightenment believed in the triumph of reason over darkness, and, as Kant expressed it, in maturing man's mind to the point where he would become of age and walk the earth proudly, free of any tutelage, whether secular or spiritual.

These ideas had first been expressed by Locke, Bayle, Leibniz, and Newton; they became intellectual currency when Voltaire spread them around the continent, when Montesquieu presented his system of politics in the *Esprit des Lois* and when the *Encyclopédie* made its appearance in 1751. As leaders of the Enlightenment, the French were better known in Latin America than the English or the Germans. Voltaire, Montesquieu, Rousseau, Diderot, were read, though how widely they were read is difficult to ascertain. All of them were on the list of forbidden books which had to be smuggled into the colonies. Obviously some copies were brought in, and it would seem that the clergy found it easier to deceive the authorities than the laymen. A study of the private libraries of colonial times has revealed that the great authors of the eighteenth century were read in many parts of this world. We can also trace the influence of scientific thinking in the curricula of the universities, though in the form of compromise with the scholastic teaching of earlier times.[29]

The ideas of the Enlightenment must have come as a shock to most Latin Americans. These new concepts completely negated the medieval ideas on which the Spanish system of the church-state had been based. They promised liberty, equality, and the pursuit of happiness to a people who had been kept in their preordained place by a rigorous hierarchical order and whose minds had been stifled by the teachings of St. Thomas and St. Augustine. It was quite natural that certain works, like Raynal's *Philosophical and Political History of the Indies,* were given particular attention, since they condemned the cruelty of the European conquest and lauded the virtues of the simple Indian. Raynal's book went into many printings and influenced many of the leaders of the independence movement.[30] Rousseau likewise was widely read, though it is not so easy to divine the application of his political ideas in Latin America. Nevertheless, the idea of popular sovereignty as explained in the *Social Contract* intoxicated many minds. Individual freedom, popular sovereignty, republican government, secular education—these were just some of the new thoughts that the Enlightenment spread around the colonies.

But let us not overrate the importance of these influences. The Enlightenment in Latin America remained a shadowy reflection of its European counterpart and never had the impact that it had on the North American colonies. Latin America did not produce, during this period, such figures as Benjamin Franklin, Thomas Jefferson, or John Adams. The Enlightenment, in the southern hemisphere, was sporadic and erratic in its reach, and consequently limited in its effect. As an intellectual awakening, it scarcely disturbed the slumber that for so long had dimmed the cultural life of the colonies.[31] It is true that literary and scientific societies were formed in Mexico City, Buenos Aires and Lima, and that the new ideas were discussed with some zeal; also it would seem that certain groups, such as the Freemasons, took a special interest in their spread. But essentially it was the upper class, the *Criollos* (Creoles) as they were called, that adhered to them. For this class the new ideas represented an ideological vehicle which could guarantee their position in society and politics.

There is no evidence that the ideas of the Enlightenment in themselves threatened the established authorities of state and church; only in conjunction with other elements could they become a revolutionary force. This leads us logically into the question of whether a potentially revolutionary situation existed in Latin America at the end of the eighteenth century. There is no clear yes or no answer. There had been uprisings in Upper

Peru as early as 1730; there had been the rebellion of Tupac Amaru in Peru itself, and a similar movement in New Granada in 1781. The instigators were called *los comuneros* and numbered among their leaders a sprinkling of mestizos and even Indians. But the disturbances were directed more against old grievances than toward a new order. And of course there were isolated individuals who challenged the Spanish rule, like the famous Francisco de Miranda, and others who became intrigued with the idea of human rights, such as Antonio Nariño.[32] Yet withal, the rule of Spain and Portugal would have persisted for a longer period had it not been for the revolutionary climate that prevailed in North America and in Europe. It was the American and, even more, the French revolutions and their aftermath that brought the independence movement to fruition.

We have so far spoken of the Spanish and Portuguese colonies as though their evolution had been identical. It is essential, however, that this impression should be clarified. The Portuguese possessions in the New World, an accidental result of the treaty with Spain at Tordesilla (1494), were for a long time overshadowed by the Portuguese enterprises in India, Southeast Asia, and Africa. The discovery of dyewood, from which the enormous country of Brazil took its name, changed the situation only slightly. There were no great treasures in evidence, and all that could be expected from the domain was agricultural wealth. Sugar cane was introduced and the country was launched on an economic system that depended on native labor, very much like the Spanish colonies. Since the interior was unexplored, the coastline was divided into *capitanías* under governors who were at the same time proprietors, and it was expected that these overlords would develop the large fiefs bestowed on them by the crown. Here too we find an incipient semifeudal society which to all intents and purposes was virtually independent of the authority of the crown. However, the crown did reserve rights similar to those claimed by Castile: one-fifth of all the precious metals and stones that might be discovered, and in addition a monopoly on all the important exports, such as dyewood, spices, etc. These monopolies, however, were farmed out, since Portugal, engaged as she was in the Asia trade, was not able to handle any increase in her obligations.

Since Portugal's first attempts at colonization had not proved successful, and since Brazil was threatened by invasion first by France and later by Holland, a more centralized form of government became necessary. In the meantime, however, affairs in Brazil moved at an ever more sluggish pace. A policy of *laisser-aller, laisser-faire* was followed, not, of course, in theory, but in practice; and it was brought on by necessity rather than by intention.

This policy was encouraged by economic circumstances. It has been said that the history of Brazil is a history of migration.[33] These migrations began when Europeans first bartered for dyewood and the Indians came to the coast to traffic with them. Later, when the sugar plantations were in operation, expeditions went into the interior to capture Indians for work on the *fazendas*. But, as the Spanish had learned, Indian labor was insufficient and had to be augmented by the importation of Negro slaves. There were frequent desertions among the latter, and the runaways found work on cattle ranches in the interior. Latifundia were the prevailing type of agrarian holdings in Brazil as well as in Hispanic America. The majority of the population, however, developed a form of nomadism in an effort either to escape their masters or to search for better economic conditions where greedy landlords and constant drought did not prevail. There were the *bandeirantes* who left São Paulo in expectation of better pasturage; another stream of adventurers rushed toward Minas Gerais when gold and diamonds were discovered there. These tendencies increased a trend toward toleration and autonomy by default on the part of the European authorities; they promised a more lenient society than the one created by Spain. Gilberto Freyre has shown how the Casa Grande of the *fazenda* contributed to the mingling and fusion of the races, another characteristic of contemporary Brazil.[34]

The difference, then, between the two parts of the Iberic American world is considerable, and it has influenced their development in the nineteenth and twentieth centuries. But they remained first cousins, closely related in their outlook on life and politics, and at a good deal of variance from the Anglo-American world to the north.

It has already been said that there is no real assurance of Latin America's preparedness for independence around 1800. Without doubt, the formation of the United States from 1776 to 1787 set an example that a few individuals wished to follow. They are the *precursores,* the forerunners, whose efforts are important but should not lead us into overrating the degree of discontent and revolutionary ferment that existed. Closer to home were the events that freed Haiti from French colonial rule in 1806. However, the small republic carried little weight in the western hemisphere; it was impoverished and almost entirely populated by descendants of Negro slaves. And the attempts by certain Englishmen to wrestle the provinces of the La Plata from Spanish rule seemed to augur the continuous stability of the ties between colonies and mother country. The British general, Beresford, and his companion, Sir Home Popham, were repulsed and eventually ousted from Buenos Aires (1806–1807). Miranda's attack on Venezuela in the same year was a complete failure. In addition, the prospects of free trade, religious liberty, or even political autonomy held little lure for the colonials. Yet they could not fail to recognize that their role in the defense of the empire was more important than it had ever been before. A *cabildo abierto* met in Buenos Aires and chose a new viceroy; here were the seeds of a degree of political autonomy. The attitude of the colonies is best summed up in the words of the Argentinian patriot Belgrano: "*Queremos el viejo amo o ninguno*" ("We want the old master or none").[35] In other words, they wished either to be free, or to remain Spanish.

CHAPTER II

The Independence Movement

THE APPEARANCE of a group of independent nations, surging forth from the colonial embryo where they have been lying inert, which with new elements give new individualities to history, and which, of course, intervene in the historical processes of the world; the unification of an entire continent that occupies half of the world, and which has proclaimed by instinct the logical principles of democracy as natural law and universal rule of the future; the establishment of a new type of international law and of a new type of constitutional law in opposition to the law of conquest and servitude and to the dogma of monarchical absolutism that had triumphed in the old world; the partition of the world in two portions which established a balance of destiny for the world; the creation of organic societies with equality for the native population, without special privilege yet with comprehensive concepts and a tendency toward cosmopolitanism; the opening of new fields to experimentation, free of all obstacles, for the unfolding of the physical and moral faculties of mankind; finally the amplitude of man's mobility and his large projections in space and time, constitute, without doubt, one of the most fundamental changes in the human condition which has occurred at any time."[1] In this hyperbolic manner, the Argentinian historian

Mitre describes the significance of the Latin American independence movement. Not everyone will agree that the foundation for these claims has been fully established, but few would refuse to concede the grandeur and heroism accompanying the movement that brought seventeen independent political societies into existence.

The Latin American independence movement was not one of autocombustion; it was sparked from without. The occupation of the Iberian Peninsula by the armies of Napoleon provided the opportunity for this revolutionary event. The Braganza family escaped from Lisbon on British ships and in due time landed in Rio de Janeiro, where they set up court. By so doing, they were very likely instrumental in preserving the territorial integrity of Brazil when independence finally came. The Spanish Bourbons, on the contrary, surrendered abjectly to Napoleon and became his prisoners, albeit *de luxe.*

Thus the enormous overseas empire was left to itself, and the old legal theory that the colonies were the possession of the crown of Castile and not of the mother country was put to the test. Within a short time a three-cornered struggle developed between the colonial administrative authorities representing the Spanish monarchy, whose default they refused to recognize; the native-born upper-class white population, called *criollos,* who claimed the right of self-government and self-determination in such extraordinary circumstances; and the great mass of those whose interests and sympathies wavered between one side and the other. The situation deteriorated into a state of civil warfare between those loyal to Spain and those members of the aristocratic class who openly or covertly favored independence from Spain.

It seems doubtful, however, that this latter group was motivated by nationalistic considerations. They were patriots, and were so called by friend and foe alike. The concept of the fatherland, *la patria,* loomed large in their vision of the future. But the greater number of independence fighters were inspired by *la patria chica,* or *la patria boba,* a kind of guileless, provincial patriotism, the protection of hearth and home. The sectionalism to which we have already referred asserted itself with increased vigor. Although the revolutionaries from Mexico to Buenos Aires and from Bogotá to Santiago de Chile had a feeling of solidarity, there was no single nation totally committed to the idea of independence. Instead there was a marked tendency to set up the old administrative units of Spanish rule as sovereign states. The leaders of the independence movement recognized the principle of *uti possidetis* which would suggest that the new republics retain the boundary lines they had held for three hundred years under colonial rule. There were, it is true, the notable exceptions of Bolivia, Uruguay, and Paraguay, which set up their boundary lines after the beginning of the independence movement.

It is difficult to assess the amount of national feeling *per se* that went into the war for independence. The generation that fought the war was made up of a small group of leaders and a large mass of the populace. The latter had no impulse of loyalty to the new order; if they entered the fight, it was with reluctance, and only after promises of personal recognition or aggrandizement. The leaders, on the other hand, were markedly unselfish in their desire to serve a great cause. In the letters and proclamations of such men as Bolívar, San Martín, Hidalgo, Santander, Sucre, Morelos, there are passages which testify to the highest ideals of patriotism. Bolívar wrote: ". . . the earth of the fatherland above all. It has fashioned our being from its substance. Our life is nothing but the essence of our poor country. It is there that we have the witnesses to our birth, the creators of our existence who gave us our souls by rearing us. There are the graves of our fathers that demand security from us. Everything reminds us of our duty. Everything evokes sweet memories and gentle feelings in us. This was the stage of our innocence, our first love, our first impressions, and everything that influenced us."[2]

San Martín and Sucre made similar declarations, yet all these dedicated men learned to their chagrin that the essentials of social cohesion, of political experience and mutual trust, were sadly lacking in Latin America. Each one received his full measure of what Bolívar called *la ingratitud de las cosas americanas* (the thanklessness of American affairs). And even though we find many expressions of exalted patriotism, we are also obliged to recall the frequent occasions when these champions of a new order despaired of ever being able to forge their people into coherent bodies politic. It must also be remembered that their pessimistic expressions concerning the future stability of the Latin American countries were uttered long before tragedy had befallen the leaders of the independence movement. Bolívar wrote in 1819: "I am more and more convinced that neither liberty, nor laws, nor the best instruction, can transform us into decent people . . . even less into republicans or real patriots . . . in our veins flows not blood, but evil mingled with terror and fear."[3]

It was the horrifying spectacle of impending anarchy, internecine struggle, bloodshed and lawlessness that directed Bolívar and San Martín to search for solutions that might bring some sort of stability to Latin America. San Martín favored constitutional monarchy in the realm of domestic policy; Bolívar aimed at an authoritarian republic with a lifetime president. In international relations San Martín preferred a system of close alliances between neighboring republics such as Argentina and Chile; Bolívar dreamed of a federation of the Andes and a league of Latin American republics. Both men were in search of international cooperation between the countries of Latin America, and here we touch upon a theme which, since the early days of the nineteenth century, has never been absent from the Latin American scene: the idea of solidarity, or at least fraternity, between the severed parts of the former colonial empire. The battles of Maipú, Boyacá, Carabobo, Ayacucho, were won by the combined efforts of several republics, and the sentiment of continental brotherhood has never completely disappeared.

Professor Whitaker has recently observed that Bolívar's continentalism was not a denial but an affirmation of nationalism. "The issue he raised was not whether the former Iberian colonies should be turned into nation states, but simply how many such states there should be."[4] I should judge that continentalism was in reality more important than nationalism in Bolívar's ideological makeup. However, the fact remains that both Bolívar and San Martín soon became nationalistic idols. We will have more to say about this subject later on.

There are other aspects of the Latin American independence movement which must occupy the student of nationalism. They concern the social and economic characteristics of this great struggle, and not all of them have been sufficiently explored.[5] To begin with, the independence movement shattered the mercantilistic walls which Spain and Portugal had constructed to protect their possessions. Many of the Latin American countries adhered to the idea of free trade and established relations with Europe and North America. At first trade was indispensable for the maintenance of the patriotic armies; later it was continued as part of the liberal creed of most of the new republics. Furthermore, the new governments were immersed in financial difficulties attending the aftermath of a disastrous war and were forced to borrow heavily from the powerful capitalistic countries, especially England. It has been estimated that Peru, Colombia, Chile, and Argentina contracted loans totaling 17 million pounds sterling, thus setting the pattern for the strained relations between creditor and debtor nations which has so greatly colored the nationalistic sentiments of Latin America. Moreover, Europeans and North Americans were busy entering the fields of mining, railroad building, and steamship navigation. With the entrance of foreign commerce and industry, there came quite naturally a flood of ideas and ideologies that brought an element of fermentation into the life of Latin America. In addition, there were social changes wrought by the independence movement which made their effect felt throughout the century. In Mexico, Colombia, Venezuela, and Peru the revolution had initiated measures toward greater justice for the Indians and the classes made up of mixed races. The tribute which the Indians had paid for so many years was abolished; mulattoes and mestizos entered the national armies and, in exceptional cases, even the higher ranks of government.

The emancipation of the slaves was likewise set in motion, proceeding at various speeds in the different nations. By mid-century most of the new republics had freed their Negro populations without the turmoil that the same measure provoked in the United States. Thus one might safely affirm that a minimum of political equality was accomplished by the independence movement, accompanied by a new degree of social mobility unknown to the inhabitants of the former colonies.[6] Such steps, however, were rarely followed by legislative measures to establish a greater degree of social and economic equality. The latifundium, or large estate, continued to be the basic agricultural characteristic throughout Latin America. Bolívar envisaged a distribution of land to the soldiers of the patriotic armies, but this dream like many others did not become a reality; only officers of rank seem to have benefited. And thus we come logically to a significant question: To what extent was society transformed by the breakaway from Spain?

Any attempt to answer this question must be carefully qualified. The hierarchical order that Spain had established disappeared legally, but the idea of a stratified society was maintained in practice, albeit with certain modifications. Needless to say, the Spaniards had been eliminated as the highest-ranking class; in many instances those who had not been driven out of the country were penalized by new legislation. The aristocratic colonial society had suffered numerically during the war, since it had borne the brunt of the fighting. Its ranks were replenished by the acceptance of some of the military leaders who had distinguished themselves in the service of their country, but also by admitting members of the merchant class and a motley group of both Europeans and North Americans who had come to Latin America to make their fortunes. But it must be emphasized that society was no longer sealed off from the Indians, the mestizos, the mulattoes, and the Negroes. Their ascent could be delayed, but ultimately not prevented. The nineteenth century witnessed the rise of individuals from these groups in many parts of Latin America. Still, the old social order yielded only slowly, and the rise of entire groups and their integration into the class structure did not take place until the twentieth century.

Textbooks on the history of Latin America take up the years following the independence movement under the heading of "the national period," setting forth the independent development of some seventeen republics. But instead of young nations asserting the shape of their destinies, we encounter only sovereign political entities endeavoring to achieve nationhood. It would, therefore, seem fitting to compare the Latin American "nations" with their European or North American counterparts, and to ask whether internal communication and cohesion had been achieved to an extent that might qualify them as nations. If we take the year 1830 as our yardstick, it becomes clear that the difference is considerable.

By 1830 the European nations had already developed a wide range of varied nationalisms. The French took the lead with what may be called liberal or democratic nationalism, hoisting the ideas of 1789 as their standard. Edmund Burke had laid the foundation for a nationalism of conservative cast on which the German romanticists elaborated with theories of *Volksgeist* and organic growth. Herder's culture nationalism had blossomed into a messianic philosophy which Fichte was the first to expound in his famous *Addresses to the German People*. And this line of thought was soon to be adopted by the Russians.

Nationalism was an ideology pointing toward the future and promising greatness and meaning to the particular nation in which it arose. However, there is also an element of history in each of these nationalisms; the European countries affirmed their past at the same time that they exalted their future. It is not accidental that the historical disciplines flourished concurrently. The French found their destiny described in romantic color in Michelet's *History of France;* Hegel and Ranke performed a like service for Germany and Macaulay for England. Great historical figures took over the ordinance of national symbols; Joan of Arc and Martin Luther are examples of this tendency. In Latin America the situation is essentially different. Certain observers have noted that Latin America did not possess these lofty national symbols which were the support of European and North American nation-states.[7] In Europe the achievement of nationalism was the result of a long preparatory process: first the engendering of a national sentiment, then the creation of a national state which would eventually become a nation-state. In cases where the process had not reached completion, as in Germany and Italy, the movements toward consummation were well under way.

In Latin America there was no similar period of preparation. The attitude of the young countries toward their past was opaque and insecure. One might say they were searching for an identity of their own. The most important ties linking them to Europe were language and religion; Latin America confessed to only two languages and but one religion. Such uniformity might seem to predispose the new nations toward unity, especially when we compare it to the many languages and religions of the nations of Europe. But the political fragmentation that befell the continent after 1830 easily canceled out these possibilities of unity. There were several causes for this fragmentation, but without doubt the severance of ties with Spain and Portugal increased it. Latin America felt obliged to turn its back on the Iberian heritage, but there was little to take its place. European ideologies, such as liberalism, conservatism, romanticism, and later socialism, poured into the void but failed to fill it. In many instances the reception of European thought was more of an imitation than an adoption; the lack of great national symbols remained. The Latin American past as it appeared to the men of 1830 offered only the confused picture of indigenous civilizations destroyed by the

conquering Spaniard. It required more than a hundred years
to sort out the perplexities of the past and to reassemble them
in a convincing world vision.

There was, of course, the heroic generation of 1810, the
próceres, the great national and continental leaders, Bolívar,
San Martín, Sucre, Santander, Hidalgo, and Artigas. Although
during their lifetimes they had suffered cruelly at the hands
of the very people they had sought to deliver, they now became
the rallying points for much that goes under the name of
nationalism in Latin America. But for many years it was
patriotism rather than nationalism that was aroused by their
names. Moreover, there were many instances when the cloak
of prestige and power worn by heroes such as Bolívar and San
Martín was assumed by self-seeking *caudillos* as a cover and
an excuse for taking over the leadership of countries vacillating
between anarchy and despotism.

Whether the phenomenon of *caudillismo* can be traced back
to the early Spanish conquistadores or whether it was a result
of the wars for independence with their ensuing preponderance
of the military, *caudillismo* must be recognized as one of the
most persisting features of the Latin American world in the
nineteenth century and even in the twentieth century. And it is
not surprising, in a layered society with little intercommunica-
tion, that the military should deal with crises. In a manner of
speaking, the *caudillos* themselves were an expression of the
drive for national identity in a perverted way; their rule offered
a transition from the Spanish paternalism of the past to the
coveted nationhood of Latin America's future. There were even
caudillos who made open appeals to nationalism, such as
Rosas in Argentina, and thus won support for their often foolhardy actions.[8] The native population was accustomed to
overlordship; the Indians had respected and obeyed their
caciques, and the Negroes could remember the chieftains who
had directed their lives in the distant African jungles.

The independence movement freed Latin America from the
political domination of Europe, but it was a freedom that

closely resembled anarchy. The new nations were made vulnerable to the financial, economic, and cultural domination of other countries. The colonial society had been shaken and loosened but not revolutionized; caste remained enshrined and society continued to be stratified for generations. The years from 1830 to 1910 envisage but do not experience a national period. In some cases the vision has now been realized; in others the unsolved problems still harry the capitals of the Latin American countries.

CHAPTER III

The Road to Nationhood

WE HAVE SAID earlier that every study of nationalism must be functional; it must take into consideration the unique conditions of geographical location and economic development in which nations are established. In the case of Latin America this would include a recognition of the unfinished business bequeathed to the former colonies by the independence movement. Once more, a comparison with Europe may be helpful.

From the outset we should take note that territorial struggles such as those between France and Germany and borderline disputes or ethnic rivalries such as occurred in the Balkans are assigned a minor role in the nationalizing process of Latin America. Likewise, the significance of war as a means of cementing nationhood in the southern continent was, on the whole, negligible. Wars did occur, it is true, and their importance should not be minimized. Mexico lost half of her territory to the United States, but this land, now occupied by Texas, Arizona, New Mexico, and California, was not yet settled and was not an integral part of Mexico. The war of the Pacific and the war between Brazil, Paraguay, and Argentina likewise had little connection with the evolution of these countries toward nationhood. This difference of pattern between the Old World and the New World is not difficult to explain. It is caused by Latin America's geographical configuration: The population is distributed over vast areas; great empty spaces, unnavigable rivers, impenetrable jungles, and towering mountains separate the nations from each other and make any struggle over boundary lines either impossible, superfluous, or merely ridiculous. Many observers have commented on the population picture of Latin America. Cities, towns, villages, isolated dwellings are scattered over some nine million square miles. Most frequently, however, people are found in clusters, and some sections reach a high degree of density while others remain vacant and unvisited. These clusters may actually date back to pre-Columbian days, when the majority of Indians settled on the high plateaus of Mexico, Bogotá, Quito, Cuzco, etc., leaving the great steaming river valleys, the inland jungles, and the coastal strips to the alligator, the monkey, and the cormorant. The tendency toward cluster formations was increased by the Spanish conquest, adding nuclei of urban settlements which thinned out or even disappeared entirely as they approached frontiers.[1] The term "frontier" is a euphemism, since the continent was largely unexplored and frontiers were only vaguely drawn. After the liberation, however, the colonial frontiers between different parts of the Spanish empire and between them and Brazil had become international boundaries. As we have said, these frontiers led through uninhabited valleys, forests, or mountain passes. Clashes over frontiers might and did occur, but their historical significance is slight.

What actually characterized the existence of the Latin American people in the nineteenth century was isolation—from each other and from the rest of the world. To a large degree South America was a forgotten continent where seventeen countries which, in the words of the English historian Seeley, had obtained independence in a moment of distraction, lived in ignorance of their neighbors. The isolation was aggravated by the difficulties of travel and the tenuous lines of communication. In this respect, Latin Americans were a century behind their European contemporaries; a modern airplane covers in one hour the travel of four to five weeks in 1830. As a result, the budding nationalism in Latin America rarely focused against a neighboring country. It concerned itself with domestic problems which grew out of geographic and demographic circumstances.

To most students of Latin America, the internal struggle of the young republics over principles of federalism versus centralism, or liberalism versus conservatism, may appear to be nothing more than shadowboxing or hairsplitting. However, behind the verbal battles, which often led to bloody strife, lay the need to grapple with the problem of space, or rather man in a space not yet subdued by civilization.

The great achievement of the independence movement was the severing of the ties between the colonial territories and the mother countries. No inwrought ideology had been developed, and the young nations were obliged to work out their own answers to the problems of political organization. Spain and Portugal had practiced centralism, mitigated only by the inefficiency of its political apparatus. For many, therefore, centralism was discredited as a system of government, and various regions asserted their right to self-determination, acknowledging only nominal control by a national government. These individuals called themselves federalists and looked to the Constitution of the United States as an inspiration to local autonomy. But their radical federalism invited chaos, leading to anarchy and political fragmentation and the complete negation of political order. A reaction against the attitude of the federalists was supported by the more farsighted elements of society, who realized that a radical federalism would forestall any progressive efforts. This group was backed by the army and the church, both of which tended toward greater unity. The federalists and centralists were not divided along class lines and were even less divided by color or racial distinctions. Centralism was favored by the merchant class of Buenos Aires and federalism by the great estate owners of the hinterland. In Mexico, on the other hand, the wealthy aristocrats spoke out against the liberal autonomy of the provinces and in favor of a strong central government.

In general, it can be maintained that the emerging nations of the Latin American world were held together by personalities rather than by institutions or ideas at this incipient stage of their development. *Caudillos* like Rosas of Argentina or Santa Anna of Mexico became the embodiments of their nations for great numbers of their fellow citizens. *Personalismo* was the rule of the day. This holds true even for Brazil, which, after the abdication of Pedro I in 1831, was threatened by the same danger of fission that confronted the Hispanic American nations. When Pedro II assumed the throne with his famous dictum "*Já quero*" ("I want it now"), the enormous country was once more reunited, the centrifugal forces were checked, and a foundation for national development was established. In Chile it was an oligarchy rather than a *caudillo* that took over the reins of government, ended the frantic turnover of constitutions, and brought the country under a class rule of the *criollos*, by the *criollos*, and for the *criollos*.

But not all the countries achieved even this transitory stability. In Colombia, Bolivia, Ecuador, Uruguay, and in Central America, political life continued to be anarchic. Their histories have the erratic upsurge and downward plunge which doctors observe on the fever charts of their patients. Social and economic ailments continued to plague the young and harassed countries. The probing historian will find it difficult, if not impossible, to see traces of nationalism in bodies politic so often convulsed to the point of disruption.

In those countries where unity had been preserved or had been reestablished, nationalism did appear, though frequently in foreign disguise, a fact which further complicates our study. Latin America borrowed freely from England, the United States, and France to express its own national aspirations and emotions. The result is confusing and forces a distinction between substance and form. Furthermore, problems of national growth varied and presented different aspects according to the ethnic foundations of the young nations. Countries having a large Indian or Negro population, or both, faced problems essentially different from countries mainly populated by a constantly replenished white European stock; this was especially true of Argentina, Uruguay, Chile, and Costa Rica. Having in mind the days of San Martín, the Argentinian Juan Bautista Alberdi drew up a program for these countries which presaged nationalism: "It is not the military alliance of our continent . . . which is called upon to organize this time. America's interests have changed. . . . The illness that the great curative council is called upon to treat is not the sickness of foreign oppression, but the sickness of poverty, underpopulation, backwardness, and misery. The present enemies of America are . . . within it —its roadless deserts, its enslaved and unexplored rivers, its coasts underpopulated through the poison of selfish restrictions, its tariff and customs anarchy, absence of credit . . . these are the great enemies of America."[2] Here then, the idea of the melting pot was applied to merge the Americans of Hispanic descent with European immigrants.

On the other hand, the Indian population of the Andean countries had to be integrated into the political sodality by means of a slow process of education, economic rehabilitation, and political enfranchisement, projects which were spread out over a century and are still by no means completed. In other countries, like Brazil, where a large slave population of African origin expected its freedom, the evolution followed still different lines to achieve racial democracy and a kind of peaceful co-existence of heterogeneous ethnic groups. Economic tensions and class conflicts between racial groups were an added complication. Small wonder that the growth toward nationhood was slow and circuitous.

It has been said that Latin American nationalism was liberal and benign in character, that it was introverted and domestically oriented.[3] There is a qualified truth in this observation. However, we cannot overlook the fact that some of the Latin American nations entered into conflicts with the European powers and even more with the rapidly expanding United States, and that these conflicts shaped, for better or worse, the character of the countries involved.

A glance at the international relations of Latin America during the nineteenth century shows that the great powers, especially England and France, did not recognize the new countries as fully independent states and were easily tempted to encroach on them. However, what conflicts there were, such as those between Argentina and England, or between Argentina and France, or those resulting from British attempts to gain a foothold in Central America, remained skirmishes which revealed the military weaknesses of the Latin American world without seriously endangering its independence. It is in the turbulent history of Mexico that we find the first onslaught of American imperialism, and it is in Mexico that soon thereafter a great European power attempted to reestablish its influence in the western hemisphere.

The conflict between Mexico and the United States seemed preordained; after more than a century, it still bears all the marks of an irrepressible struggle. The actual events were not necessarily bound to occur as they did, but a clash of some kind could hardly have been avoided.

The westward expansion of the United States was an instinctive, irresistible movement, something in the line of a natural force. Certainly no country as weak and unstable as the newly independent Mexico could hope to thwart its advance. Long before John L. O'Sullivan had used it as a political slogan, the idea of a "manifest destiny," the vision of multiplying millions spreading freely across a country allotted them by a beneficent providence, was an inborn and inbred American ideal.[4] It was an ideal that had been advanced step by step, through the Louisiana Purchase, through the acquisition of Florida in 1819, and through the explorations of the early pioneers. No doubt the American government would have preferred to follow this pattern of purchase, negotiation, and peaceful infiltration when it came to the lands that became Texas, New Mexico, Arizona, and California. These were vast reaches of open land, holding great promise for the mass of farmers, ranchers, and entrepreneurs who were eager to occupy them. And this territorial settlement was forbidden to fall into the odious category of colonization: "We have not adopted a system of colonization," observed a leading member of the Jackson administration, "and it is to be hoped we never shall."⁵ Indeed, the western expansion did appear to escape the odium of colonial enterprises: it occurred in the temperate zone; it did not depend on the exploitation of subjugated people; the occupied land could be organized in a form provided for by the American constitution.

On the other hand, it was to be expected that the Mexicans might have their own point of view and that possibly it might not conform to the attitude of the north. The Mexicans felt they had indisputable rights in the southwestern lands; they asserted that the settlers who had come into Texas had recognized the sovereignty of the Mexican republic; they argued further that the continued immigration of Anglo-Saxons would increase the spread of Protestantism and slavery, both of which institutions were repugnant to the young state. It might be protested that the Mexican government would have displayed more political prudence had she accepted the offer from Washington and avoided a hopeless conflict. But the powerful emotion of national pride had been aroused on both sides of the border, and in Mexico the avenue to compromise was closed by the vanity and overconfidence of Santa Anna.

The story of the years from 1836 to 1848 needs no retelling in this context. Mexico became the victim of its political system —anarchy tempered by *caudillo* rule. When the final documents were drawn up, Mexico had lost half her territory and had suffered a rankling defeat. Certain powerful influences in the United States used the weakness of the Latin American world as an excuse to push their claims still further; the greedy eyes of the expansionists swiveled in many directions—toward Cuba, Santo Domingo, and the northern provinces of Mexico. But in 1861 the outbreak of the Civil War foreclosed all these ambitious plans.

The Mexican War had, however, clarified some important points, notably, the strength of the expansionist forces in the United States and the weakness of the Latin American republics. This variance remained a constant in the international relations of the continent and hence a constant in the development of Latin American nationalism. The fear of the *coloso del norte* was real enough and well founded. It was further strengthened by the continued and growing penetration of Latin American countries by American venture capital, which often used piratical means to its ends. Moreover, there seemed to be no effective defense against the American encroachment. The Monroe Doctrine had been used by the United States to further its own aims, and European assistance even if obtainable (which seemed less than likely) might very well be worse than the ill it sought to remedy. All attempts at federation or cooperative alliance were either outright failures or treaties without teeth.

As for the history of Mexico, the war with the United States had a catalytic effect. In its aftermath came the ban on the military *caudillo* and the rise of leaders from a different layer of society, namely, the Indian. The redemption of the Indian had been envisaged even in the days of Hidalgo and Morelos, but the forces of reaction and traditionalism had overpowered it. Now it rose again, and for the first time in Mexican history leaders appeared whose very features confirmed the claims of a race that had been subjugated for three centuries. Benito Juárez and Juan Álvarez were the most notable of these new men of authority.

La Reforma, as the great movement was called, represents a peculiar mixture of liberal ideas of European origin and native aspirations that sprang from the soil of the new continent. Liberal ideas had made their appearance as early as 1833 and had been embodied in a series of laws to which no heed was paid by anyone. The year 1848 had brought a revival of European liberalism that had a marked influence on the Mexicans. There was a literary renaissance which had its center in the Academía de San Juan de Letran and gave voice to a romantic nationalism of liberal coloring. Its literature has been called "public service literature" by Pedro Henríquez Ureña, literature *engagé*, destined to kindle the flames of revolutionary patriotism.[6]

The program of La Reforma singled out two groups as its foremost targets: the church and the army. Both institutions in reality enjoyed a status of immunity under Mexican law, since they had their own courts of law and were therefore exempted from the jurisdiction of the state in important matters. Two famous laws, La Ley Juárez and La Ley Lerdo, were attempts to remedy the situation by abolishing the *fueros* (special courts dealing with affairs of the church and the army) and by cutting through the economic foundations on which the church based its position.

The Roman Catholic Church was, at this time, the largest landowner in Mexico, with control of an estimated fifty percent of all real estate. La Ley Lerdo obliged the church to forfeit all land not specifically delegated to the exercise of religious duties. The liberals hoped that this land would be used to convert the landless peons into peasants. These ideas of secular reform, which were both anticlerical and antimilitaristic, were accompanied by the reaffirmation of human rights, parliamentary power, and states' rights. These concepts were put forth in a new constitution, drafted in 1857. The men of La Reforma did not realize that their action had turned the key in a Pandora's box. All of the vested interest of Mexican society (the church, the great landowners, and the officers of the armed forces) stood to lose, or stood in fear of losing, their predominant position. The church lost no time in employing the weapon of excommunication, which in semifeudal Mexico was still a powerful threat. A civil war was initiated, which degenerated into an international affair, albeit with unique features. The "war of the reform" is not just another episode in the tortuous history of the Latin American people. It is a turning point, even though its implications in the history of the continent were not immediately evident.[7]

We have already noted that the conservative groups pooled their aversions to liberal reform—the church supported the cause of the landed aristocracy, the aristocracy backed the army, and so forth. But they were now guided by a new intention, namely, to find added support for their cause among their peers in church, army, and society in the Old World, especially in France and Spain. These were crucial years for the Catholic conservatives of Europe; they were threatened by the liberal movements in Italy and Germany, and they were also fearful of the rising tide of social movements engendered by the industrial revolution.

Napoleon III, who posed as the defender of the papacy in Italy and as the pacifier of the bourgeoisie in France, seemed to be the natural choice as a leader of the conservative forces in search of outside help. His empire might likewise profit from overseas acquisitions which could, perhaps, be gained at a minimum expenditure of gold or lives. The American Civil War offered a unique opportunity to disregard the Monroe Doctrine, and Napoleon gave himself over to dreams of an empire stretching from the Mason-Dixon line to the Isthmus of Panama.

The French intervention occurred in the backwash of a dispute over Mexican customs. Three European powers were determined to seize the revenues from Mexican customs in lieu of payments on loans which Mexico had been unable to meet. But by 1860, Juárez had become president under the new constitution and was fiercely resolved to put the anticlerical legislation into practice. When Napoleon finally chose a Hapsburg prince as a candidate for the Mexican throne, the conflict was heightened to the point of a tragic encounter. The unfortunate Archduke Maximilian, though well disposed toward the Mexican nation, was nevertheless a descendant of Charles V, whose name was a sanguinary reminder of the conquest of Cortés.

At the beginning of the conflict, Juárez could muster very

little in the way of an opposing force and withdrew from the capital, leaving the French in possession. Maximilian and Carlota entered Mexico City in 1864, and their new empire was speedily recognized by the European powers. But Maximilian soon learned that there is little repose for him who rests on bayonets. With the close of the Civil War, the United States was again free to act, but contented herself, for the time being, by supporting Juárez with arms while impressing the French emperor with the danger of open intervention. Napoleon, now faced with the far greater danger of a united Germany on his eastern frontier, withdrew the French forces in 1867, breaking, by this act, his solemn promise to Maximilian, who became the first victim of the Mexican fury. Juárez took over at once, and the "empire" collapsed like a house of cards.[8]

It may, perhaps, be an exaggeration to say that the shots that killed Maximilian in June of 1867 were heard round the world. The struggle between the ill-fated emperor and the native leader, Juárez, does, however, seem to take place on the same historical plane where Montezuma and Cortés played out their roles in the destiny of Latin America. This time it was the Indian who triumphed. Juárez deserves the title "father of his country" even more than Hidalgo; he had defended the existence of Mexico as an independent nation, and as such, she was never again to be threatened.

The year 1867 marks the high point of Juárez's career. The aftermath of La Reforma was an anticlimax. Once more Mexico proved that it is an easier task to defend independence against external enemies than to establish freedom at home.

The basic problems which Mexican liberalism had promised to solve had not been tackled. Although the church and the military had been discredited, no elite had emerged that could shoulder the destiny of Mexico in an age of industrialism and capitalism. Nor was liberalism more than a hollow ideology; its tenets of *laisser-faire* and *laisser-aller* did not meet the pressing needs of the devastated country. *Personalismo*, this curse of the previous period, continued to poison the emancipated state;

ironically, the age-old habit of government by man rather than by law found in Juárez a new idol. And finally the problems of land distribution remained unsolved, except in the case of some church lands which were shifted from the hands of the clergy into those of a new class of *hacendados,* a class composed of mestizos and whites.

Mexico had defended its existence as a nation, but the breach between ruler and ruled had not been closed. The constitution of 1857 was still on the books, but it was evoked only at the pleasure of the seated powers.

After the death of Juárez, in 1872, *caudillismo* became once more the order of the day, and militarism asserted itself anew. Porfirio Díaz, mestizo by origin and soldier in bearing, became the president in 1876 under the slogan "effective suffrage—no reelection." Díaz held the power until his downfall in 1910! He preferred the tangible results of economic development imposed from above to the idealistic hopes of the generation of reform. Under his rule, Mexico became a stable and prosperous country. The *Pax Porfiriana* came as a relief after fifty years of anarchy, bloodshed, and civil strife, but it demanded its price.[9]

A new ideology now came to the fore, that of positivism. In accordance with the theory of Auguste Comte, the leaders of the regime called themselves *los científicos* (the scientists). They were the wolves in sheep's clothing of positivistic dogma, ready to devour the despised Indian. Mexico, it was said, could no more absorb democracy than a sponge can absorb a tortilla. Indians had to be treated as children, and the scientific experts assumed the role of the parent who "knows best." This attitude opened Mexico to the entrepreneur, whether national or foreign, and encouraged exploitation in the name of progress. One percent of the population controlled most of the land worked by the peons. The church was permitted to return to its policy of accumulating riches; in exchange for this privilege, she admonished the poor to "love their humble state and to work."[10]

The entire phenomenon of Porfirio Díaz, however, should

not be considered only in the context of Mexican history. Its role in the encounter between the Indo-American world and western capitalism endows it with greater significance. We shall return to this later in our study.

Let us now turn our attention to the development of certain other Latin American republics. Their histories do not parallel one another, yet there are structural analogies to be observed and considered. The primary political issue was the struggle between the forces that took constitutionalism as their goal and those that still adhered to the ancient pattern of personalism. In certain countries a balance was achieved which allowed a peaceful evolution over a fairly long stretch of time; in others, however, political and social convulsions continued to rack the land. In Brazil, Argentina, and Chile the outlook was hopeful; in Colombia, Venezuela, Ecuador, Peru, and Bolivia the horizon was darker. Professor J. J. Johnson notes that Venezuela suffered fifty revolutions during the nineteenth century; Colombia experienced twenty-seven civil wars; Ecuador set up eleven different constitutions during a period of sixty-five years, while Bolivia, in the same period, was torn by some sixty-odd revolutions and lost six presidents by assassins' hands.[11]

Shocking as these statistics may have seemed to the nineteenth century, they do not greatly vary from the course of events during the twentieth century. Their counterparts may be observed in many underdeveloped countries that have broken free from colonial rule. Nor is the struggle between constitutionalism and personalism unknown to our times.

In Brazil the problem of constitutionalism versus personalism was dramatized by the shift from monarchy to republic, but even the last Brazilian monarch, Pedro the Magnanimous (Pedro II), was not a true representative of the personality cult. He adhered to the principles of constitutional monarchy as embodied in the two houses of the empire, reserving for himself the "moderating power" of a veto which gave him the imperial prerogative of dismissing recalcitrant public servants or dissolving the chambers if he felt that conditions in the state warranted such action.

Today's generation of Brazilian historians are inclined to judge Pedro II harshly. They feel he did not understand the budding commercial and industrial interests of Brazil and hence did not take advantage of their vast potential; they accuse him of catering to the aristocracy of plantation owners and shelving the slavery problem; they condemn him for his abuse of the veto power. Whatever the truth may be, Pedro should still be given credit for holding the empire together and protecting it from the centrifugal forces which had caused the dissolution of the Spanish realm. In addition, a certain amount of industrial advance did take place, in railroad building and steamship travel, for instance. Admittedly this was a drop in the bucket when gauged by the enormity of the task.[12]

The Brazilian national anthem sings of a "giant land eternally lying in a splendid cradle." A more prosaic but more accurate statement might be that Brazil was a great land in search of a people. And here we come upon the most sensitive question to plague the empire. Pedro II was opposed to slavery and had set an example by freeing his slaves early in his reign. This, however, was a personal act that did not commit the landholding aristocracy who depended on slave labor to maintain the sugar plantations. Although officially the slave trade had been abandoned, large numbers of slaves were continuously smuggled into the country. After the Emancipation Proclamation of Abraham Lincoln, Brazil was the only country in the western hemisphere to maintain slavery. Obviously it could not withstand the increased pressure of a liberal public opinion. There was, however, still another harmful aspect of slavery. An enormous country like Brazil could only begin to fulfill its destiny when the great empty spaces became populated, but the immigrants who might settle in the plains and the valleys would be loath to make their homes in a land where "agricultural labor was equated with . . . slavery."[13]

Hence it was logical that slavery came to be considered a

corollary of the empire, and the abolition of slavery spelled the abolition of the monarchy. In May of 1888, all slaves were emancipated under the law. A year later Brazil was proclaimed a republic. This was accomplished in good Brazilian fashion, without bloodshed and without violence—one might even say, without bitterness.

The legacy of imperial Brazil and its great landowning class should not, however, be underestimated. Although the abolition of slavery went far toward ruining the old aristocracy, a considerable part of its outlook on life was preserved under the republic and has given to Brazil both the advantage and the virtue of a patrician tradition. Brazil was, in more ways than one, an underdeveloped country: it had no university; education was the privilege of the chosen few; and, as we have noted, economic advancement was slow. But, at least the bitterness and senseless sacrifice of civil war had been avoided, and the country could continue on the road to constitutionalism without a major break.

In Brazil, as in Mexico, the philosophy of Auguste Comte served as an ideological shield for the transition from colonial to capitalistic economy. The first constitution of 1891 adopted Auguste Comte's motto of "order and progress." Perhaps more important than any philosophical influence was Brazil's trend away from Great Britain's parliamentary system and her drift toward the basic concepts of the constitution of the United States. There was no doubt that federalism suited the enormous country better than a centralized monarchy. The twenty states composing the federal republic enjoyed a good deal of autonomy; the constitution left economic and social matters in an indeterminate state, and the government shelved any responsibility for administrating them. As a result, education was neglected and scant progress was made. The republic was run by a small oligarchy still dominated by the landholding aristocracy. However, important geographical shifts had taken place.[14] The northeastern region, where sugar had been king, sank into oblivion; the southern states—Rio de Janeiro, São Paulo, Rio

Grande do Sul—with their large coffee crops were in the ascendant. Moreover, the abolition of slavery had a stimulating effect on immigration. More than 200,000 Europeans came into Brazil during 1891 (most of them from southern Europe), and the flow continued well into the period preceding the First World War.

In Brazil, as elsewhere, a process of nationalization took place of which at least the enlightened Brazilians were conscious. In the words of one historian of the times, "It is the history of the formation of a new type by the action of five factors, a semiconscious formation in which miscegenation played a dominant role. Every Brazilian is a mestizo, if not biologically at least culturally. The agents which have brought about this basic situation are the Portuguese, the Negro, the Indian, the physical environment, and the imitation of foreign culture."[15] One could assert that there was already a national character in evidence, and, obviously, national character was a prerequisite to nationalism.

Argentina had reached a degree of political and social cohesion earlier than Brazil. The *caudillo* Rosas had driven some of the best minds of the country into exile, but in the long run this was a blessing in disguise. Men like Alberdi, Sarmiento, and Esteban Echeverría, and others of the generation of 1837, found in exile both the opportunity and the necessary objectivity for a thorough reflection on Argentina as it really was.[16] "Governments," said Alberdi, "are nothing more than the work and the fruit of societies; they reflect the character of the people who create them.[17] And the same thought reverberates through the writings of all the men of this period. They had absorbed the thought of German romanticists like Savigny and the ideas of such French socialists as Saint-Simon and Fourier, and they were bent on shaping the soul of the Argentinian nation. Sarmiento studied the life of the gaucho in his famous *Facundo*, and found that "space is the evil that afflicts the . . . Republic." He saw no hope for the future except in the cities, where he found everything that characterizes civilized people. He believed there were two distinct societies, two peoples, each foreign to the other. In other words, there was Buenos Aires, and there were the provinces, and the work of the generation of 1837 was to effect the conciliation of these two elements and the organization of the nation.

Since the evil in Argentina was the desert, the desert had to be conquered by whatever means possible: by filling it with people—hence Alberdi's slogan, *gobernar es poblar* (to govern is to populate)—by making the rivers navigable, by opening arteries of communication. "Which constitution," asked Alberdi, "is best suited to the desert? It is the one that makes the desert disappear."

The fall of Rosas brought these ideas to the fore. A constitution drafted in 1853 expressed the triumph of federalism moderated to the extent that it made efficient government feasible. It was the victory of what Alberdi had called *la república posible*, a victory of political realism through which alone Argentina could achieve nationhood.[18]

The incorporation of Buenos Aires into the republic presented the most thorny problem. The port had a long tradition of privilege and leadership which it was loath to surrender. But the matter was solved in 1862 when Bartolomé Mitre, himself a *porteño*, became president of the nation. From 1862 to 1880 the country was led by three powerful figures, Mitre, Sarmiento, and Avellaneda, each devoted to national unity and the prevalence of liberal principles. These men realized that development of the country had been too long delayed, and that it could be hastened only by Argentina's participation in the main element of nineteenth-century western life—economic expansion.

The way to accomplish this was to open the country to European immigration. It was necessary to develop a policy of colonization and to direct the incoming population to those regions where agriculture promised a glorious future. Argentina turned to the production of wheat and meat, which in turn brought about the construction of railroads and the modernization of the harbor facilities of Buenos Aires. New agricultural centers sprang up, but Buenos Aires continued to be the nerve center of the new commonwealth.

Every liberal of this period was convinced that both European immigrants and native-born Argentinians must be educated. No one recognized this more clearly than Sarmiento, who had written about popular education long before he had become president. He had studied the educational systems of Europe and the United States and had accepted education as the most effective tool to suppress the "barbarism" of the desert. As a result, primary and secondary schools multiplied and became one of the elements in the forging of a nation, leavened with both new and old components.

In retrospect, it can be said that the experiment was successful up to a point. Without a doubt the liberals achieved what Romero has termed "conciliation and organization of the nation." Yet the barriers of class remained unscaled, and the organization of society continued to reflect the hierarchical structure whose basis had been laid by Spain. A landed aristocracy retained the reins of power. It was an elite, an oligarchy as it was later called, separated from the masses not so much by title as by wealth. And land was still the symbol of consolidated wealth, the only thing to bring prestige and recognition to a man and his family.[19]

But the masses, as we have called them, were not an undifferentiated sea of people. The immigrants presented no problem at first; their impact on Argentinian nationhood came later. But there were the inhabitants of the pampas, the gauchos, who seemed to be separated from the life of the times and for whom the advancement of a capitalistic civilization could only mean the destruction of their own way of life. It was during this period that the poet José Hernández created the myth of the gaucho in his famous epic *Martín Fierro*. The hero belonged to a bygone era; he might be called a fighter for personal independence, a rebel against society and conformity. But was he the man of the future; would he fit into the framework of legal life and the complexity of technical advancement?[20]

Perhaps it was not an accident that the gaucho reached the elevation of a national legend at the very time that new economic forces put an end to his carefree existence. The Argentinian past was poor in symbols of a national character, and it was only natural that the country turned to the courage, the independence, and the arrogance of the gaucho for the warp and the woof of her national personality. The gaucho element thus became an integral part of the Argentinian character.

Early in our century, one of Argentina's presidents described the quality of his country as follows: "Argentinians refuse to accept any truth which might make them inferior to anyone else. Theirs is the greatest city in the world; their frontier mountains are the highest, and their pampas the widest; theirs the most beautiful lakes, the best cattle, the richest vineyards, and the loveliest women . . . perhaps it is this overwhelming pride of the Argentinians that leads them to believe that they can live aloof from any interdependence of nations; that they are self-sufficient."[21]

There is, however, an additional significance of the gaucho ideal and its projection onto the national scene. For here was an ideal to which the immigrant, perhaps especially the immigrant, could cling. Argentina entered into a period of rapid population growth in 1880. The first national census, taken in 1869, notes 1,830,214 inhabitants; by 1895 the population had more than doubled. The percentage of foreigners climbed to 25.4. This is the Alluvial Era in which Buenos Aires rapidly became one of the great metropolises of the world.[22]

Argentinian society was thus transformed under successive waves of immigration. Ortega y Gasset formulated this process in the following words: "Thousands and thousands of new men arrive on the Atlantic coast of Argentina with no other spiritual possession than a fierce individual hunger; men abnormally lacking in all interior discipline, men uprooted from their native societies . . . But the immigrant is not an Italian, nor a Spaniard, nor a Syrian. He is an abstract being whose personality has been reduced to the exclusive aim of seeking a fortune."[23] They sought not only a fortune, but a new social and communal identity. It should not seem surprising that they adhered to the ideal of national pride and self-sufficiency and "forthwith found salvation in surrender."[24]

Shortly before his death, Sarmiento, the great advocate of immigration, issued a warning that the ever-rising tide of strangers might endanger the foundation on which Argentina was built: "One does not construct a homeland," he said, "without patriotism as its cement, nor does one build as the soul and glory of a nation a city without citizens."

The great influx of immigrants tended at first to harden the class structure rather than soften it. The growing wealth of the young nation transformed the elite into an ostentatious upper class that considered itself entitled to live off the fat of the land. Many of the great landlords did not even know where their properties were located; speculation in land was rampant, as was the exploitation of immigrant labor. Industrial establishments began to appear, credit expanded, and foreign loans accelerated the pace of economic activities. As in other parts of the world, the railroads and the telegraph helped to strengthen national unity. In spite of foreign immigration and economic transformation, Argentina offers a picture of political stability at the close of the nineteenth century. The members of the ruling class were responsible for this fortunate state of affairs; they considered themselves entitled to preserve their leadership, and they ran the country with a "conservative liberalism" which, at the time, excluded the enfranchisement of the popular elements of society. The office of the president became all-important, far outweighing the other two branches of government. There was no organized opposition to check the power of the oligarchy, who exercised control to suit their convenience. Only after the first generation of immigrants had been incorporated into the body politic was there a demand for popular

democracy. We will not concern ourselves here with the formation of parties and sub-parties in Argentina. It was the Radical
Civic Union that was finally victorious and achieved power
under the leadership of Hipólito Irigoyen in 1916.

Three other republics are pertinent to our study of the growth
of nationhood in Latin America. They are, in order of importance, Chile, Uruguay, and Costa Rica.

The aftermath of the independence movement in Chile had
been turbulent, but brief. By 1832 a degree of political stability
and social order had emerged which lasted until 1919.

Two factors are basic to Chilean history: its geography and
the composition of its master class.[25] Chile's geography is that of
an island country. It is separated from its neighbors by high
mountain ranges, deserts, and dense forests. On a map of South
America, Chile looks like a shoestring lying along the edge of
the continent. It has 3,000 miles of coastline, but it has little
depth of land mass. The development of a merchant marine was
essential for Chile and was started early in the life of the republic. Only a small portion of Chile's land is arable, but in isolated spots there was considerable mineral wealth, which helped
support the national economy. The exploitation of these minerals, however, presented a considerable problem. Chile has coal,
nitrates, copper, and sulphur; nitrates held the greatest promise
in the nineteenth century. As a result of the increase in agriculture in Europe and the stepping up of the armament race before
1914, nitrates were in great demand for the manufacture of fertilizers and explosives. Chile was determined to secure the monopoly of the nitrates located in the Desert of Atacama, and in
the War of the Pacific, in which she defeated both Peru and
Bolivia, she obtained her objective. This is one of the few cases
where we can detect economic nationalism accompanied by aggressive tendencies among the countries of Latin America. Once
the control of the nitrate fields had been achieved, Chile exploited them by means of a labor population which was made to
work under miserable conditions and for starvation wages. This
leads us to the second factor: the composition of the ruling class.

We possess a penetrating description of Chile's "gentry" in George McCutcheon McBride's book on Chile.[26] The picture of master and man that he has given offers the best clue to an understanding of Chilean society. Chile had, and still has, a master class which dates back to the days of Hispanic rule. It is a landholding aristocracy, well educated, highly cultured, and widely traveled. For an entire century, it was in full control of Chile's national life.

A tenant class furnished all menial work, whether in the fields, the corrals, or the households. The workers were called *rotos* (the ragged ones) and made up the fixed tenantry of the great estates. The masters were allied with the commercial interests of Santiago de Chile and Valparaiso; they also had a voice in banking and mining interests. But it was really the land which assured them their status and their political influence. Their situation was not unlike that of the English gentry of the eighteenth century. The estates were run in a paternalistic manner, masters and servants forming a great family. The master expected and received both obedience and respect. Those who served him were entitled to care and to charity if necessary.

Chilean society was agrarian, and it set the mold for the social structure of the country. The country's industrial population was descended from the *rotos*. The middle class, as it developed during the century, owed much to the gentry. The clergy, the university professors, the writers, the musicians, the statesmen, and the lawyers felt they belonged to the elite. As in many aristocratic societies, those who had once had wealth continued to maintain their status, while those who had come into riches by means of commercial ventures were not automatically accepted by the inner circle.

The upper and lower groups were not sharply divided by their racial background. Both were descendants of Spaniards and Indians, although the majority of the masters passed for white and a great proportion of the lower class were taken for Indians. "But all were Chileans, speaking one language and claiming no marked difference of race."[27]

Chilean society of the nineteenth century presented a cultivated, intellectual profile. It received such distinguished men as
Andrés Bello, who helped shape the educational system; it gave
refuge to Sarmiento when he was exiled from Argentina; its his-
toriography was renowned. But this very aristocracy of character and outlook was poor preparation for the coming of the
industrial age. True, immigrants had been received, both from
Germany and Italy, and some from Spain, but their coming had
not changed the basic nature of Chilean society.

Chile's constitutional history during the nineteenth century
shows only surface changes. Liberals battled conservatives over
such issues as the respective virtues of the parliamentary and
the presidential systems, but these struggles were superficial, and
underneath the same group continued to rule—*plus ça change,
plus c'est la même chose*. Until 1891, Chile preferred the strong
president, though never to the point of embracing outright the
personal regime of the military *caudillo*. After 1891 the pendu-
lum swung back to congressional rule. However, political consciousness as well as political responsibility was limited to the
upper class, who controlled representation on all levels.

The First World War provoked several changes in Chile.
Sympathies were divided; the upper classes had economic ties
with Great Britain and cultural ties with France, but the German immigrants in southern Chile naturally favored Germany,
and the army was largely influenced by German experts who
had helped to reorganize the military forces.

The end of the war brought a decline in the demand for nitrates and plunged the country into an economic crisis which
was the first serious challenge to the oligarchy. It was symptomatic that the son of an Italian immigrant who had worked in
the nitrate fields himself should run for president. He was the
candidate of the Liberal Alliance, which was opposed by the
National Union. Alessandri was the first representative of the
lower classes, but he also found favor with the middle class,
who objected to permanent control by the landed interests. The
election was very close, and a special tribunal was finally ap-

pointed before Alessandri was declared the victor. His triumph parallels that of Irigoyen in Argentina. In both countries popular democracy seemed to be on the march and nationhood had passed from the dangerous phase where centrifugal forces could threaten its existence. Alessandri promised more than he could deliver—the nationalization of the mines and the nitrate fields, the enfranchisement of women—but a greater popular participation in government mark his tenure as a turning point in Chilean history.[28]

Uruguay presents the most startling case of Latin American development. Before 1810 it held no independent place in the Spanish empire, being a part of the region called La Plata. Montevideo had become an important commercial port by the end of the eighteenth century, but it was consistently denied recognition by the Spanish authorities. When the revolution began, Artigas, a member of the Creole aristocracy, took it upon himself to rouse a sense of national consciousness in the small country known only as the *banda oriental,* the eastern shore of the Río de la Plata. Although Artigas's life, like the lives of so many leaders of the independence movement, ended in despair and exile, the impetus of his endeavor prevailed.[29] Uruguay became an independent republic, not because of a feeling of nationhood, but because it could function as a buffer between its two powerful neighbors, Brazil and Argentina, both of whom coveted the *banda oriental.* British diplomacy was instrumental in bringing about this settlement.

However, diplomatic recognition did not mean true independence, and Uruguay continued to be a political football, forced to suffer frequent intervention by its neighbors. The domestic history of the small country was likewise a hectic scramble between the "whites" and the "reds" to obtain control, their distinguishing criteria, however, being almost nil. Governments were thrown out of office, officials were assassinated, all without plan or goal. It was an inglorious history; there was not even a Rosas or a Santa Anna about whom the people could boast.

Yet conditions presaging nationhood were better in Uruguay

than in many other parts of Latin America. It was a small republic, but not too small for cattle breeding on a large scale; the climate favored European immigration; and more important, there were no racial minorities to absorb. At the end of the century the country underwent a remarkable transformation. Civilianism prevailed in the government, and the vision of one man made Uruguay the first welfare state in the western world.

This man was José Batlle y Ordóñez, who, first as a newspaperman and later as the acknowledged leader of his people, brought on a change as deep-reaching as can be claimed by any statesman of the twentieth century. As one of his observers has said, ". . . in no other country . . . has any one man so deeply left his imprint upon the life and character of a people as did José Batlle y Ordóñez upon Uruguay."[30]

Batlle y Ordóñez's vision focused on one essential. If *caudillismo, personalismo,* and the evils of militarism were to be overcome, it was not enough to draft a constitution and subscribe to the motto of "order and progress." Unless the people had a stake in society, the rift between leaders and followers would remain as wide as ever. A solid social fabric could be woven only when and if the welfare of the state meant the welfare of all. It has been rightly said that every state is a welfare state in one form or another.[31] In the case of Uruguay it took the form of socialist security combined with a high measure of democratic freedom.

We have already noted that the ethnic conditions in Uruguay were propitious for the establishment of a welfare state. The country was small—it was not plagued by what Alberdi called the "desert" of Argentina; there had been no great latifundia; the wealthy did not flaunt their wealth or in other ways set themselves apart from the less prosperous immigrants. The Uruguayan intelligentsia fitted easily into this picture. The name of José Enrique Rodó comes to mind; his motto had been "To improve oneself is to live." And Rodó, the author of *Ariel,* was also the spokesman of a typical Latin idealism which defended spiritual values against the crass materialism of the industrial civilization. Thus Batlle y Ordóñez found a favorable climate when he suggested that the state could act as an agent to close "the enormous gap between the rich and the poor." A far-reaching social legislation was introduced between 1915 and 1919 which made Uruguay the chief laboratory for social experimentation in America.[32]

This secular philosophy of Batlle y Ordóñez is deeply implanted in every Uruguayan mind; the people believe that it is the business of the state to set up an equitable distribution of national income and at the same time assure the maximum well-being of the populace. It is of interest to note that this ideology was proclaimed before the Mexican or the Russian revolution set the pace for socialistic experiments.

But the egalitarian character of Batlle y Ordóñez's program must not occupy us here to the exclusion of its other aspects. Uruguay, like the greater number of Latin American countries, had developed its industries and its communication system with the aid of foreign investors, notably Great Britain. Batlle y Ordóñez hoped that the state would replace foreign influence by the nationalization of such vital services as railroads, telephones, insurance, etc. To a large extent his hopes have been realized, and one may, therefore, conclude that there is an undercurrent of economic nationalism bolstering the Uruguayan experiment. It is hardly surprising that democratic state socialism found easy acceptance among Uruguayans, bringing as it did a more advanced type of social legislation than any that existed in Europe at this time, let alone the nations of the western hemisphere.

It seems probable that these benefits have been more significant for the Uruguayans than the constitutional measures designed to put an end to *caudillismo*. The constitution of 1919 outlined a complicated system of shared responsibilities shouldered by the president, the legislature, and the majority and minority parties. Later in its history Uruguay adopted the Swiss system of government by executive council. There is no doubt that these measures kept the country from sliding back into a pattern of dictatorship and strongman rule, but the more tangible benefits of old-age pensions, child welfare, state care for mothers, and minimum wage for farm labor probably had an equal role in maintaining the democratic form of government.

Uruguay is also unique in South America for having broken with the militaristic tradition. The maintenance of a military establishment in addition to the increasing expenses of the welfare state would have put an almost unbearable strain on the financial resources of the little country. Under the circumstances, the importance of education was recognized and encouraged. The University of Montevideo became the training ground for a new middle-class elite that is proving itself in the defense and maintenance of Uruguayan ideals in that "Purple Land" where democracy is not merely a form of government and a way of life, but almost a religion.[33]

Costa Rica presents a parallel to the Uruguayan evolution. Small in size and populated in the main by people of European descent, it prides itself on its civil spirit. Its costly army has been abandoned and a police force has taken its place. Education and library facilities represent the largest expenditures, and the country's literacy rate is consequently very high. The distribution of property occupies a prudent middle ground between latifundium and small holding. In general, revolutions have been avoided or, once launched, have foundered. There are, to be sure, economic problems, since the country is still basically agrarian and per capita incomes remain low. The upper class resembles closely that of most Latin American countries and values participation in politics or literature above business activities or technical ventures. Although the distribution of property and the achievements of liberty are far from complete, it still may be asserted that the Costa Ricans have reached an unusually high degree of democratic progress.[34]

The struggle between constitutionalism and personalism in Latin America represents a momentous and indispensable step in the march to nationhood. Only in a few cases did the fight come to a definitive conclusion. The age-old tradition of searching for personalistic solutions rather than institutional ones was too deeply rooted to be overcome by constitutional debates. Furthermore, those groups that had a tendency to support dictatorships, the military and the clergy, were still powerful in many countries. Finally, constitutions were by no means in themselves a panacea for the long-standing economic ills that bedeviled the Latin American nations.

Before entering into a consideration of the economic problems, we should advise the reader that there were several republics that did not fit into the general pattern which we have sketched above, namely, Colombia, Ecuador, Peru, Bolivia, Venezuela, and some small states in Central America. Certain of these republics give evidence of the formation of that evasive quality known as "national character." There is an old saying in South America to the effect that Colombia is a university, Ecuador a monastery, and Venezuela a barracks. In Colombia the man of letters holds rank; in Ecuador it is the cleric; and in Venezuela it is the soldier. Such qualifications are not, of course, comprehensive; they apply only to the ruling elites. Indians, Negroes, mestizos, etc., were passive onlookers in a power struggle that for them was all but meaningless. We must keep in mind that these states were torn asunder by long and bloody civil wars or shaken by frequent and meaningless pronunciamentos, being saved from complete destruction only by conservative and centralistic reactions to the misunderstood application of liberalism and federalism.

Thus Ecuador was rescued by García Moreno, who held that Catholicism was the only basis for the erection of a stable society. "Civilization itself is the fruit of Catholicism," he said, "and degenerates whenever it departs from it." In the late nineteenth century Ecuador saw the establishment of a theocracy, dedicated to "the sacred heart of Jesus." The Jesuits were readmitted to the country, and the republic might have become a Jesuit utopia like Paraguay in the seventeenth century if García Moreno had been allowed to carry out his plans. Even after Moreno's assassination in 1875, the country continued to be dominated by the ecclesiastical perspective.

In Colombia a similar development took place and was marked by a personal conversion. Rafael Núñez, one of Colombia's most distinguished writers, had long been a leader of the liberal party. Convinced that the country could not be held together under federal institutions, he favored the introduction of centralized government based on an alliance with the church. Only after his election did his sympathetic attitude toward the church become known to his supporters as he began to promulgate his ideas. The liberals never forgave him and even today recall "Núñez's treason." The constitution which was drawn up under Núñez in 1886 provided for a powerful president, elected for a six-year term, whose authority should be backed by the church, which in this way regained the status it had enjoyed in colonial times.[35] This constitution remained valid until 1936, but the apparent consistency did not mean that Colombia was on her way to nationhood. Civil wars disrupted the country, some of them long and costly in human life; there was no agreement among the feuding parties about national interests, whether foreign or domestic; and the formation of a national spirit was not even shocked into existence by such traumatic experiences as the loss of Panama in 1903. Colombians pride themselves on the absence of dictators in their national history, but they hesitate to turn the coin over to see the examples of anarchy and excessive individualism imprinted there. These examples have recurred even in the twentieth century. "Our aptitude for anarchism," confessed Jorge Padilla, "is incredible . . . we are an archipelago of opinions, of theses, of contrary interests."[36]

The history of Venezuela offers a still more disconcerting spectacle. The independence movement here was truly "the last day of despotism and the first day of the same."[37] One dictator followed the other with disturbing monotony: Páez, Antonio Guzmán Blanco, Cipriano Castro, and finally Gómez. If we look for an analogy to the developments in Colombia and Ecuador, we find it in Antonio Guzmán Blanco, who established himself in Caracas in 1870 and became the dominating influence in Venezuelan history for a period of more than two decades. In contrast to Núñez and García Moreno, he professed liberal ideas and even anticlericalism. The church was disestablished and education was made free and compulsory. In other respects, however, his administration resembles the careers of Núñez and García Moreno. He brought financial stability to his country and strove for fiscal honesty. But his liberalism and Freemasonry were little more than a veneer. At the very best he was an enlightened dictator, given to bestowing benefits on the people as he saw fit, so that something was done for the people but nothing by the people.

In these three countries, where no individual profile was yet recognizable, and even more in Peru and Bolivia, the chasm between the rulers and the ruled remained unbridged. It mattered little who was in and who was out, since the ins were twin brothers of the outs. Thus we can hardly assert that these various countries experienced the phenomenon of national will or popular sovereignty. The populace was an illiterate mass, whether enfranchised or not, living in substandard conditions that were mitigated only by the bounty of tropical nature. Their plight was worse than desperate; they were indifferent and accepted their future with apathy.

CHAPTER IV

Latin America and
World Economy

O UR SURVEY has now brought us into the twentieth century.
Some of the republics were on their way to nationhood; others
had not yet contrived the minimum stability essential to national
development. We may conclude that during the nineteenth
century the Latin American countries were deeply involved with
problems of political organization, even though much of their
struggle was mere sound and fury. However, Latin America lay
in the path of those great trade winds that swept the seas of
commerce throughout the century, and its social and economic
life was inevitably and profoundly altered.

We have noted that geographic obstacles made communication between the different republics and between different parts
of the same republic exceedingly difficult. This enforced isolation of certain sections began to yield to the technological
forces that the industrial revolution had set in motion. More
exchange became possible, but it should be held in mind that
this exchange was limited to Latin America and the United
States or Latin America and Europe. We may discount as
negligible any influence from other civilizations, such as the
Asian ones. Innovations in the production of coal and steel
revolutionized transportation and industry in all parts of the
world; Latin America was no exception.[1] Many regions of Latin

America which before the middle of the nineteenth century had been only loosely linked with western Europe acquired an effective association thanks to these developments.

The functioning power of a world economy during the period 1850 to 1914 was based on three conditions: freedom of international trade, freedom for population migration, and a large flow of capital from the western European countries to the underdeveloped regions of the world. Latin America was affected by all three; her economy was stimulated, quickened, and transformed.[2]

During the period we are considering, economic life changed with a swiftness hitherto unknown in history. Latin Americans until then had geared their activities to a subsistence economy rather than to market production. But now many adopted a new outlook since the production of foodstuffs, various raw materials, and tropical crops, such as tobacco, for consumption by the industrialized nations became a profitable venture. In turn, changes in the domestic markets of the Latin American countries took place. The growth of foreign markets brought an expansion of the domestic markets and a demand for industrial goods. Subsistence production continued in agriculture and in many crafts, but the production of goods destined for export was necessarily carried out by those who were divorced from the subsistence economy. This also held true for the transportation of goods. An increase in supporting industries, a broadening of governmental functions, and the encouragement of urbanization were notable effects of the changed economy.[3]

We are thus brought to an essential question: who reaped the benefits of this contact with the industrial revolution of the western world? Given the hierarchical structure of Latin American society, it was logical for the new economic activities to benefit the already existing elite, that is, the landholding class and the patrician bourgeoisie in the big cities—Buenos Aires, Bogotá, Mexico City, Santiago de Chile, etc. Actually the acquisition of foreign markets led to an increase in the number of large holdings. Hence the impact of high capitalism tended to strengthen the stratified society rather than to moderate it.

Different methods were used to build up large estates. In some countries great holdings were fashioned out of the public domain, and these were sold sometimes to individuals, sometimes to companies. Occasionally the transfer was made in return for services rendered—military service or the surveying of virgin lands. Such procedures were followed in Mexico under Díaz and in Argentina under several administrations. Sometimes grants were given on the assumption that colonization would follow; unfortunately, settlement did not always take place, and the land frequently fell into the hands of the great landholders.[4]

However, public domain was not the only foundation for rural empire. In Mexico and in Bolivia land was alienated from Indian communities, even though in some cases the titles dated back to pre-Columbian days and had been confirmed by the Spanish crown. The building of roads and railroads sometimes had a destructive effect on the Indian communities, forcing them to yield to the pressure of "progress." Still another method of creating large landholdings was the confiscation of church lands, which could be bought for a low price and consolidated into extensive haciendas. Obviously this process could only result in strengthening the landholding class already in power in most of the Latin American countries. In no case did the laboring classes benefit from this change. Actually, great estates, managed with a backward technology, demanded a greater number of laborers, and peonage rose as landholdings increased.

There were other aspects of Latin America's involvement in the world economy. One may be noted as the division of labor between the industrialized nations of Europe and the United States on the one hand, and the nonindustrialized countries toward the south, on the other. The latter, either because of inertia or because of the dynamics of the world market, specialized in a limited number of products—coffee, tobacco, nitrates, copper, rubber, cocoa, bananas, wheat, and, later, oil. A *monocultura* system resulted in which the entire economy of a country depended on one product so far as its exports were concerned. Under such a system a country becomes extremely vulnerable to poor crops, "acts of God," fluctuating prices in the world market, and the inevitable ups and downs of business cycles. The European capitalists took advantage of the one-product economy, as, for instance, in the boost given to the Peruvian guano trade, or the exploitation of nitrates in the Desert of Atacama, or the propulsion of the rubber boom in the Amazon Basin.

Throughout the nineteenth century Latin America maintained itself by means of an economy of extraction—from its mines, its fields, its forests—with high profits for the owners of these commodities and a substandard living for the workers. Here we can note a direct line of development from a colonial economy supervised by mercantilistic bureaucracies to a colonial economy directed by capitalistic interests.

Latin America had its full share of European and North American investments during the nineteenth century. The building of railroads and roads, the development of utilities and communications, the construction of harbors and refrigeration facilities, the excavation of mines, the provision of steamships for the great rivers, all called for a substantial outlay of capital —which was sadly lacking in Latin America. The gap was first filled by British capital, with the United States, France, Germany, and Belgium running a close second.[5] There was, moreover, considerable foreign money invested in agriculture, such as banana plantations for the United Fruit Company, the Cuban sugar plantations after 1898, and the great ranches in Argentina and Mexico.

Latin Americans viewed these commercial affiliations with mixed feelings. There were some, like Porfirio Díaz, who welcomed foreign capital without discrimination or limitation because they felt that only in this manner could their countries advance, and they were unconcerned about the exploitation of the Indians, whom they considered hopeless in any case. Others, like the shrewd Juan Vicente Gómez of Venezuela, insisted on their fair share of the royalties from the foreign companies in their lands.[6]

Still another attitude became noticeable and gradually increased throughout the late nineteenth century and into the twentieth century: a feeling of hostility toward the foreign capitalists who exploited the country for their own good with little thought for the future of Latin America. This has contributed greatly to Latin American xenophobia and is, in reality, one of the basic ingredients of its rising nationalism. As early as 1896, Juan Bautista Justo, the founder of the Socialist Party in Argentina, wrote in *La Nación:* "English capital has done what their arms could not do. Today our country is tributary to England. Every year millions of gold pesos leave here and go to the stockholders of English enterprises that are established in Argentina. No one can deny the benefits that the railroads, the gas plants, the streetcars, and the telegraph and telephone lines have brought to us. No one can deny to English companies the right to possess vast expanses of land in our country, since the Argentine lords of the land have the right to live on their income wherever it most pleases them. But the gold that the English capitalists take out of Argentina, or carry off in the form of products, does us no more good than the Irish got from the revenues that the English lords took out of Ireland."[7]

The overtones of this tirade will not be wasted on the reader; they were echoed in many Latin American countries and can be detected in the speeches of Juan Domingo Perón. But economic complaints were not the only ones. Many Latin Americans had an uneasy feeling about the outcome of the Spanish-American War. To be sure, they welcomed the independence of Cuba, but they questioned whether it was independence or a new form of vassalage backed up by American capital and the Marines.

As the United States became more imperialistic and more menacing at the end of the century, the Latin Americans, especially their writers and poets, became ever more alarmed, finally coming out openly in their opposition to the growing influence of an alien civilization. The "generation of 1898" in Spain found its counterpart in South America. Pan-Hispanism became its watchword.[8]

The writer who articulated this new awareness was the Uruguayan José Enrique Rodó in his famous essay *Ariel*, written in 1899. Rodó declared the Latin Americans to be the heirs of the Mediterranean culture of Greece and Rome, of France, Portugal, and Spain; they were the brothers of Ariel, the spirit of light, joy, and poetry, as opposed to the spirit of science, utilitarianism, and materialism that dominated the Anglo-Protestant world, the world of Caliban. Rodó did not deny that the Anglo-Saxons had certain virtues, but he felt they could not be grafted onto the Latin tree. *Ariel* became the gospel of the new movement. It was a call to arms to maintain in its full integrity the cultural heritage that Spain and Portugal had bequeathed to the Iberic American world. Be conscious possessors of the power you contain within yourselves, said Rodó; America needs to maintain its original duality. There should not be the imitation of one race by the other, but a reciprocity of influences.

Rodó's *Ariel* is a seminal book in the history of ideas in the western hemisphere. Its significance lies less in its originality than in its symptomatic value; it is the beginning of Yankee-phobia, a movement that became almost universal as the century progressed. Rodó's criticism of the United States as boisterous, clumsy, lacking in tradition, admiring bigness rather than greatness, and aiming at a world made in its own image has been repeated in numberless conversations and editorials. Who would deny that more than a grain of truth lies here? On the other hand, Latin America was soon faced with a dilemma which Rodó did not foresee: How was it possible to live in an age of technology and industrialization without adhering to the standard of values that he derided? How could poverty, misery, and peonage be overcome without the production of material wealth and its concomitants?[9]

There were other contradictions inherent in Rodó's thesis.

His position could be interpreted as both nationalistic and internationalistic. His dual definition of the role of the Americas could give rise to a Latin version of "manifest destiny," an exhortation of the greatness of the western hemisphere from the southern point of view. Bolívar had already stressed this view in many of his orations and letters and had advanced the idea of an American league of nations with executive organs of its own, a court of justice, and arbitration for all conflicts that might arise between the republics of the hemisphere.[10] Even though Bolívar's efforts had been unsuccessful, his idea did not die, and it was rekindled by Rodó. In essence, it was a kind of "continental nationalism," the grouping of all Latin American countries along a front that would serve to defend their right to live their own lives, choose their own leaders, depose them if they wished, and reject any form of interference from without. This "continental nationalism" found its expression in Latin America's "matchless devotion to the rule of nonintervention," a defensive rather than a constructive attitude designed to preserve the Latin American procedures against unwarranted advice or action from its powerful neighbor.[11] The *coloso del norte* was both admired and hated. It was rich, great, and enterprising; but the Latins had no wish to become its victims.

There is another aspect of Rodó's exaltation of the spiritual superiority of his world. It gave a great incentive to the growth of a cultural nationalism in each of the members of the Latin American family. The Spanish writer Miguel de Unamuno was quick to take note of this. He wrote to Rodó about *Ariel:* "There is work to do. Your work is the greatest, to my knowledge, that has been undertaken recently in America. The sleeping people must be aroused, and their depth penetrated. . . ."[12]

Rodó's admonitory words were not likely to intimidate so powerful an imperialist as Theodore Roosevelt. The events of President Roosevelt's administration and his tremendous impact on the hemispheric scene need no retelling. From the Spanish-American War to the secession of Panama, there is a direct line of American intervention. Roosevelt claimed for the United

States the right to police the entire hemisphere. As he expressed it in 1904: ". . . chronic wrongdoing, or an impotence which results in a general loosening of the ties of civilized society, may in America, as elsewhere, ultimately require intervention by some civilized nation, and in the Western Hemisphere the adherence of the United States to the Monroe Doctrine may force the United States, however reluctantly, in flagrant cases of such wrongdoing or impotence to the exercise of an international police power." That the United States was, in such a case, to be judge, jury, and executioner did not dismay Roosevelt, nor did it trouble him that the police action he recommended seemed to coincide in a convenient way with the economic interests of his nation.

This pronouncement of President Roosevelt's was known in diplomatic language as the Roosevelt corollary, a thinly disguised justification for making Latin America the hunting ground of North American imperialism. Compared with some of his contemporaries, Albert J. Beveridge for instance, Roosevelt might still be called a moderate, but his highhanded action in severing Panama from Colombia sent a tremor of apprehension through most of the countries south of the Rio Grande. That it engendered a violent reaction in Colombia is easily understood, but Colombia was not the only country to feel misgivings. In Argentina the foreign minister, Luis María Drago, attempted to draw up a doctrine which would take the western hemisphere out of the imperialistic race and protect it from encroachment either by the European powers or by the United States. Drago hoped that a multilateral inter-American policy would benefit small and great powers alike. However, Roosevelt felt no inclination to abandon his program, and the Drago doctrine was rejected.[13]

The most eloquent voice to be raised in defense of the rights of Latin America was that of a poet, Rubén Darío. Although a cosmopolitan who belonged to the group of symbolists in Paris, he felt moved to express the fear and the anger which had convulsed "our America": "Our vast America, the land of Montezuma, the Inca's mighty realm, of Christopher Columbus, the fair America, America of the Spanish, the Roman Catholic . . . this land still lives." Darío brings in the name of Roosevelt, characterizing him as the fear-inspiring rifleman and champion of the chase who thought he was God himself, but who lacked one thing—God.[14]

Thus Latin American nationalism, whether continental or individual, found an easily recognizable target, the materialistic Yankee, who in his pursuit of earthly happiness seemed to be the opposite of the Latin American ideal.

In perspective, Latin American nationalism appears to be a by-product of the encounter with Western capitalism. In this encounter the Latin American countries had been for the most part passive partners; they shared the feeling that they had been the objects of foreign encroachment. In reality, of course, the process was both inevitable and irreversible.

The changing social and economic character of Latin America between 1900 and 1930 was the seedbed in which nationalism germinated and grew. As we have noted, the impact of the capitalistic system had at first enhanced the stratified society already in existence and consequently strengthened the colonial character of the economy. All of the Latin American countries were debtor countries. But there were still other changes which must be taken into account.

The constant stream of immigration to the ABC countries and to Uruguay hastened the cultivation of thousands of acres of wasteland. Railroads multiplied; telegraph and cable facilities were expanded. Cities were modernized; gaslight was introduced; streetcars were set in motion; even a subway was built. Obviously these innovations would have been impossible without financial and technical assistance from abroad, and Latin America speedily became the prize market for investment capital and skilled technicians.

It must be borne in mind that the complexities of the capitalistic process were not clearly understood in Latin America, but this also held true for many European countries before and even after 1914. Capitalism seemed to be in the nature of an intrinsic force which swept everything along in its wake; only the Great Depression awakened man to the possibility of controlling the dynamics of the economy.

One aspect of the economic expansion has recently been given special attention and is of particular interest to our study of Latin American nationalism: It is the rise of a middle sector in Latin American society.[15] The members of this group came mainly from urban backgrounds and were employed in transportation, communications, finance, or other industrial enterprises. Also to be found in their ranks were government officials and professionals in medicine, law, and engineering. By the very nature of their occupations these individuals were less castelike than the landholding aristocracy and sooner or later would open their doors to immigrants, or, at least, the sons of immigrants. Moreover, life in the cities had a leveling influence and tended to equalize national and class differences.

The rise of the metropolis in Latin America presents a remarkable phenomenon, and it is of special interest to our study, since nationalism is stronger and more pronounced in urban areas. The growth of the cities was spectacular. Montevideo's population increased threefold from 1887 to 1914; Buenos Aires shows the same picture over a period of only twenty-two years; in Brazil, São Paulo and Rio de Janeiro grew at the same rapid pace.[16] This urban expansion was not limited to the great cities, but affected the entire demographic structure of Latin America. In Chile, 43% of the population were living in cities as early as 1907; Uruguay was 35% urban; and Argentina reported 53% urbanized by 1914. Mexico and Brazil, on the other hand, remained predominantly agrarian. Nevertheless, in each country the capital, whether national or provincial, began to play an important role.

These cities were not homogeneous. The old patrician families lived side by side with the newly arrived immigrants or the laborers who had drifted to the city from rural areas. The differences in wealth and living standards were often fantastic, but new patterns of class life and association slowly began to emerge. Immigrants and laborers learned to read and write, or, if this was beyond their ability, they at least sent their children to school. In many instances, ties with the Old World were continued, and ideas that had been alien to Latin America began to take root. Socialism made its appearance, and among those immigrants who had come from Spain and Italy, anarcho-syndicalism found its supporters. The working forces in the cities must have realized that their chances of obtaining political influence on their own were slim. Their hope lay in a political democracy which could be achieved only by allying themselves with the bourgeois element. There was a constant ground swell increasing the rank and file of the middle sector. These people were less tradition-conscious than the old elites; they were more sensitive to outside influences, whether European or North American; they were more willing to recognize backwardness at home and to search for new models of social advancement.

It was this new middle sector that led the movement toward nationalism in Latin America, and between 1910 and 1930 its members began to reach for power. Let us, however, beware of generalizations; conditions vary so greatly in Latin America that any true or realistic composite is impossible. The parallels are there, nevertheless, and they are unmistakable.

CHAPTER V

The Mexican Revolution

THE YEAR of the Mexican revolution, 1910, is more decisive in the chronology of Latin America than the year 1914. Although the First World War revealed many cleavages in western civilization and affected the economy of some of the Latin American republics, it does not constitute as marked a watershed as the Mexican revolution. This conflict became the pivotal experiment that in one form or another has influenced and set the pace for most of the Iberian American world.

In 1910, Porfirio Díaz was an old man, as were most of those to whom he had delegated power. The question of his succession had kept the country in a state of suspense for some years, and the old fox played off one possibility against another with irritating skill.[1] The wealth of the country was in few hands; only four percent of the population were enfranchised; the program of material prosperity which Díaz had embraced had been fulfilled only for those who enjoyed the confidence of the almighty dictator whose slogan was *pan o palo* (bread or the stick). Nearly seventy percent of the people were still illiterate. There was a deep feeling of alienation corroding the inhabitants whose land had been taken away and given to capitalists, whether national or foreign, who controlled the railways, the mines, and the oil. Several movements were beginning to voice the general feeling of protest; the agitators were socialists, anarchosyndicalists, Freemasons—young men, in general, thirsting for power. Of these, the most promising was Francisco Madero, a young intellectual of often confused ideas who had been educated in France and the United States.[2] He belonged to the landowning class (his holdings were in Coahuila), but he sensed the necessity for reform. Madero's program was modest: He ran under the slogan "effective suffrage, no re-election." Thus the Mexican revolution began with a moderate platform, only to become more radical as time went on, the classical progress of revolution.

Díaz, however, did not choose to take any chances with Madero and threw him into prison for the duration of the elections. At his release, he went to Texas, where he proclaimed the *"plan de San Luis de Potosí,"* in which he promised to destroy the regime. That the country was ripe for insurrection became evident when guerrilla bands began to spring up here and there throughout the land. Emiliano Zapata gathered around him the *campesinos* from Morelos under the cry *"tierra y libertad."* Yucatán became a scene of terror, and farther to the north roamed the adventurer Pancho Villa, whose sole aim was to ravage and to plunder.

Eventually the capitulation and removal of Díaz were achieved, and in 1911 Madero became president. He had a gift for awaking enthusiasm among the masses and sincerely believed in Mexico as a nation, but he had very little comprehension of social and economic problems. He lacked the cynical realism of the politicians and the military, whose victim he became. Almost symbolically, Madero represented the conflict between the ideal and the real which typifies the entire revolution. With his goatee and his high-pitched voice, he was hailed as the "semidivine deliverer of the masses from bondage."[3] Like many a savior, he did not understand that his country was a cauldron, that a social revolution to free the masses from economic slavery was imminent, and that political freedom was the least of their worries.

The historian who contemplates a multifaceted phenomenon like the Mexican revolution is easily led into oversimplification and is tempted, like any good Hegelian, to assert that "the real is reasonable." Thus it has been said that the goal of the revolution was "the achievement of national unity and racial homogeneity through thousands of small internally unified communities."⁴ Without doubt this aim existed, but the picture of the revolution was more kaleidoscopic. The land problem was paramount, but the task of developing the industrial resources of the country was almost as important. Furthermore the relation between church and state demanded clarification, as did the question of whether military or civilian leadership should prevail. The constitutional issue was obscured for many years until Mexico found a solution suitable to its society. Each of these problems presented its own difficulty. Assembled and assailed *en masse,* as they were from 1910 to 1940, they produced volcanic eruptions and a revolutionary heat that seemed purely destructive. For thirty years Mexico was a country of passion, violence, and chaos. The tendency toward *caudillismo* appeared to have been strengthened rather than weakened. Commanding personalities sprang up everywhere and had their followings; together they formed a new class of revolutionaries, cruel, self-seeking, often boldly nihilistic. The peasant leader Zapata felt the plight of the peons most deeply. In a letter to Venustiano Carranza, then the head of the state, he wrote: "As a revolutionary . . . who has had an opportunity to know the national soul . . . with its miseries and its hopes . . . I address myself to you . . . since you first had the idea of rebelling . . . since you first conceived the project of making yourself chief and director of the misnamed "constitutionalist" cause, you . . . have tried to convert the revolution into a movement for your own gain and that of a little group of friends . . . who have helped you to get to the top . . . it has never crossed your mind that the revolution was for the benefit of the masses, for that great legion of the oppressed which you have aroused with your preachings . . . in the agrarian reform [you have betrayed your trust]; haciendas have been given or rented to [your] favorite generals . . . the people have been mocked in their hopes; the *ejidos* [public lands] have not been returned to the villages . . . nor have the lands been distributed to the workers, the poor peasants, and those truly in need."[5] This letter gives a good picture of the warring factions in Mexico: constitutionalists versus agrarians, socialists versus militarists. In the words of Anita Brenner, "a blur of rebel yells, dynamited trains, dust clouds of guerrillas, fire, chaos, desolation, and high exhilaration, became ten years of utter and complete upheaval."[6]

To make the events comprehensible, we will be obliged to separate the strands of the revolution according to the problems that were at stake. The reader should keep in mind, however, that the issues were not isolated; they were discussed and fought for simultaneously. From our point of view they all converge on the idea of nationalism; they have this common denominator, that they were to be solved, or not solved, in and for the Mexican body politic.

The Mexican revolution had no universal message, as had the French and the Russian revolutions, though lessons could and would be drawn from it. A society composed of superimposed layers had to be melted down and a new one forged in the revolution. The history of Mexico had to be rewritten; its pre-Columbian greatness had to be rediscovered and reinterpreted; Mexican art had to be evaluated, its folklore in dance and music reinstated; the problem of the two races, European and Indian, living in the same space and framework, had to be faced. And in addition to all of this, there were the pressing issues of the revolution itself. If solutions were to be found, it could only be through a slow and tortuous process of integration.

The name "integral nationalism" was coined by members of the French rightist movement.[7] However, it fits as well or better in the framework of the Mexican revolution, and we venture to adopt it in describing the phenomenon of contemporary Mexico. In reality the process of integration is much more marked in

Mexico than in France, where it continued to reside in the domain of wishful thinking.

Throughout its first decade the Mexican revolution presented the familiar spectacle of Saturn devouring his children. Madero was overthrown and killed by Huerta, a *caudillo* in whom the American and British ambassadors put their trust. Huerta, however, was forced into exile and was replaced by Carranza. Carranza was a landowner of the old school and a Díaz senator, but mounting pressures forced him to make concessions to the agrarian socialists and to issue a decree in which he promised redistribution of land under a national agrarian commission. He also called a constitutional convention, which met in 1916; its draft for a new constitution was adopted in 1917.

This constitution is a remarkable document. Some of its provisions date back to earlier liberal statutes, particularly those concerned with church and state. In other aspects the liberal doctrines were left far behind, and a new era in the social history of the western world was initiated. Article 123 guaranteed the rights of labor and was tantamount to a "declaration of national emancipation from foreign tutelage."[8]

The article covered both industrial and agricultural workers and guaranteed the eight-hour day, minimum wage, social security, and other matters important to labor. Although it far outran Mexico's industrial development, it was a charter for the evolution and organization of a free labor movement which has gradually become a reality.

For our purposes, however, the most important article of the constitution is Article 27. By its terms the nation would at all times have the right to impose on private property whatever rules might be dictated by the public interest. The constitution claimed for the nation direct jurisdiction over "all minerals, or substances in veins, masses, or layers . . . such as minerals from which are extracted the metals and metaloids used in industry, precious stones, salt deposits from seawater, mineral or organic materials to be used as fertilizers, solid mineral fuels, petroleum; and all solid, liquid, or gaseous hydrogen carbide."[9]

Article 27 was a summation of all the grievances that the revolutionists held against the great soil and subsoil interests in Mexico, whether foreign or national; and it gave a promise of redress. In essence the article confirmed the national ownership of all subsoil rights, a tradition dating back to Spanish days which Díaz had allowed to lapse during the period of his regime. The provision set forth three aims: to define the nature and limitations of private property; to define ownership by both individuals and corporations; and to introduce a formula for the solution of the agrarian problem.[10] The concept behind these stipulations was that of "conditional ownership" limited by the higher goal of social welfare. The Uruguayan constitution of 1917 and the Weimar constitution of 1919 present similar ideas.

The problem of subsoil rights was the most controversial, since it affected a large group of foreign investors, especially the American and British interests in Mexican oil. The immediate question was whether or not Article 27 would be made retroactive; in other words, would it annul leases and deeds that had been registered before 1917. The United States government supported the interests of its investors in Mexico with the threat of nonrecognition or intervention. Either could have seriously jeopardized the success of the Mexican revolution. As a result, the chief executive of the Mexican government, at this moment the general Álvaro Obregón, threw his weight behind the plea of the foreign investors and forced the Mexican supreme court to exempt the oil companies from a forced compliance with Article 27.[11] This was not the last word in the struggle over subsoil rights, but the decision of the supreme court did not endear the Americans to the Mexicans.

For many Mexicans, Article 27 became the focal point of the revolutionary mystique, which they considered essentially defensive in character. As Vasconcelos expressed it, "Many of our recent reforms are a safeguard for the future of Mexican prosperity and Mexican democracy. Such a policy not only serves the Mexicans, but it serves human progress."[12] The Mexican Labor Code parallels this attitude. It implemented Article 123, in 1931, and the Law of Cooperatives, which was passed in 1938. Not all laws were strictly enforced, but at least a beginning had been made which, decades later, made way for industrial peace in Mexico.

Other aspects of national life that the constitution of 1917 attempted to solve had similar destinies. The relations between state and church, for instance, went through a phase of violent struggle until a final balance was reached. In the end the country preserved its Catholic profile, but adhered to the separation of church and state, which had been the creed of Mexican liberalism since the days of Juárez.

Land reform, likewise, did not end in an outright victory for the revolution, nor was this in any way surprising. Twentieth-century history has shown that there is no problem more difficult to solve. In Mexico the question was not only what land to distribute, but how much and to whom, together with the initial difficulty of finding a way to prepare the peasants to work the land successfully. Today, Mexico is still an agrarian country.[13] Two-thirds of all Mexicans live on the land. The proportion was even higher during the days of the revolution. The revolution chose to solve the land problem by establishing, or rather reestablishing, the *ejido*, the village community, with communal holdings and communal production. Revolutionaries like Zapata did not find that this solution fulfilled all they had expected of it, but the agrarian reform movement has, nonetheless, continued on a trial-and-error basis. A six-year plan was introduced and an agrarian code passed in 1934. The zigzag course of land reform in Mexico need not delay us here. Suffice it to say that all those who have remained faithful to what may be called the spirit of 1917 profess their belief in land reform, because, as Silva Herzog remarked, land hunger was the original cause of the revolution.

One of the greatest obstacles to land distribution was the lack of education among the *campesinos*. But the educational problem was a national one and really involved all classes.

The most difficult hurdle along Mexico's course toward nationalism was the chasm between the past and the present. Should the revolution recognize the Spanish conquest as part of Mexico's history, and should it, at the same time, try to redeem the Indian? Furthermore, how could the Indian be redeemed? One out of seven Indians spoke an Indian language, and one out of fourteen spoke only an Indian language. The *maestro,* the teacher, became the unknown soldier of the revolution. The master strategist in the field was José Vasconcelos; he established the ministry of education in 1920 and headed it until 1925. Vasconcelos aimed at the regeneration of the Indian through education, believing that only along this path could he reach equality with the European and fit himself for a place in society in proportion to his numbers. The program was in the line of a cultural nationalism which would redeem and incorporate the Indian into the life of the nation.[14] This step marks the beginning of a most important phase in the nationalism of Latin America, especially for the nations along the Andes, where the ethnic stock includes large numbers of unredeemed Indians.

The process of integration covered all fields of enlightened endeavor. It began by resurrecting the Aztec mythology and the pantheon of the Aztec religion, whose cruel beauty had never been completely forgotten. This was not an artificial attempt to restore a pagan religion, but a serious effort to work back into the past of the Mexican nation. Archaeology received a tremendous impulse, and gradually the monuments of the Indian past were unearthed. Here, as in Israel, archaeology became the key to the country's early history.

The scholars who worked in the ruins of Teotihuacán and Yucatán have made great contributions, but perhaps the Mexican artists have done even more to acquaint their own nation and the world with Aztec history. The first heroic wave came in the twentieth century, following closely on the heels of the revolution: Orozco, Rivera, Siqueiros, Juan O'Gorman, Tamayo, and many others. They discovered monumental painting for themselves, either in frescoes or in stone murals. They turned toward national subjects: the battles between Indians and Spaniards, between the peasants and their exploiters, between Juárez and foreign invaders. They glorified the Indian, both men and women, in their earthy beauty; great sheaves of Mexican corn, the basic food of the country for thousands of years, marched across their canvases. The Indian was exalted as the forgotten hero of Mexico's history. Their art fulfilled a function similar to its counterpart in the Middle Ages, when the Bible was interpreted in stone and wood for those who could not read. In Mexico there were no great cathedral doors for this purpose, but there were the National Palace, the Mexican National Museum of History, and the National Institute of Social Security, and later there would be the great enterprise of the Ciudad Universitaria (University City).[15] The message conveyed by these frescoes and murals was often anticlerical and anticapitalistic, but the humble virtues of the Mexican nation never lacked emphasis.

The Mexican art of this decade fulfilled two functions. It interpreted Mexican history to the Mexican people, thus creating a visual memory which aided in establishing a new national identity, overcoming the alienation which had disturbed Mexico since the days of Cortés. In addition, Mexican art made the world aware of Mexico's struggle and in the process obtained universal reach, becoming an integral part of contemporary art.[16] It was, therefore, no exaggeration to say that "the Mexican Indian who stands at the center of the current revolution . . . is sure to give ensuing culture its dominant qualities."[17] In frescoes such as those by Orozco in the library of Dartmouth College, the western world was called upon to witness the renaissance of the Mexican Indian.

A parallel development in literature, expecially in the novel, can also be noted. The revolution provided the Mexican writer with an epic theme of inexhaustible variety. There were the heroes like Zapata and Villa; there were later the new rulers, the bosses, who emerged victorious from the fight; and there were the "underdogs" described by Mariano Azuela in *Los de abajo*, one of the great novels of this era. The literary work of the revolution reflected the lives and the problems of the Mexican people—their bravery, their complex psychology, their fanaticism, and their superstition.

The value of these novels is documentary and descriptive rather than aesthetic, but there was also an upsurge in literary criticism, represented at its best by Alfonso Reyes. The attempt to create a Mexican music based on the tradition of dance and folklore motifs fell short of expectations and cannot be rated on the level of the Mexican paintings.[18] In the realm of poetry the fruits of the revolution are more promising. A host of names come to mind: Jaime Torres Bodet is most interesting to our particular study.

Torres Bodet, born in 1902, witnessed as a child the overthrow of the Díaz regime and some of the cruelties of the revolution, giving him a distaste for all things military. In 1921 he became the private secretary of Vasconcelos, thus combining the careers of poet and educator. Later on he was asked to find a solution to Mexico's serious problem, illiteracy. He implemented a four-point program which, in August of 1944, culminated in the famous law whereby every educated Mexican took on the obligation of teaching one illiterate Mexican; the slogan was "each one teach one." Torres Bodet, poet and public servant, despises the intellectual who hides in cold egotism. "One of the highest obligations of the . . . writer is the struggle for law and freedom."[19]

Mexico's tremendous cultural effort resulted in a philosophy of history which has been outlined by Vasconcelos. He renewed Rodó's and Darío's claims that Latin America holds a unique position among the great branches of humanity. He baptized his native land in the name of the *raza cosmica* (cosmic race), which reconciled European, American, and African strains in its blood and in its culture. Obviously, the idea that Latin America, and Mexico in particular, is the protagonist of a cosmic race involves much wishful thinking; yet an impartial observer is obliged to admit that it holds a modicum of truth. Racial democracy was first expressed in the western hemisphere, and most

Latin American countries abide by it. Furthermore the ideals of Iberic culture, the Spanish Mediterranean heritage, have not been abandoned in favor of an artificial "Indianism"; rather Mexico, and the nations which follow her example, aim at a symbiosis of European, Indian, and Negro traits which would make them unique in our western civilization.

The achievements of cultural nationalism in Mexico were considerable; they represented communication between Mexicans, one of the true criteria of nationhood. Yet the cultural superstructure was based on profound changes in the basic structure of Mexican economy and society. We must now consider these changes.

As we have noted, the Mexican revolution, like all true revolutions, attacked the great national problems on a broad front. The participants do not seem to have realized that few of these issues could be solved overnight. As a result Mexico was plunged into a war of all against all, a class war in which the workers were fighting the entrepreneurs, the peasants the landowners, the believers the liberal intellectuals, and so forth. Few understood that the constitution of 1917 was a commitment, a pledge to the future, that might take a hundred years to fulfill. The workers fared well during the twenties, and the peasants had their day in the thirties, but slowly the middle class gained control of the revolutionary movement.[20] This was a gradual shifting of the gravitational center that to many looked like a betrayal of the revolution.

In the period between 1915 and 1940, the revolutionary groups showed a decided preference for *caudillos* who had distinguished themselves on the battlefield. Many a man who had grown up as a farmer, a teacher, or even a bartender had joined the ranks; Obregón, Calles, Cárdenas are only a few of the names. The Mexican revolutionary general, with sombrero and six-shooter, smelling, as Miss Porter observed, of tequila and fornication, became a cartoon figure. The core of the movement was, well into the thirties, a military clique, with all the rivalries, the violence, and the corruption that usually accompanies military rule.

The revolution had been the particular enterprise of this group, and they knew how to make it pay. In the breakup of the great latifundia, they became rich themselves. A new class appeared: the profiteers of the revolution. Some were pure Indians, some mestizos. There were labor leaders, officers, politicians, businessmen, all now enjoying a wealth and prestige they had not known under Díaz. They moved into the urban centers, especially Mexico City; they came into contact with the middle sector; they developed new tastes and broader understanding. Once more the old saying "Jacobins, when ministers, are not Jacobin ministers" was proven true. Holding office had a sobering effect on many who were now confronted with the responsibility for their nation. Moreover, it became increasingly clear that the revolution depended for its victory on an alliance with the intelligentsia, with writers, technicians, administrators, doctors, engineers, etc. The distribution of land meant little if the peasant was not taught how to put it to use.

There were other lessons that had to be learned. Most of the problems that the revolutionists were determined to tackle had international aspects, and they could not be solved without involving the country in international conflicts. The church-state problem reached out toward the Vatican and toward the millions of Catholics all over the world. Land reform affected the foreign investors, especially those to the north, whose government would frown on expropriation. The question of subsoil rights jeopardized the privileges that the great oil companies had enjoyed. While conflicts with other nations slowed the revolutionaries or even caused them to retract, they also strengthened the nationalistic undercurrents. Eventually the conflict with the oil companies became the test case of Mexican economic nationalism.

We have already seen that Obregón was forced to interpret Article 27 in a manner that allowed the foreign oil concessionaires to continue their operations in Mexico. This led to the recognition of the Mexican government by the United States, France, and Great Britain. But Mexico did not relinquish its claim to national control of all natural resources nor to complete jurisdiction over all litigation that might arise from the holding of property in Mexico by foreigners. The entire problem had been shelved rather than solved, and it was bound to come up again.

Consequently, foreign and domestic interests conflicted in several areas when the backwash of the Great Depression flooded across Mexico. One of the most important silver producers in the world, Mexico had gone off the gold standard in 1931.[21] The mineral industry was declared a public utility, and all interests engaged in this branch of the economy were forced to comply with Article 27. The implementation of Article 123 brought Mexico into additional conflict with foreign entrepreneurs. The eight-hour day, the right to strike, and the compulsory arbitration of labor disputes had been made law in 1931. In 1933 a six-year plan was adopted as the basis for the industrial development of the country. Obviously inspired by the Russian Five-Year Plan, it was socialist rather than communist in outlook and can best be described as a form of national socialism.[22]

With these planks in his platform Lázaro Cárdenas became president in 1934. He was a true revolutionary who believed in state intervention as the cure for the ills that afflicted his land. His impact on Mexico is undeniable; even today he is the acknowledged Grand Old Man of the revolution.

Cárdenas speeded up the process of land distribution, more than doubling the acreage previously allotted to the small farmer or the village community. The operations were not always successful, but the indomitable Cárdenas was not discouraged and can rightly claim that he broke the hacienda system in Mexico.

Even more important was Cárdenas's attack on the alienation of national industries. He had already undertaken the nationalization of the railroads when he began his concerted assault on the oil companies. He well knew that his support in Mexico depended on the peasants and the workers. In 1937 the Mexican Federation of Workers went on strike at the foreign oil fields. The government sided with the workers and ordered the companies to raise wages and to increase the percentage of Mexican employees on the management level.

Juan Vicente Gómez had insisted that the oil companies pay at least 25% royalties of the gross production, and Cárdenas may well have been guided by Venezuela when he gave voice to his convictions: "How many of the villages near the oil fields possess such things as hospitals, schools, social centers, water supply, or purification plants, or athletic fields, or electric plants? . . . Who does not know, or is not acquainted with the irritating discrimination that governs construction and layout of company oil camps? Comfort of all kinds for the foreign staff; poor accommodations, misery, and unhealthfulness for our nationals."[23] When the oil companies refused to comply with the government orders, Cárdenas directed the nationalization of the Mexican oil on March 18, 1938. The industry was henceforth to be administered by a national agency, Petróleos Mexicanos (Pemex). The response to this move of the president was overwhelming in Mexico. It was Cárdenas's most popular act. And it seemed as though the Mexican people were either oblivious to or unmoved by the price they might have to pay.

The flame kindled by the Mexican oil dispute furnished considerable heat to the already rampant nationalism. It actually worked as a catalytic agent to draw all Mexicans together. Even the devout Catholics who had opposed the anticlerical policy of the revolution felt that they were obliged to support Cárdenas in his fight against foreign interests. They made large contributions to a fund from which the oil companies would eventually be compensated for the properties that had been nationalized. A committee representing the entire number of higher Mexican clergy issued the following statement in May of 1938: "No exhortation has been necessary to induce Mexican Catholics to contribute generously to the government of the republic to pay the debt contracted with regard to the nationalization of petroleum companies . . . this contribution will be an eloquent testimonial that the Catholic doctrine is a stimulus to carrying out citizenship duties and gives a solid basis to true patriotism."[24]

Great Britain and the United States were the countries most affected by the nationalization of the oil industry. Under Franklin D. Roosevelt, the United States would not consider direct intervention, but economic sanctions were discussed. Cárdenas was willing to compensate the oil companies, but his estimate of proper compensation and that of the oil companies were miles apart. What saved the Mexican president from the possible results of his daring gamble was the coming of the Second World War. Mexico threatened to turn to Italy and Germany for a market, though the sympathies of Cárdenas were certainly not with the fascist countries, as shown by his statement of July, 1938: "We prefer to trade with the United States, but we cannot pay too great a price for this preference. It is also true that greatly increased commerce with Germany might tend to heighten German political influence here. This is something we take even more seriously than the loss of trade with the United States. In such matters we need the help of our neighbors, and if our neighbors do not help us, we will manage as best we can."[25]

The task of making peace with the United States fell to Cárdenas's successor, Manuel Ávila Camacho, who became president in 1940. With Ávila Camacho a new phase of the revolutionary cycle began. Whether he himself was the innovator, whether he was merely the executor of social changes long in the making, or whether the Second World War with its economic demands and technological transformations was responsible cannot yet be asserted. Very likely all three factors combined to bring about the turn of events. Various interpretations have been advanced. The prevalent one is that the revolution had become institutionalized. Howard Cline thinks that the revolution matured.[26] This writer suggests that the revolution entered the period of "routinization," to use Max Weber's expression. Whatever the label, the change was significant.

The Mexican revolution did not produce a Cromwell, a Napoleon, a Lenin, or a Stalin. On the contrary, a nucleus of men emerged who felt themselves committed to the creed of the revolution. Many of them came from the middle sector of society, which by 1940 was definitely in the ascendancy. This was a new generation; its members had few if any personal involvements in the sanguinary period of the earlier struggle. But they were determined to preserve the legacy they had received and to increase the value of its provisions. A renewed force was given the movement through the PRI, the Partido Revolucionario Institucional (Party of the Institutional Revolution), which became the official party of the movement. The military wing was subdued without apparent upheaval. Ávila Camacho was the last military figure to occupy the presidency; it now became bad taste to glorify the *caudillo* as a symbol of the national history. Painters like Rivera and Orozco had already ridiculed the military in their murals; now as important a writer as Vasconcelos took the same stand.[27]

As the official party, the PRI wins all elections; the president and all the important officers of the republic are drawn from its ranks. Supposedly it is permeated with the "mystique of the revolution," and it is called upon to direct the destinies of the country. The ideals of the revolution are constantly interpreted by it, not as dogma but as living potential; they represent a goal rather than a doctrine. There is, therefore, no paradox in the recent remark of a Mexican president: "A true revolutionary is known by his respect for the law."[28]

The PRI is a self-perpetuating group. It chooses from its members those whom it thinks most likely to succeed in office. In general these men have been bureaucrats with government experience; in comparison with Obregón, Zapata, or even Cárdenas, they lack color and dash. There seems to be some resemblance between the government of the *científicos* and the PRI, except that the basis of PRI rule rests on broad foundations. The new class which has emerged since 1940 deserves to be called a middle class; it ranges all the way from wealthy landowners and rich industrialists to small shopkeepers and the proprietors of launderettes and gas stations. Their undisputed support goes to the PRI.

Religious issues in Mexico have lain buried since Ávila Camacho's famous confession: "*Soy creyente*" (I am a believer). The PRI tolerates other parties, such as the Partido Popular Socialista and the communist-backed Frente Electoral del Pueblo, but these parties know that their chances are nil. Campaigning is often vigorous and presidential candidates act as if their triumph were hanging in the balance, but no one is really fooled.[29] The system is one of "modified democracy," which may shock those who think that the Anglo-Saxon two-party system is the only one to guarantee freedom, but so far Mexico has been satisfied with its political arrangements.

The routinization of the Mexican revolution put a floor under the social turmoil; the torrent that had overflowed the land is now channeled and tamed. The agrarian program has continued, but it is paralleled by a policy of industrial growth which holds greater promise for erasing or at least mitigating the scourge of poverty. Ávila Camacho initiated this program during the Second World War when he overcame the resentment against the United States and led his country into the war on the side of the Allies. Just as he had shelved the problem of anticlericalism, so did he overcome xenophobia and class struggle. Harmony and balance became the keynote.[30] The Indo-agrarian phase of the revolution was now considered an indispensable prelude to the industrialization of the nation. Private enterprise was encouraged, though with reservations. Article 27 remains valid, and the national welfare and sovereignty are still the overriding principles from which the PRI cannot and will not depart. Public utilities have been purchased from their Canadian and United States owners without fanfare; the steel industry is nationally controlled, but private capitalists, whether national or foreign, strive and prosper. The total volume of industrial production rose dramatically during the war years, as did investments in industry. The tax system in Mexico had always laid a heavy burden on the consumer, and it continues to do so, but by the same token, it now allows the accumulation of private capital which the country needs. American capital began to return to Mexico, but the government has taken care that the process of capitalistic alienation shall not be repeated. About 90% of all capital invested in Mexican enterprises is national.[31].

Among thirty of the largest firms the distribution of ownership is as follows: government-owned 82.2%; domestically owned, 13.9%; privately owned by foreigners, 3.9%.[32] The industrialization of Mexico has wrought important changes in the population structure and the class system. Mexico is still a long way from the classless society, but it would be unfair to deny the existence of a much more equitable distribution of the national wealth. During the days of Porfirio Díaz, the upper class numbered only 1.5% of the population; the middle class was represented by 7.78%, and the remainder were the poor. In 1960, according to Howard Cline, the upper class reached 6.5% of the population; the middle sector of varying income groups had risen as high as 30%, and those still on the subsistence level were some 40% of the total population. The gap of about 20% in these statistics is accounted for by persons of a transitional status who had not yet reached middle-class standards.[33]

Like most Latin American countries, Mexico has many other problems which lie outside the pale of our discussion. Its population has increased from 20 million to 36 million in 1963, and this explosion threatens to wipe out many of the gains of the revolution.[34] Although 100 million acres have been distributed among the peasants since 1915, available and productive land is in short supply. There have been illegal land seizure, migration to the city slums, and the lure of *bracero* work across the U.S. border. These maneuvers present no solutions, and the problems remain and are likely to become more serious. Nevertheless, Mexico should be equal to the task. The revolution was a success, and for almost three decades Mexico's political life has been normal within the framework of its own constitution.

President has followed president without bloodshed or violence; the army is under civilian control. The original slogan of the revolution, "effective suffrage, no reelection," has been realized so far as the latter part is concerned; the president remains the soul of the administrative body. Designated by the PRI, the presidents' personalities may differ, but their ideologies remain much the same—witness Miguel Alemán, Ruiz Cortines, López Mateos. Some are "of the extreme left, within the Law"; some are more to the center; but all pay homage to the mystique of the revolution.[35] Mexico's economic progress has likewise been extraordinary. Her international credit is good, and so is her international posture, both within the hemisphere and beyond. Her relations with the United States are those of friendly independence. No longer does one hear the old saying: "So far from God, so near to the United States."

In the process of routinization, the flaming colors of the revolutionary beliefs have grown dim and some of its cultural features now lack their original luster. Mexico City is rapidly becoming a counterpart of other great cities; there are skyscrapers and supermarkets, elegant shops and international hotels. But the old Plaza Major is still there, and the great cathedral is as imposing as ever. Communication, which we have used as a yardstick in measuring the achievements of nationalism, has vastly increased among Mexicans because of the economic ties binding them together. However, 3 million Indians do not speak Spanish, and 40% of the population is illiterate. Progress in this field is hampered by the sudden growth of the population, which has led again to scarcity of schools and teachers, especially in rural areas.[36] A federal building program for schools is under way, accompanied by a teacher-training effort, and education receives the largest share of the federal budget. The National University is an imposing creation, both artistically and intellectually, but it has few sister institutions in the outlying states.

There is a great deal of freedom in Mexico, freedom of the press and freedom of speech and thought, both of which will be respected as long as they do not lead to "social dissolution." This attitude is the shield used to ward off attacks from the extreme left and the extreme right against the "establishment." In Mexico, as in the Soviet Union today, there is a "revolutionary establishment" determined to stay in power.

Mexico has achieved political stability after three decades of political turmoil; with it have come economic advances that have moved the country out of the columns of underdeveloped countries. Its political leaders recognize that the road to economic stability lies in industrialization: $750 million have been earmarked for the expansion of the steel and chemical industries during the next six years. Foreign investments are encouraged as long as they do not jeopardize national control of the economy.

Exports have risen from $170 million to $931 million in a period of thirty years. Income from tourism has increased from $30 million to $655 million over the same span. The country's monetary reserves have grown from $29 million to $464 million.

Agriculture remains the most aggravating problem; it is here that the government has suffered the most serious criticism. The peasants insist that there is still much land that could be distributed, and they complain of "lack of government planning." But the newly elected president has left no doubt that he will maintain the economic rhythm he has inherited. Stress will be laid on the national production, which reached a growth of 6% in 1963, and which may reach a peak of 7%. Parallel to the industrial growth, there has been a rise in consumer purchases, which reflects the economic power of the middle sector. Labor likewise is expected to participate in the national cornucopia as a result of the new profit-sharing law.

All in all, the Mexican revolution has converted the country into a proud example of industrial democracy, even though political freedom remains restricted. In international affairs Mexico goes her own way, not unaligned, but still independent.

CHAPTER VI

The Andean Countries: Indian Renaissance

THE MEXICAN REVOLUTION was a crucial event in the history of Latin America, and many of the other countries considered it an experiment from which they could take heart. This was especially true of republics with a large Indian population which was not integrated into the body politic. Mexico's state socialism later inspired Brazil and Argentina, and it was actually anticipated in Uruguay. Neither Argentina nor Uruguay, however, are troubled with racial problems of any significance, and Brazil was well advanced toward racial democracy. We therefore get the most resounding echo of the Mexican revolution from the countries along the Andean range: Colombia, Ecuador, Peru, and Bolivia. These republics have been called the "Bolívarian block," because it had been Bolívar's dream to unite them in a Federation of the Andes.[1] They are also referred to as Andean America, with Chile included in the grouping.[2] Venezuela has an evolution all its own, as do the Central American republics; these countries will be dealt with later in our study.

The Andean bloc presents a mosaic of problems, largely due to its ethnic structure. About 40% of the 25 million Latin American Indians live in this region, some still in tribal primitivism, many speaking no language but their own and hence unable to communicate with the government officials, who speak and read only Spanish. These republics have other structural features in common. Their turbulent history, studded with revolutions during the nineteenth century, has already been noted. They were dependent on the *monocultura* system; the land problem was a festering sore in all of them; they were ruled by small elites, sometimes under military dictatorship, sometimes by a pseudo-parliamentary regime.

Chile was the first of these countries to embrace the doctrine of the welfare state. Alessandri's second term, 1932–1938, brought about Chile's membership in the New Deal family, a movement much in vogue in the Americas after 1932.

Colombia adhered to the same creed when the liberals returned to power in 1934 after thirty years of conservative rule. But Ecuador, Bolivia, and Peru followed an erratic course for many more years. A characteristic of all these countries seems to be the attempt, however furtive, to combine the features of the welfare state with a rehabilitation of the Indian. *Indianismo* became a watchword among the Andean nations, and no one has done more for its propagation than Raúl Haya de la Torre, the leader of the Peruvian radical party.

Haya de la Torre is a perplexing figure in the Latin American world. For two decades he appeared to be an outstanding leader of Indo-America; lately, however, he has seemed weak in the face of Peruvian power politics. His career began in the years following the First World War. It was a period of fermentation for many of the Latin American countries. The European image had become tarnished in the great carnage; many of the intellectuals looked now to Mexico and to the Soviet Union for new hope. A youth movement took shape, the first in the history of the continent. Student strikes became the fashion, first in Argentina and soon in Peru. Haya de la Torre considered the movement a vast intellectual renaissance. In reality it was the birth of a new political operation, Aprismo, named for Haya de la Torre's political party, the APRA, or Alianza

Popular Revolucionaria Americana (Popular Revolutionary Alliance for America).[3]

The Aprista movement had its roots in Peruvian history, which had been marked by a chain of failures during the nineteenth century, the country vacillating between revolutionary and dictatorial forces. Jorge Basadre has described the atmosphere of disillusionment that spread through Peruvian society. Uppermost were four problems: the ruling aristocracy and its outlook, the land tenure system, the position of the church, and the neglected position of the Indian. All of these issues reverberated in the Aprista program. In addition, Marxist thinking had made itself felt. It had been communicated to Haya de la Torre by the brilliant and tragic José Carlos Mariátegui (1895–1930), whose book *Seven Essays of Interpretation of the Peruvian Reality* was one of the few original attempts to adapt Marxism to the Indo-American situation.[4]

Haya de la Torre rose from the leadership of a student movement to the position of speaker of the opposition against the militaristic and bigoted dictatorship in Peru. His activities brought imprisonment and exile. He founded the APRA in Mexico in 1924. This was a broad and utopian socialist movement based on five points: action against United States imperialism, the political unity of Latin America, nationalization of land and industry, internationalization of the Panama Canal, and, finally, solidarity of all people and all oppressed classes. The vague nature of the program and the professed note of internationalism may make us wonder whether Haya de la Torre deserves a place in our studies. However, it seems certain that Aprismo influenced Latin American nationalism in two significant ways: It strengthened the continental nationalism with which we are already familiar, and it enhanced revolutionary nationalism in at least two countries, Peru and Bolivia. Further, it inspired the expectation in the countries burdened with a large Indian population that a form of agrarian socialism might be built. The trials and tribulations of Haya de la Torre's career need not delay us here. His party grew both inside and outside of

Peru; meanwhile its progenitor spent his time inside and outside of prison. More important to us is the ideological content of the party's program.[5]

What is Aprismo? According to a kind of catechism prepared for the movement in 1941, it is ". . . the great movement of the people and of the Peruvian youth, it is the popular coalition of the manual and intellectual workers, who have as a patriotic and social ideal, a Peru renovated by Justice, Culture, by Liberty, and by a democratic respect for the rights of all Peruvians to live, to work, to govern themselves, and to argue without foreign imperialism or internal tyranny."[6]

Karl Marx would probably have snorted at this program, but it might have pleased such men as Michelet or Mancini. In any case, it attracted many a young Peruvian writer, and was echoed in Colombia, Ecuador, Venezuela, Guatemala, and Panama. Haya de la Torre liked to think of himself as the voice of 130 million Latin Americans, and we should give him credit for at least one thing: he tried to come to grips with a single problem, the nature of Latin American reality. As mentioned, he came under the influence of Marx, but he realized that events in the socioeconomic realm had not come to pass according to Marx's predictions, nor were the beneficiaries those whom Marx had designated.

As far as Latin America was concerned, the Marxist faced a very perplexing program. Should Peru, or any other backward country, follow the pattern outlined by Marx, that is, the progression from feudalism through capitalism to socialism? If so, certainly patience was of the essence and the Apristas would be obliged to welcome imperialism, even Yankee imperialism, as the first stage of capitalism. This was a conclusion which Haya de la Torre was loath to admit. Closely linked to this problem was that of the Indian. Just what was his place in the picture of historical development as painted by doctrinaire Marxism? The Apristas could cite the Inca past as an example of native socialism. But it was a past that had been disrupted, a myth that had been shattered. The Spaniards had superimposed their own civilization on that of the Indian; two cultures now existed, the culture of the conqueror and the culture of the conquered. Aprismo thought of itself as part of a renaissance in which this situation would be reversed. Not only were the followers of Aprismo proud of their Indian stock; they saw, or thought they saw, a completely new perspective in the history of the New World.[7]

Luis Alberto Sánchez, one of the most serious and intelligent of Haya de la Torre's partisans, presented this picture in outline. America, he said, was a New World only to the Europeans; to the Americans it was an old world in which the Indian had lived for many centuries. This attitude toward the native heritage brought to the fore a new historical consciousness in the light of which the old controversy about Europe versus America could be viewed from a different angle. For the Apristas, the true America was that of the Indo-American. They took up the ideas of Rodó and Darío, though with a difference. Whereas Rodó and Darío had defended Latin America against Anglo-Saxon America, the Apristas defended Indo-America against Pan-America, Anglo-Saxon style. The emphasis on the Indian as the building block of the future leads us into one of the most discussed problems of Andean America: the psychology of the Indian. This subject has been the basis of debate ever since the days of Columbus and Las Casas, and its heat has not abated with independence. Could the Indian become a part of the white man's technological and dynamic civilization? Some observers felt that it was futile to expect anything from the Indian; they argued that he had given up the fight centuries ago; the power of the Inca empire had not been able to withstand the first contact with the civilization of Europe. Following the conquest, the Indian had contributed nothing to the conduct of modern life. "The Inca Indian is useless. But by some monstrous deformity the Indian is indeed a living force in Bolivia, a passive, inert mass, a stone blocking the viscera of the social program."[8]

Anyone who has lived in Andean America will recognize this

line of argument; he will be familiar with the description of the Indian as stoic, melancholic, treacherous, lazy, patient, enduring, etc., ad infinitum. He may also remember the lines of the Peruvian poet Chocano:

> *O raza antigua y mysteriosa*
> *De impenetrable corazón*
> *Que sin gozar ves la alegría*
> *Y sin sufrir ves el dolor.*

> (O ancient and mysterious race
> With heart impenetrable
> You look upon joy without pleasure
> And upon suffering without pain.)

Many a Latin American repeats this stanza when contemplating his country's destiny. Leaving amateur psychology to the amateurs, we can at least maintain that a gulf separated the Indian from the white man, and even from the mestizo, a gulf that represented a cultural lag of some thousand years. Was there any possibility of bridging such a gulf? The missionary educator and the cultural behaviorist were inclined to believe there was. They advanced the idea that it was the responsibility of the upper classes to undertake this change and to break the "cake of custom." They referred to Mexico, where a movement to redeem the Indian was under way. The ruling class had been in control of the Indian for decades; theirs was the obligation for his regeneration. It was a white man's burden—with a guilt complex.[9]

According to Aprista opinion, the Indian should be regenerated by following forty-eight rules of clean living: by avoiding alcohol, tobacco, and the chewing of coca, by being punctual, and by telling the truth[10]— in other words, by breaking habits predating historical record. It was utopian in concept and could hardly be expected to succeed. But Aprismo was successful in a more general way. *Indianismo* became a program to which many adhered with pride throughout Andean America.

Eventually the indigenous novel appeared in Andean America. Some authors glorified the land of tropical America in contrast with the tamed nature of the Old World, describing in glowing terms the lush forests, the wide sweep of the prairies, the towering Andes. The most famous of these are Romulo Gallegos's *Doña Bárbara* and José Eustasio Rivera's *La vorágine* (*The Vortex*), both written in the twentieth century. More pertinent to our interests are the Indian novels, for example, *Huasipungo*, by the Ecuadorian Jorge Icaza, or *Nuestro pan* by Gil Gilbert. The Bolivian writer Alcides Arguedas exposed the unhappy situation of the Indian in *Raza de bronce* (*Race of Bronze*), and the Peruvian Ciro Alegría wrote a book that has received wide attention: *El Mundo es ancho y ajeno* (*Broad and Alien Is the World*).[11] But it was not the novel alone that carried the message of the Indian. The Chilean poet Pablo Neruda, a convert to communism, protested against American capitalism, one of its most helpless victims being the Indian. "When the trumpet sounded, everything was ready on earth, and Jehovah distributed the world among Coca-Cola, Anaconda, Ford Motors, and other such corporations. The United Fruit Company reserved for itself the juiciest part, the central coast of my fatherland, the sweet waist of America."[12]

Benjamin Carrión Mora, the Ecuadorian writer, produced a biography of the Inca chieftain Atahualpa, who was taken captive and murdered by Pizarro; under the pen of Carrión he becomes a symbol of the oppressed Indian. The Colombian government published a magazine entitled *Revista de las Indias*. In the same republic politicians like Armando Solano and the fiery Jorge Eliécer Gaitán asserted with pride, "We are Indians."[13]

However, one should not overrate the depth of the Indian renaissance. Much of it was a romantic pose; some was based on a shrewd calculation aimed at winning the support of the Indian masses. Nonetheless, the movement presents a significant about-turn in Latin American affairs. Many countries started campaigns to wipe out illiteracy, to introduce hygienic living, to improve the dietary habits of the people, etc. But results were slow in coming. Only a visionary like Haya de la Torre could say that the movement was a force pressed onward by a completely pure people.[14] In all the republics which attempted to make *Indianismo* the backbone of democratic advancement, political stability has been sadly lacking; instead, pronunciamentos and dictatorships, personal quarrels and civil war, have been the order of the day.

There is still another side of the Aprista movement which deserves our attention. It concerns Haya de la Torre's international ideas. Haya de la Torre was a fervent advocate of the projected Latin American Union. "The basis of all effective democracy," he said, "and of all possible social justice in our nations is to be found in their political and economic union . . . we live Balkanized." One of the remedies he suggested was the internationalization of the Panama Canal, or as he put it, the joint ownership and control of the canal by all the nations of America. He believed such a step would help to unite the republics of the hemisphere against the imperialism of the United States.

The impact on Andean America of Haya de la Torre's ideas is not easy to gauge. In some instances, as in Peru and Bolivia, he sparked a genuine revolutionary movement with the color of national socialism. In Venezuela and Ecuador, on the other hand, he increased the tendency toward social democracy or the New Deal. And in Panama, he stimulated a wave of nationalism.

Panama's nationalism has been in the limelight recently and should be accorded some attention at this juncture. Here is a unique case in Latin American affairs, since the republic of Panama came into existence with the encouragement and aid of the United States. Yet today the United States is the prime target of Panamanian nationalism. The existence of the Panama Canal complicates the problem tremendously, because the canal is the economic foundation of the "nation" and its pride, yet also the object of Panamanian hatred and resentment. Inhabitants of the republic began to display the attitude of "my country right or wrong" during the same period that Mexican nationalism reacted against American superiority, national socialism appeared in Germany, and fascism triumphed in Italy. Panama protested and at times revolted against an international status which closely resembled the structure of a protectorate directed by the United States.

In 1903, the United States had obtained by treaty a *de facto* sovereignty over the land strip through which the canal was to flow; it had been assigned to the United States in perpetuity. Thus Panama became an independent nation through an event which, from the start, deprived her of the jurisdiction over her territory. The canal had made her existence possible, but had at the same time poisoned it with hatred of the great power in whose shadow she now lived. A political life of sorts had developed, but parties were mostly personal factions, and the leaders belonged to the small clique able to trace their ancestors back to colonial times. Most administrations were laced with graft and inefficiency. *Coups d'état* occurred frequently, without effecting the peculiar social structure of the dwarf republic.[15] Under Article 136 of the constitution the government could ask the United States to supervise elections or to keep order. It was a provision which served only to confirm the status of protectorate, and when used it was a source of popular anger.

A revision of the treaty of 1903 was undertaken under President Franklin D. Roosevelt. The convention of friendship and cooperation of 1936 ruled that the United States must relinquish the right of intervention in the domestic affairs of the republic. In return Panama promised to collaborate in the defense of the canal. Secretary of State Hull accompanied the agreement with a note which promised the Panamanians equal opportunities with the United States citizens who resided in the Zone. Whether this agreement ended the status of Panama as a protectorate and set up the two countries as partners is problematical.[16] The republic continued to be divided into the Canal Zone and the territory of the republic proper. There was and still is a vast difference in wages, living standards, and general outlook on life between the "Zonians," the citizens of the United States, who often display an ardent and sometimes imprudent nationalism, the Panamanians who work in the Zone for the Americans; and finally the Panamanians who share the general poverty and misery that Latin Americans have been heir to. It was only to be expected that certain Panamanian politicians should fall under the spell of the German national socialist movement, and that, in consequence, the republic was looked upon as a potential danger spot in hemispheric defense. Nationalism centered on the question of control of the canal as well as on such subjects as national symbols, the display of the flag, etc. In the thirties Panamanian nationalism was easily controlled or at least appeased by concessions from its powerful "protector."

In Latin America as elsewhere, the decade of the thirties was a crucial period. The Great Depression struck at many of the republics. The interruption in world trade was particularly painful to countries still dependent on a one-crop economy. Currency crises occurred, further increasing the obstacles to trade and travel. A tendency to fall back on the methods of mercantilism developed; many of the Latin American countries raised their tariff rates and tried feverishly to fill their industrial needs with improvised manufacturing. A new mystique, that of industrialization, began to permeate the land.

The decade spelled more than economic tribulation for Latin America. Set in motion by the Great Depression, two new political systems made their appearance: the New Deal, originating in the United States, and national socialism, born and bred in Germany. These ideologies soon extended their influence to Latin America, where communism had already gained some momentum, affecting some of the younger politicians, such as Rómulo Betancourt in Venezuela, Gerardo Molina in Colombia, and Luiz Carlos Prestes in Brazil. However, communism made no heavy inroads in Latin America until the close of the Second World War.

The old European democracies like France and England were

in disarray, and the young democracy of the Spanish republic was so unstable that her downfall seemed imminent. When it came in 1936, a host of Spanish intellectuals invaded the Latin American countries and contributed to the general ferment of ideas that had begun in 1929. The main contenders and pace setters were, however, the New Deal and national socialism.

The example of the New Deal was especially noticeable in Colombia. Here the liberals under the leadership of Alfonso López returned to office in 1934 and introduced a series of sweeping reforms, including a revision of the constitution, a secularization of education with greater emphasis on free instruction of the poor and dispossessed, and a social security system to which, it was hoped, the country would eventually adjust. Many of these reforms remain on paper, but they marked a beginning. The government was still in the hands of the old families—the Lleras, Sampers, Restrepos—but members of the mestizo and mulatto groups penetrated the almost hermetic ruling class in ever increasing numbers. Not all of these politicians became members of the Jockey Club or joined the polo-playing crowd, but they did find it possible to rise to the rank of cabinet minister or ambassador as did Gabriel Turbay, the son of a Syrian immigrant. In Chile too we find evidence of New Deal influence in the second term of Alessandri, 1932–1938, and in the administration of his successor, Pedro Aguirre Cerda.

Alessandri introduced a labor code of 618 articles. The eight-hour day and the forty-eight-hour week became standard, likewise the stipulation for a labor contract with detailed information as to what was required of the worker. Syndicalism, or unionism, was also prescribed for all but the very small enterprises. There was an elaborate apparatus for solving labor disputes. Even profit sharing became law.[17] Chile's social security system went further than Colombia's, and decidedly further than the organizational set-up in the United States. It provided for medical care, maternity care, and a pension plan. Although it was an expensive and somewhat cumbersome program, it unquestionably extended social benefits to a much larger number than had previously enjoyed them. Education was made free and compulsory, with the result that Chile can claim a high literacy rate, about 80%. There was also a determined effort to develop the industrial resources of the land, which gained momentum during the Second World War, when industrial imports were hard to obtain. Considerable progress was made, but there were also handicaps and setbacks. Aguirre Cerda had formed a government of the *Frente Popular* (Popular Front), following the example of Léon Blum and Manuel Azaña. This gave impetus to the left-of-center groups. Strikes and a vicious inflationary cycle have plagued Chile ever since the thirties. Other countries affected by the New Deal policies were Venezuela, Brazil, and Ecuador, but the results became more apparent after the termination of the Second World War.

The influence of national socialism on the Latin American world has not yet been fully investigated; it warrants a study of its own.[18] There were many German immigrants in the Latin American countries, and quite naturally they became the carriers of Nazi propaganda. They were given support by the active program beamed to Latin America from the Third Reich. In some instances military or educational missions were instrumental in introducing the propaganda of Hitler and Goebbels. The entire relationship of the Nazi movement to Latin America was paradoxical. Its racial theory, the overlordship of the master race over the slave races of the world, should have been offensive to Latin Americans, and in many instances it was. Yet there was inherent in this ideology an appeal to the ruling elites which in some cases found a sympathetic response. The elites could use Hitler's racial mania as a justification of their own privileged position; they could explain and exonerate their exploitation of the Indians, Negroes, and mixed races, with the pseudo-Darwinian argument that served the Führer in Germany.

The claim of Mussolini and Hitler that the hour of the "have-nots" was at hand seemed clearly applicable to the Latin American countries. All of them were still on the list of debtor nations, and they naturally resented the powerful Anglo-Saxon bloc which had financed their development at the price of high interest rates and a controlling hand in their economies. Hitler's struggle against *Zinsknechtschaft* (enslavement by interest) was taken up with enthusiasm by many Latin American countries. Moreover, the Nazi government, under the guidance of Dr. Schacht, worked out a series of economic devices that suited the economies of many of the republics which were suffering from the blows of the Great Depression. Dr. Schacht did not demand a cash-and-carry commerce. Instead he designed a barter system whereby Germany would purchase coffee, tobacco, tin, oil, etc., and pay for these goods in industrial manufactures. There were such financial innovations as the "coffee mark," which had a higher exchange rate than the Reichsmark and was, consequently, an incentive to increased trade with Germany. German industry virtually controlled the markets for optical instruments, pharmaceuticals, electrical appliances, and chemicals. And the Reich was willing to extend long-term credits to Latin American buyers, which helped to stimulate German commerce.

There were other considerations. Some of the airlines in Latin American countries had been founded by German pilots after the First World War and were now manned and serviced by German personnel. Many Germans had married into *Criollo* families and had made pleasant adjustments to the customs and manners of their guest country. Many Latin Americans viewed Hitler's timing, shrewdness and successful rise to power with awe. Having themselves lived for so long in the *caudillo* tradition, they found the rise of the dictator less alarming than those who had been reared in the democratic tradition. When they compared Germany with the western democracies, they observed that the latter had an ideal but lacked the idealism to support it, whereas Germany without an ideal still had the proper amount of idealism to defend her cause. The first Latin American country to experience the influence of national socialism and to adhere to it was also the most unlikely one: Bolivia.

CHAPTER VII

The Bolivian National Revolution

THE ONLY WAR to make its appearance in Latin America during the twentieth century was the Chaco War; in its wake came the Bolivian revolution. There had been border disputes between Peru and Colombia and Peru and Ecuador which were the cause of considerable nationalistic pyrotechnics, but the Chaco War was the first full-fledged affair.

El Gran Chaco is located deep in the center of South America. It lies in the angle between the Pilcomayo river and the Paraguay river and borders on Argentina, Bolivia, and Paraguay. It is a low alluvial plain, mostly swamp and jungle, and was considered a worthless piece of real estate, fit only for the savage Indians who inhabited it. Like many territorial disputes in Latin American history, the Chaco War had its roots in colonial times. As we know, the boundaries between the administrative divisions of the Spanish empire were ill defined. In this early period, Bolivia was known as the *Audiencia de Charcas,* while Paraguay belonged to the viceroyalty of La Plata. Bolivia's claim to the limits of the *audiencia* and Paraguay's right to the limits of the original *provincia* overlapped, and this circumstance was responsible, at least in part, for the ill feeling between the two countries.[1] But there were other reasons. Bolivia and Paraguay were the only land-locked countries in South

America. Both republics are in great majority composed of Indians; the Bolivian Indians are quite different from the Guaraní who form 90% of the Paraguayan population, but they are Indians just the same. Both countries had their share of famous and infamous dictators. Dr. Francia in Paraguay and Melgarejo in Bolivia became synonymous with cruel, personal rule. Both republics had been the victims of international conflicts in the nineteenth century. Bolivia's defeat by Chile in the War of the Pacific (1879–1883) cut her off from any outlet to the Pacific except through territory under the jurisdiction of Chile. She was obliged to look toward the east, hoping to establish a port on the Paraguay river which, through the Río de la Plata, would furnish her with an outlet on the Atlantic. She did not expect Paraguay to oppose this project, since Paraguay had just been through a ruinous war and was weak and unstable.

The war Paraguay lost is known as the War of the Triple Alliance; Paraguay had been fighting against the combined forces of Argentina, Uruguay, and Brazil (1865–1870). The conflict had been the enterprise of one man, Francisco López, a Guaraní Indian who hoped to become the Napoleon of his country. He dreamed of a greater Paraguay with access to the Atlantic, and he trained an army of 60,000 men to realize his dream. But the project came to naught; Lopez was defeated by the powerful Triple Alliance and died in the Paraguayan jungle. Paraguay lost territory to Brazil and Argentina. A large part of the region known as El Gran Chaco was awarded to the latter.

Accordingly, both Bolivia and Paraguay had an interest in the province. A period of litigation followed during which the interested parties appealed to arbitration by foreign powers. In 1878 President Hayes decided in favor of Paraguay against Argentina, a decision which Bolivia did not feel bound to respect since she was not a party to the agreement.[2] There were other treaties; there was even an attempt to divide the Chaco into three zones. And the Chaco problem dragged on into the twentieth century, with both countries insisting on their rights.

Two factors prevented a peaceful settlement of the rival claims, one economic, the other military. Early in the 1900's foreign capital began to pour into the Chaco. *Estancias* were set up for the purpose of breeding cattle and producing quebracho, a product used in the tanning industry. A little later, surveyors for foreign oil companies spotted deposits; the Royal Shell Company and Standard Oil of New Jersey took a dominant interest in these. In the meantime both Paraguay and Bolivia were slowly moving into the disputed territory, endeavoring to establish their rights by building *fortines,* small outposts from which each side hoped to repel the other. Inevitably incidents occurred. The American sister republics made several attempts to reconcile the dispute, but were unsuccessful. In June of 1932, Bolivia took the offensive, and in May of 1933, Paraguay declared a state of war between herself and Bolivia. There can be little doubt that Bolivia was the aggressor.

What prompted the unhappy country to act as she did is a matter of conjecture. The entire history of Bolivia had been a series of misfortunes, wherein, as Goethe might have said, folly and violence were mingled. She had lost large portions of the national territory to her neighbors; she was in many ways far behind her sister nations, Argentina and Chile; a nationalistic movement cannot be detected before the 1920's, according to Guillermo Francovich.[3] One of her own writers had called her the *pueblo enfermo,* the sick people.[4]

During the decade of the twenties, Bolivia's mining industry grew so rapidly that she was soon the largest tin-producing country in the world. But the Great Depression proved disastrous, producing revolutionary upheavals in which a military junta gained control. If, as has been suggested, Bolivia launched the war with Paraguay to avoid further domestic troubles, the stratagem misfired.

The Chaco War has been described as the "war of the green hell," and the great oil interests have been accused of being the prime culprits. Few of these suspicions can be substantiated.

In the end, thousands had died on both sides, and Bolivia had lost another 20,000 square miles of territory. The war has been called one of the most senseless conflicts in history. Certainly for Bolivia it was meaningless except for triggering further revolutionary developments. When the people began to realize how they had been misled, labor demonstrations took place, and the president was ousted in a bloodless coup. Its mastermind was the chief of staff of the army, Colonel German Busch, an officer of German descent under the influence of national socialist thinking. A party calling itself the National Socialist Party appeared, demanding the abolition of monopolies, labor conscription, and national syndicates for all workers. Most of the members were students who had been inflamed by the program of Haya de la Torre; others were veterans of the Chaco War. Eventually Busch became president of the republic and set about establishing a totalitarian regime. There were violent street demonstrations directed against United States imperialism, the oil companies, and foreign monopolies. Bolivia came to be viewed as the Nazi bridgehead in the western hemisphere. Such an encroachment could not be considered with equanimity by the United States, and Busch was overthrown in 1939. He committed suicide, anticipating his hero, Hitler, by six years. Nevertheless, a train of events had been set in motion which led twelve years later to a successful revolution of national socialist coloring.

Two groups of Bolivian society were brought to the fore by the Chaco War. On the surface diametrically opposed in their sociological structures, they nevertheless coincided in many of their aims. One group was an outgrowth of the military and called itself the Radepa (*razón de patria,* or reason of the fatherland). Their ideals were borrowed from Germany, and their goal was a blend of nationalism and socialism. However, they lacked popular support and various other parties sprang up; among them the MNR (Movimiento Nacional Revolucionario) was the most promising. Its founder and leader, Victor Paz Estenssoro, a professor of economics at La Paz University,

combined the popular themes of nationalism and revolution
with the ideals of the military, emphasizing the necessity for a
strong state and a centralized government. Paz Estenssoro became minister of finance in the 1940's, but was forced out of
office when the president of Bolivia was assassinated. Paz
Estenssoro fled to Argentina, and the MNR went underground.[5]

Although Bolivia had enjoyed a transitory prosperity during
the war years, when tin was in great demand, the period which
followed revealed once more the perennial crisis Bolivia had
endured from the beginning. Government followed government,
and one political incompetent after another showed his in-
ability to cope with the most basic issues.

Bolivia's society and its power structure had not changed
since Bolívar had called the country into existence. Many of
her institutions went back to colonial times, some even to the
days of Inca rule. More than half of the population were Indian,
continuing to speak their Quechua or Aymara and apparently
impervious to the influence of their white conquerors. If, as we
have asserted, a nation is composed of people who communicate
with each other more intensely than with others, Bolivia cannot
be called a nation before the twentieth century. Bolivia has
been called many names, all denoting an unhappy land.[6] The
Bolivian Indian is described as useless, mysterious, enigmatic,
uncommunicative, silent, immutable, living in a closed world, a
passive inert mass, a stone blocking social progress, etc. There
are, of course, a few optimistic people who continue to believe
in the Indian potential,[7] yet there can be little doubt that the
Indian has been the great retarding factor in the tragic history
of Bolivia.

The country's advancement is hampered in other ways. It is
sharply divided between the *altiplano,* the highlands, where
may be found the highest plateaus known to man, and the
yungas, the valleys. The capital, La Paz, is located in the high
country; here also is the famous Lake Titicaca. Life here is
harsh and unbending; only the Bolivian Indian would have
chosen this brown earth, without trees and with little green to

refresh the eye. East of these forbidding heights are the tropical valleys, where there is an abundance of fruit, a region still unexploited. Still another division, the Oriente, is an untouched wilderness which includes more than half of the national territory. It may some day be opened to man, but so far has remained in isolation because of the lack of transportation.

Like many other Latin American countries, Bolivia is an example of the scourge of the *monocultura* system. In colonial times it was the treasure house of the Hispanic empire. From the silver mines of Potosí flowed the wealth by means of which Philip II hoped to conquer the world. When the silver mines had no more to give, tin made up the lack. The tin barons were a small group representing monopoly capitalism in its purest form: the Hochschild, the Patiño, and the Aramayo interests exercised an almost complete control over the production of tin. The effects of the monopoly were aggravated by absentee ownership. Any revolutionary agitation would inevitably find these families a popular target. But conditions in the mining industry were not the only grounds for revolution. Agriculture showed the familiar outlines of the latifundium. The *campesinos* were condemned to live in a state that closely resembled the medieval serf; they worked the land of their masters for a compensation below subsistence level. Small wonder that alcoholism was prevalent among the Indians. With their unusual headgear, their ponchos, their inscrutable expressions, they seemed the relics of a neolithic culture. They had little or no faith in the white man, or the mestizo for that matter, and remained outside the pale of urban life.[8] An anecdote heard frequently in Bolivia explains their position. A young man, a member of the elite, got into a discussion with an Indian. Trying to impress him, he said, "I am the son of the president." Inquired the Indian, "And who is president now?"

It is interesting to ponder the possibilities for revolutionary movement in Bolivia. There was, of course, the communist solution, revolution by workers and peasants, and the establishment of a socialist state. Marxism still has a large number of followers in Bolivia, but this ideology did not carry the day. Bolivian socialism has no international alignments, nor can it be termed a branch office of the Moscow organization. We noted that the military looked for guidance to Nazi Germany, but the result of the war was enough to discredit the national socialist movement. The climate of the MNR, however, is both national and socialist, though it bears little resemblance to the German movement. For the inspiration necessary to revolution, no doubt the Mexican revolution would suffice, and there are many indications that the young revolutionaries took a leaf out of the Mexican book.[9] But conditions in Bolivia were less propitious than in Mexico, and it is a measure of the stamina of Paz Estenssoro, the revolutionary leader, that he did not abandon the struggle nor choose an extremist solution after the manner of Fidel Castro.

We have said that the MNR was driven underground and its leader forced into exile. In 1951, however, Paz Estenssoro returned to Bolivia and was elected to the presidency. A military junta prevented him from assuming office, but popular feeling was strong enough to resent and resist the use of arms, and on April 9, 1952, the Movimiento Nacional Revolucionario swept the country. By then, it had become clear that if Bolivia were to emerge from her state of anarchy, the MNR would have to take over the government. Even the military conceded this, or at least most of the military. The actual fighting was brief and not unduly bloody. The *ancien régime* showed little vitality in defending its position.

Was this just another *coup d'état* like so many that Bolivia had suffered? After thirteen years it seems safe to say that the revolution of April 1952 will have lasting effects, whatever the fate of its protagonists. A return to the prerevolutionary order is well-nigh impossible.

Paz Estenssoro has taken great pains to deny that the MNR owed anything to the Nazi movement. "We are," he said in 1944, "the Revolutionary Nationalist Party. . . . We have seen that a country with a semicolonial structure like Bolivia, in a revolutionary period, and within the present realities, must insofar as possible achieve a socialist regime which will permit the realization of social conquests appropriate to any nationalist policy."[10] But there can be little doubt that the Nazi influence had been strong, though it did not prevent the MNR from borrowing with a free hand from other ideological sources. This national socialism or Titoism was, of course, given its own particular color by the Bolivian reality.

The MNR faced three problems of first magnitude: nationalization of the mineral wealth, the tin mines in particular; agrarian reform; and finally control of the military, which had been Bolivia's *bête noire* since 1825.

The nationalization of the mines was the most spectacular action undertaken by the MNR, and it is difficult to judge it impartially. The mining industry had been in trouble before the revolution. A United Nations report of 1951 had predicted imminent decline unless confidence could be restored and considerable capital invested.[11] The Patiños, the Hochschilds, and the Aramayos, who controlled the country's principal source of foreign exchange, could not resist the temptation to interfere in internal politics, which made their monopoly doubly obnoxious. Obviously, a movement dedicated to economic nationalism could not tolerate a condition of this nature. The MNR, however, failed to take into consideration the singular traits of Bolivian mining at great altitudes, with high accident rates and with a low rate of productivity.[12] And it was an example of revolutionary naiveté to imagine that the nationalization of the mines would be a panacea for all the ills that beset the Bolivian economy.

Paz Estenssoro was anxious to divorce his policy of nationalization from any wholesale policy of expropriation or confiscation. The mines were placed in the hands of a government trust, Corporación Minera de Bolivia, and the former owners were offered what the MNR considered an equitable compensation, which was to come out of the revenues from the mines.

At this writing, the results of the nationalization have been far from satisfactory. The payroll of the new mining trust has increased as production has decreased. Furthermore, the labor force of the mines became a source of political intrigue and has been used by the left wing of the MNR to sabotage any government action that did not meet with its approval. Foreign experts were summarily dismissed, but replacements from among the Bolivian nationals were hard to find.

Thus the Bolivian mines have been operating in the red. Production sank from 30,000 tons in 1950 to 16,000 tons in 1961. While the cost of production rose, the price of tin on the world market fell. To add to the sorry picture, many of the mines have reached their point of exhaustion.[13]

Objective observers maintain that the "principal factors which contribute to the cost of mining operations are largely the result of social and political conditions."[14] In other words, it has proved easier to destroy capitalistic management than to replace it. Such failure does not necessarily prove that the Bolivian experiment must be considered a complete failure; it does show, however, that economic nationalism in Latin America is confronted with tremendous obstacles.

One method of overcoming the failure to nationalize the mines would be to diversify the national economy and to make a resolute break away from the *monocultura* system. This, of course, is easier said than done, since an underdeveloped country like Bolivia could only turn to agriculture for diversification. And here the national revolution entered the same vicious cycle that had plagued it in the nationalization of the mines. From the beginning the MNR had demanded legislation whereby every Bolivian would be made a landholder.[15] But the obstacles in the path of land reform were formidable. The latifundia were the prime target of the reformers, but the root of the troubles lay deeper. Before the MNR took over, United Nations observers had made the statement that Bolivia lacked an integrated market economy; the reasons for this lack they traced back to the conservatism of a primitive society. Agriculture was stagnant, and foodstuffs that could have been produced within the country were, perforce, imported. Of the land in cultivation, 90% was worked in a semifeudal fashion, that is, it was worked by the Indians for absentee landlords who took the largest share of the crops, leaving the worker the meager remains for his substandard living. To these grievances must be added the systematic land theft from Indian communities that had been going on since colonial days.

The revolutionary movement listed three objectives of agrarian reform: the distribution of the arable land to peasants who had no land; the restoration to the Indian communities of the lands that had been taken from them; and the termination of the serfdom under which the rural workers had been crushed.[16] The revolutionists also hoped to increase production and to make the rural population more mobile.

The government went to great lengths to emphasize that the land reform was not communist-inspired, that it respected private property, and that it in no way emulated the Russian example of basing agrarian production on the collective farm system.

However, the latifundium was officially outlawed. It was defined as rural property which remains unexploited or insufficiently exploited. On the other hand, holdings where the proprietors had invested in modern machinery or modern methods of cultivation were exempt from the process of redistribution. The government also encouraged the establishment of cooperatives, which, it was hoped, might eventually supersede the Indian communities.

The reform was a necessity, and the legislation which tended to bring it about is praiseworthy, but enforcement was quite another matter. Latin America is not alone in discovering that land reform is fraught with difficulties. Distribution is useless unless accompanied by a credit system for financing the newly created farms until such time as they become self-supporting. Perhaps even more important is the availability of technical advice and technical implements so that the peasants may be educated in new methods of production. In the case of Bolivia, these facilities were sadly lacking. In addition, there was the psychological problem. The Indians are not easily educated. Accustomed to living on a subsistence economy, weakened by alcoholism and the use of coca leaves as a stimulant, they are antagonistic to all technological instruction. The language barrier formed a further block. The government agents who undertook to teach the Indians were obliged to learn the Quechua or Aymara vernacular, which supplied no equivalent for the technical terms to be explained. Age-old superstition resisted the most basic notions of personal welfare and hygiene.[17] The task of converting a great number of people who have been living all their lives in the Stone Age into the twentieth-century image of a progressive community is likely to prove as impracticable as grafting a grapevine on a eucalyptus tree. Mere technical education will not suffice. Only a complete rehabilitation of the Indian can overcome the neglect of centuries.

The MNR is quite aware of its obligation to educate the Indian and to mold him into a responsible and active citizen, but only a determined optimist would expect this to be accomplished during our lifetime. The problem of illiteracy among the Quechua and Aymara Indians is staggering; more than 80% can neither read nor write. In the course of their rehabilitation, they would be obliged to abandon their native tongue in favor of Spanish, and where would the government procure the necessary teachers to train these people in the speech of Cervantes? Campaigns for literacy have been essayed in other parts of Latin America; they give rise to a great skepticism as far as early results are concerned. In Bolivia, moreover, there exists no large fund of folklore and tradition, which helped to support the educational campaigns of the Mexican revolution. Neither in music, nor in dance, nor in the visual arts can Bolivia hope to emulate Mexico. The mystique which quickened and continues to quicken the Mexican revolution can hardly be reproduced in Bolivia. And another objection should not be taken lightly: critics of the Bolivian revolution have argued that it tends to promote racial intolerance and hatred. "The purpose of this revolution," says one of its opponents, "is neither economic nor social, but political: to supplant an energetic and cultured citizenry of European extraction with an illiterate Indian electorate. In order to gain the Indians' support, they have been handed the land seized from its rightful owners."[18]

While such accusations may be inspired by class resentment on the part of those who feel that their rights have been infringed, they cannot be altogether discarded. Xenophobia has been an element of Latin American nationalism from its inception. The attempt to rehabilitate the Andean Indian at the expense of the ruling white or mestizo oligarchy could easily lead to discriminatory action against the white man, perhaps to the point where his participation in the nation's fate would be denied. It may be recalled that Bolivia's neighbor, Paraguay, essayed such a course early in its history. El Supremo, the almighty Dr. Francia, prohibited marriages between Europeans and white women in an attempt to build a nation of Indians and to expedite the homogeneity of the Paraguayan people.[19] Whether Bolivia will go to such lengths will depend to a large extent on the fate of the MNR.

Paz Estenssoro has declared repeatedly that he may be counted in the western column; he has resisted any attempt by communist and fellow traveler to sway him by Marxist promises. Nevertheless, labor plays a large and important role in Bolivia; workers and peasants have been unionized, and a consolidating union has been established, the Central Obrera Boliviana. The workers have proved to be the most efficient supporters and, in the case of need, the most resourceful defenders of the government. Attempts to influence the Central Obrera Boliviana toward the far left have not been lacking. The Marxists in the Bolivian labor movement are making every effort to explain certain economic facts by means of their own dialectic: "The Bolivian revolution," they assert, "must have the character of a combined revolution—bourgeois-democratic in its immediate objectives and socialist in its uninterrupted results. It is quite impossible to separate the two phases of the revolution.

This means that the workers in power must not halt at bourgeois democratic limits, but must strike ever more deeply at the rights of private property, going over to socialist methods and in this way giving the revolution a permanent character."[20]

The responsible leadership of the MNR has, however, been shying away from Trotskyism as well as from Stalinism. There is more reliance on the workers, mostly because their backing was needed in the fight against the discredited army. The old military force was dissolved by decree on July 24, 1953, and replaced by a militia. Regular and noncommissioned officers were retired. "With the power of the state in the hands of the people through its political vanguard, the MNR had to replace the old massacring army, organized and educated for the defense of the oligarchic interests, and to substitute for it a new one destined for the defense of the political and economic sovereignty of the Fatherland."[21] Whether the new militia will be less dangerous than the old army remains to be seen. The tradition of the military and of revolution by *golpe de estado* (*coup d'état*) has been long and consistent in Bolivia; time alone will determine whether it has been erased.*

The main reason that the MNR has hesitated to throw its lot in with the communist movement is, however, an economic one. Its leaders realized that the United States could be of greater assistance to their program of economic independence than the communist bloc, and consequently they decided to cooperate with the power that had inspired their jibes against Yankee imperialism. The United States, on the other hand, fearful of a revolutionary volcano deep in the heart of Latin America, decided to trust the assurances of Paz Estenssoro and to take his professions of faith in the democratic ideal and in the sanctity of private property at their face value. United States policy in Bolivia has been considerably more successful than in Cuba. The United States has given substantial economic aid and technical assistance to Bolivia, and, working through the International Monetary Fund, has advanced large sums to

* Paz Estenssoro was overthrown in 1964 by a military coup.

the republic with the stipulation that the financial recommendations of the IMF should be accepted. These aimed at the stabilization of the currency, together with the freezing of wages, and the restriction of credits and subsidies, which the government was wont to lavish on certain pet projects. The MNR was forced to heed the counsel of the International Monetary Fund, but the reforms fell short of their goal. They relieved some aspects of the crisis, but aggravated others; economic stability could be gained only by economic expansion, and economic expansion was all but throttled by the control of subsidies, credits, and currency.[22]

The United States has advanced to Bolivia about a billion dollars in support of an experiment that runs counter to the basic philosophy of its own citizens, but the international situation gave the government little choice. The Soviet Union would be all too willing to pick up the tab. Other nations, such as West Germany, have also aided Bolivia, but the economy of the republic remains shaky.

In the Cuban conflict, Bolivia has sided with the United States. When the Organization of American States voted to sever diplomatic relations with Cuba and join the economic blockade against Castro's island, Bolivia was one of four countries to vote against the resolution, but on August 21, 1964, she announced that she would bow to the will of the majority, and the Cuban envoy was asked to leave La Paz.[23]

Paz Estenssoro knew that this action would receive the bitter criticism of the opposition. Consequently, he announced that he would send an "observer" to the conference of the unaligned nations to take place in Cairo in October of 1964. Bolivia had been represented at the Belgrade Conference in 1961, and President Tito had paid a visit to Bolivia in 1963. The philosophies of the two governments are indeed similar; both try to reconcile nationalism and socialism and steer clear of any commitment that might jeopardize their independence.

A final assessment of the Bolivian national revolution is not yet possible. To call it the most profound movement toward social change in Latin America since the Mexican revolution seems an overstatement.[24] But it does have significance even if the significance is only symptomatic of the social energies that are stirring in Latin America. There has been a remarkable kinship between the Mexican and the Bolivian revolutions; both were American; both have refused to join the international trends of socialism; both have been striving for agricultural and industrial independence. But Bolivia would have foundered without the help she received from the United States, and her accomplishments to date are far from impressive.

It is interesting to analyze the nationalistic current that flows through the Bolivian revolution. A country so deeply divided by social and geographical cleavages could hardly be expected to become a breeding ground for nationalism. Nevertheless, the nation is the rallying point for most of the revolutionary measures that have been introduced. Social justice and economic independence are evoked in the name of popular and national sovereignty. Perhaps the leaders of the MNR envision a future Bolivian nation rather than engendering an enthusiasm for the one already in existence. One might call it a visionary nationalism.

The success of any such visionary nationalism will to a large extent depend on the response that the MNR will provoke in the American Indian. If the Indian is converted into an active, responsible citizen, able to find his place in a technologically determined world, the Bolivian revolution will have performed a miracle.

Other features of the Bolivian revolution demand attention. It has followed no hard-and-fast rule of revolutionary dialectic. There has been little bloodshed; there has been no class struggle; and moderation has been the keynote.[25] A stratified society has been leveled. The upper class has suffered greatly, not only through the loss of prestige and power, but through nationalization and inflation. The peasants and workers have moved up, but they are still a long distance from the top. Should the revolution succeed, a middle sector would necessarily emerge which would include politicians, managers, engineers, physicians, and other professionals. Only a Bolivian elite could implement the mandates of the revolution.

One final paradox may be mentioned before we leave the Bolivian scene. What an ironical circumstance is presented when we see a national revolution adhering to the tenets of national sovereignty and independence, and at the same time submitting to the supervision of the *coloso del norte!*

Future historians will probe into the ideological affiliations of the MNR. They will question its debt to Haya de la Torre, to his slogan of *tierra y libertad,* to his *Indianismo.* An additional irony stems from the fact that Haya de la Torre has not been able to play a decisive role in his own country. The APRA (Alianza Popular Revolucionaria Americana) continues to be a force in Peru and to gain partisans. Haya de la Torre himself had a change of heart during the Second World War and made his peace with the United States, the country that had been the target of his most bitter criticism. Yet all attempts to integrate APRA with the political life of Peru were met with opposition from the economic and military forces that had blocked Haya de la Torre and his movement.

Although the Aprista movement commanded a large following, Haya de la Torre was persecuted by the military, who were backed by the famous "forty families" controlling the country. In 1948 General Odría overthrew the constitutional government of President Bustamante, which had been favorable to land reform.

Haya de la Torre has been in and out of prison several times since the ousting of President Bustamante Rivero, and his right to asylum has become a *cause célèbre* that finally reached the International Court of Justice at The Hague. However, the Peruvian aristocracy had become increasingly aware of the Bolivian example and may have come to the conclusion that it might be wiser to initiate reforms from above rather than wait for revolution from below. The government of Manuel Prado, who became president in 1956, showed signs of moderating its opposition to the Aprista movement. As of late the government of Belaúnde Terry has taken certain steps indicating a recognition of the necessity for agrarian reform. Belaúnde's party, the Acción Popular, is striving for a peaceful revolution that would break the present power structure, diversify the economy, and open up the jungle areas as escape valves for the great masses of increasingly restive Indians. It has been said that Belaúnde represents the concern of the new middle sector for the welfare of their country, supported as they now are with new money and new hope.[26] If this is true, Peru might follow the Bolivian example, though perhaps at a slower pace. Ecuador likewise has been promised an agrarian reform, a term that had been an anathema to the Ecuadorians. Here, as elsewhere, results will speak louder than words.

CHAPTER VIII

The National Revolution
in Brazil

THROUGHOUT THIS STUDY we have maintained that an analysis
of nationalism must be functional and must comprehend the
factors which condition the appearance and the impact of this
phenomenon in the place where it becomes manifest. Although
nationalism in Latin America has certain features which permit
us to consider it a common trend in the western hemisphere, it
differs from country to country according to geographical conditions, ethnic components, cultural and political traditions, and
the degree of economic development which has been achieved
since independence.

We have noted that Brazil's evolution during the nineteenth
century was atypical when compared with the Hispanic American countries. Its history had been more peaceful, its transition
from monarchy to republic less violent, its break with slavery
almost unopposed by the old regime. As we have said, a feeling
of national identity was evidenced as early as 1889, when the
country embarked on its career as a republic.

The young giant, no longer an empire and yet not a nation,
shows a picture characteristic of the Latin American world:
surface struggle at the political level, and far-reaching social
and economic changes in depth. Between 1889 and 1930 there
was constant conflict between the military and the civilian

forces for the control of the government, with indeterminate results. At the same time the center of gravity moved to the south, from the "colonial sugar-cotton-tobacco-cacao plantations of Bahia and Pernambuco to the coffee-cattle-industrial lands of São Paulo, Minas Gerais, Rio de Janeiro and Rio Grande do Sul."[1]

Brazil became the world's largest coffee producer. But though there was prosperity, there was also unrest. Brazilian intellectuals in the majority still looked toward Europe, captives of the fascination of the Old World. But at least one writer sensed the plight of his people, especially the tragedy of the humble peasants in the interior. Euclydes da Cunha's book, *Os Sertões*, published in 1902, may rightly be called the beginning of Brazilian political thought.[2] The *Sertão* is a semiarid highland region populated by frontiersmen of mixed Portuguese and Indian blood. These people did not adjust to the exigencies of modern life, and in 1896 they revolted against the young republic in the hope of restoring a theocratic regime. They were crushed by the federal army of Brazil, but their resistance brought to light one of the country's greatest problems: regionalism.

Da Cunha described the dramatic experience of the man of the interior and revealed to the intellectuals of the Atlantic coast the sterility of their continued veneration for European values. This perspective led to a new national awareness. Gilberto Freyre has recently defined its inherent polarization as *sertanejismo* versus *oceanismo*, the interior versus the coast.[3] We are, he states, a "constellation of regions," and it is as a constellation of regions that the Portuguese-speaking part of the New World achieved nationhood.

Os sertões was published in a decade when the great majority of Brazilian thinkers were under the influence of either Catholicism or positivism, but neither seemed equipped to answer the cry for social justice raised by the peasants of the interior. Only an understanding that was both compassionate and realistic could focus efficiently on the enormous problems facing the country. Three issues stood out in clear relief: the constant interference of the military, the centrifugal forces produced by an anarchic regionalism, and an economy that relied exclusively on one product for its connections with the world market.[4] Coffee constituted the axis of the national economy; it had helped make Brazil prosperous and it had allowed a modest amount of industrialization. In the process some of the characteristics of colonial life had been overcome.[5] Essentially, however, Brazil continued to maintain a colonial economy, depending for her survival on the consumption by other countries of her greatest product.

The First World War upset the economic balance on which Brazilian prosperity depended. The world transformation, with its weakening of the great empires of the past, with the adoption of new political ideals in Europe, with its revolutionizing of technology and transportation, left its imprint even on a country that was but slightly affected by the European struggle. A revolutionary mood came over many of the Brazilian intellectuals, but such a change in attitude would not have produced a national revolution; the intellectuals turned their attention to social and economic changes; together they produced a revolutionary climate culminating in the national revolution of 1930.

Brazil's monopoly of the coffee market had led to overexpansion and overproduction. She had not taken into consideration that other countries, both inside and outside the western hemisphere, would claim their share of this lucrative trade. Secondary products on which she had counted, such as rubber from the Amazon Basin, were likewise being produced in greater quantities by her Asian competitors. From the end of the First World War to the beginning of the Great Depression, Brazil lived in an economic crisis that may be called endemic. The culmination of the crisis was only delayed by the illusionary prosperity which the world enjoyed between 1919 and 1929. American loans tided Brazil over its most pressing predicaments, but the problem remained unsolved. In fact, the loans tended to aggravate the situation by contributing to the atmosphere of extravagant speculation in which the nation moved.

The military, never completely subdued, became restive and allied themselves with the wave of communist expansion then sweeping the world. A former army captain, Luis Carlos Prestes, gathered around him a motley force of enthusiastic partisans and tried to seize power. The undertaking failed; Prestes and his men retreated into the lowlands, where they continued their resistance for more than two years. This marks the beginning of an organized communist movement, which, to this day, draws its support from the impoverished peasants of the northeast. But political power had long since moved away from the northeast; in practice, the two largest states, São Paulo and Minas Gerais, controlled the fate of the country. A gentlemen's agreement existed allowing for an alternation of the presidency between the politicians of these two powerful regions.

São Paulo was more influential than Minas Gerais; it produced the largest part of the coffee crop, and, by the same token, controlled Brazil's export trade. By the late twenties, coffee prices were tumbling, and Brazil's ability to pay for industrial goods was impaired. São Paulo resorted to extreme remedies; large portions of the coffee crop were destroyed in an effort to raise the value of the remainder.

In the end, it was this issue that tore the country asunder, and caused São Paulo to abandon the standing agreement concerning alternating presidents. The incumbent, President Washington Luiz Pereira de Souza, decided to support the governor of São Paulo as his successor. The politicians considered this a breach of the traditional agreement and threw their support to the governor of a third state, Rio Grande do Sul. Their candidate was Dr. Getúlio Vargas, chosen by the Liberal Alliance and running for office on a program of social and economic reforms. The elections favored the São Paulo candidate, but the opposition maintained that the elections were fraudulent and installed Vargas by force. He assumed office on November 3, 1930. With his accession begins the era of the national revolution. Vargas is the first *caudillo* in the history of Brazil; his presidency marks "the crossroad at which the preponderance of an elite of ivory tower academicians, dilettantes, and confused amateurs fades away." A new generation took over which tried to meet the economic challenge of the depression head on.[6] This could not be done without taking stock of the true Brazilian condition.

Brazil had reached national awareness through the work of one man, Euclydes da Cunha, but by 1930 there was a group of writers, painters, sociologists, and anthropologists whose works centered around Brazil's destiny and whose goal was the revising and reshaping of the national consciousness. National sources, wrote one of them, may not inspire us to reach the highest peaks, but they will lead us to an ultimate future of inventiveness and independence. There were other evidences that Brazilian society was undergoing changes which would supersede the semi-feudal outlook she had known for centuries. Marxist unions had been founded as early as 1918, anarchists and communists had established nuclei throughout the industrial centers. And all these foci of unrest converged in the revolution of 1930.[7]

Regardless of how well the nation had been prepared for a revolution which was, of necessity, both national and socialistic in character, the uprising might have fizzled out or prolonged itself through years of turmoil (as in Mexico's case) had there not been an organizing center. The name of Getúlio Vargas will forever remain associated with the renovation of Brazilian society that took place between 1930 and 1950 and that continued even after his death in 1954.

Vargas was born in São Borja, Rio Grande do Sul, in 1883, to a family of prominence in this most southern state of Brazil. There has been some speculation to the effect that the gaucho tradition of his native land gave him the drive and aggressiveness which made him one of the most spectacular figures of twentieth-century politics. He entered the Brazilian army as a private at the age of sixteen and turned to politics in 1908, after graduating from the University of Pôrto Alegre. He served in the national congress for four years and became minister of finance in 1926. In 1928 he was elected governor of Rio Grande do Sul. From the position of governor, he made his bid for the presidency and led the revolution which ended the first republic. For the next fifteen years he was the chief executive of Brazil.[8]

Personal as well as general factors contributed to his remarkable career. He was a man of indomitable courage, a fact readily admitted even by his foes. He was also a fervent nationalist whose slogan was "Nationalism is my banner; no one shall ever snatch it away from me." However, this stocky, inscrutable little man cherished also a sympathy for the underprivileged. He wanted to be "the father of the poor." In a country with a long tradition of paternalism, where the relations of "masters and slaves" had been abolished but not forgotten, such an avowal struck a welcoming chord in the hearts of many Brazilians. Some observers believe Vargas to have been lacking in charismatic appeal, yet charisma is as charisma does, and no one can deny that when Vargas took office, Brazil was a confederacy of bickering states, and when he left it had become a republic with many attributes of modern nationhood.

To comprehend the Vargas regime we must first make some assessment of the situation in which Brazil found itself. The Great Depression revealed Brazil as a country afflicted with many social ills. The Brazilian sociologist M. A. Teixeira has drawn up a list of twenty-seven grievances; we will take note of only the most serious of these: excessive dispersion of the population, often leading to complete social isolation; lack of urban and personal hygiene, and extreme misery among a part of the agricultural proletariat; frequent outbreaks of banditry; wasteful devastation of the forests; illiteracy among the rural and urban population; lack of proper credit institutions; poor administration of the municipalities; lack of harmony in the undertakings of the various branches of the public administration; and deficient selection, discipline, and remuneration for the whole body of public servants.[9] In many ways the list is typical of grievances in other Latin American countries, but in the case of Brazil the wrongs were multiplied because of the country's magnitude; lack of communications made remedial action almost hopeless.

Getúlio Vargas, however, was undaunted. He proved his political dexterity by the manner in which he gradually wrested the power from the hands of his lieutenants, to whom much of his victory was due. Eventually the Vargas regime became a one-man show.[10] This may be regrettable; perhaps some of Brazil's later tribulations can be attributed to this lack of party organization. Yet it must be admitted that Vargas faced pressing problems and that time was of the essence.

Oswaldo Aranha, one-time foreign minister in the Vargas regime and one of Brazil's outstanding authorities on international affairs, made the following comment on his country: It was without money, without exchange, and legally in a moratorium, with pressing promises to be met abroad, due or to become due within a few days; with a floating debt, federal, state and local, which had never been calculated; with coffee in three crises—price, overproduction, and large stocks in the warehouses; with its economy, industry, and labor in ruins; and with an unemployment crisis.[11] This reads like a typical description of the economic disaster brought on by the Great Depression in the United States, in Germany, in Austria, and elsewhere. And let us not forget that the economic disruption of society in many of these countries was the vehicle that carried the champions of totalitarianism to victory.

The Vargas regime had its veneer of totalitarianism, or possibly it was more than a veneer. But in essence a dictatorship of the Nazi type could not have succeeded. To quote a pun heard frequently in Brazil, it was a *dictablanda* (benevolent despotism), not a *dictadura* (dictatorship). Of course, racism would have been impossible to conceive in a country that prided itself on its racial plurality, but even a monolithic party organization was hardly feasible in a nation with so little cohesion.

A complete overhaul of the administrative machinery was imperative, and Vargas proceeded with all deliberate speed.

Indolent, incompetent, or corrupt officials were removed from government service and replaced by *interventores* (supervisors), frequently from the Brazilian army. It amounted to a purge of the old aristocratic elements which had usurped the privileges of the ruling class far too long. The reaction was not slow in coming. Since the army stood behind Vargas, his enemies had to depend on state police, especially from São Paulo, which stood to lose most from the Vargas reforms. The Paulistas were unwilling to give up their position without a fight, and two years after Vargas had taken office, they started a rebellion and marched on Rio de Janeiro. This civil war was, however, of short duration; in October of 1932 Vargas was once more firmly established. In 1934 a constituent assembly was called and promulgated a new constitution, electing Vargas to the presidency for a term of four years.

This constitution represents a compromise between states' rights supporters and the advocates of strong centralized government. In some respects it was more reactionary than Vargas had desired; in others, it leapt far ahead of the social and cultural development of Brazil.[12] Thus it did not satisfy the *caudillo*-president, who made it understood that he would be the first to revise it. This he did in his own fashion.

The Communist Party showed signs of preparing for revolution, and a fascist movement, called Integralism, stood ready to launch a revolution of its own. This double menace forced Vargas further on the road toward authoritarianism; there can be little doubt, however, that such action suited his temper well. As the term of his office drew to a close, and the question of presidential succession arose in November of 1937, he adopted measures gleaned from Mussolini and Hitler. All parties were dissolved, the national congress was dispersed, and the election was called off. A new constitution was published, closely following the fascist example. It placed no limits on Vargas's continuance in office and transferred many of the responsibilities of the states to the federal government. The press was placed under strict control, either by nationalizing the newspapers or by censorship. But the gratification expressed by Rome and Berlin concerning the *coup d'état* of 1937 was premature; the Vargas revolution was a complex affair, and like its wily leader, it does not seem to fit into any mold. Vargas's Estado Novo is not easily categorized.

The constitution of 1937 declared a state of national emergency and promised ratification by plebiscite at a later date.[13] This promise was never fulfilled, and since the constitution had also declared that all acts attempting to solve the national emergency were outside the jurisdiction of the courts, the Estado Novo was, if not totalitarian, certainly authoritarian. The president was empowered to rule by decree.

Some Brazilians questioned the existence of any constitution at all, speculating on whether the whole thing was not a legalistic camouflage for the ambitions of the dictator. The question seems academic, however, since there could be no doubt that a state of emergency did indeed exist, that it was not of Vargas's making, and that he was determined to end it.

A cursory reading of this constitution makes it clear that Brazil's socioeconomic problems are at its core. It was a declaration of intentions which have since become an integral part of the national expectations in Brazil and which are regarded with respect by every statesman.

Private property was preserved in the constitution, but the central government was granted the right to intervene for the purpose of stimulating or coordinating production and curbing competition. Work was declared a social duty; minimum wage and the eight-hour work day were introduced; child labor and night work were restricted, and, most important, social security and medical care for workers and expectant mothers were decreed. These measures represented everything that was revolutionary for a country that had followed the habits of unrestrained capitalism tempered only by tropical indolence. Once again, it would be hard to say which countries had served as models for Vargas and the framers of the constitution. Some provisions seem to have been taken from Italy's corporate state, while others could have been copied from the Soviet constitution of 1936. It matters little, since the essence of the Brazilian revolution was nationalistic and socialistic at the same time. Articles 145 to 153 of the constitution deal with the utilization of national wealth, making special reference to subsoil rights and mineral deposits. They give a promise of nationalization, but nationalization Brazilian style.[14] The important thing was not the transfer of private property into the hands of the state, but the prevention of foreign control and foreign ownership of key industries, such as oil and steel. Here too, the seeds for further development were planted: Since 1937 the concept of "nationalization" has spread to many other branches of the economy. It is more than likely that the Mexican revolution with its famous Article 27 was the inspiration for Article 143 of the Brazilian constitution, which stated that utilization of mines, subsoil rights, and water power are, in principle, reserved to Brazilians or enterprises composed of Brazilian stockholders. This ordinance was later extended to cover banks and insurance companies, and since many of these were controlled by foreign capital it is not difficult to understand the implications. The nationalistic fervor went so far as to stipulate that Brazilians married to foreigners were restricted in the free disposition of their property if it fell in the category of minerals or subsoil wealth.

Many other nationalistic measures were introduced. Concessionaires of public enterprises, whether federal, state, or municipal, had to be Brazilians, and this ruling applied also to administrators in the bureaucratic machinery. Nationally registered ships had to be owned and commanded by nationals, and their crews had to be two-thirds Brazilian. Even the liberal professions were closed to foreigners, and diplomas from abroad could not be revalidated in Brazil. (It is an evidence of the nationalistic fury that this law was laid down at a time when many nations were reaping the benefit of the exodus from Nazi Germany.) Labor unions could be headed only by Brazilian nationals. A fear of foreign aggression also seems to have existed,

though from whom remains a mystery; industries located at a
distance of 150 kilometers or less from the border were ordered
to employ only Brazilian workers.[15]

In the light of this patriotic frenzy, it is surprising that the
affairs of the country did not come to a standstill. Vargas, however, proceeded to draw the Brazilian economy out of its doldrums. A mixture of public and private enterprise emerged,
much like that to be found in many other countries during the
thirties. The intervention of the government in the management
of the coffee crop continued to be a necessity. Vargas bought
large quantities of this commodity and ordered it to be dumped
in the sea or burned in the furnaces of Brazilian locomotives.
Institutes for research in sugar and alcohol were set up in order
to stimulate consumption of these products. Since foreign exchange was in short supply, manufacturing was encouraged
and took a great leap ahead. Raw materials and equipment for
these industries were given priority by the government, and
almost overnight there appeared a rash of new industrial centers. Great numbers flocked to these urban centers, and, as a
result, housing, public utilities, transportation, and medical care
had to be improvised.[16] Most of the new towns were situated in
São Paulo, Minas Gerais, Pernambuco, Bahia, Rio de Janeiro, Rio
Grande do Sul, and Santa Catharina. The new cities demanded
new plants for drinking water; sewer systems had to be laid out;
power lines for the additional consumption of electricity were
needed; and in general, basic industries, such as steel, coal, and
oil, had to be stimulated. But the development of new industry
required a heavy outlay of capital, and this was lacking in
Brazil. Vargas did not invite foreign capital to come to the
rescue. A large part of Brazil's electrical industry was controlled
by Canadian and British interests, and Vargas did not wish to
repeat this pattern in other branches of the national economy.

Although it is not difficult to understand and to sympathize
with Vargas's motives, it must be admitted that his program
slowed up the process of industrialization and delayed even
more the full use of the national resources. But Vargas ob-

viously feared that a large influx of foreign capital would alien-
ate the working and middle classes from the body politic, and
it was on these two groups that he relied. Therefore, it was
toward their interests that much of the legislative effort of the
Estado Novo was directed.

During the first years of his tenure, Vargas had created a
ministry of labor, industry and commerce. Not much later, he
took the necessary steps to legalize the existence of trade unions.
Until then, labor had largely been "a problem for the police."[17]
Now unions could register with the new government agency.
The Vargas regime offered recognition of the trade unions in
exchange for the unions' recognition of government supervision
and intervention. Labor accepted the proposition—not, however, without some hesitation, since it had been greatly under
the influence of anarchistic and communist elements. But the
economic advantages overcame the ideologic resistance; employers could not refuse to bargain with unions that had been
recognized by the government. Furthermore, a social security
system covering white- and blue-collar workers promised protection for illness and old age; and everyone realized that social
security could not be established without government help. As
a result, relations between labor and management under the
Vargas dictatorship were satisfactory.[18]

In general, the economic policy of the Vargas regime was
ardently nationalistic. There was the famous "two-thirds act"
which demanded a minimum quota of two-thirds for nationals
employed in each enterprise.[19] No Brazilian was to receive a
smaller salary than a foreigner who did the same type of work.
Moreover, these guarantees were surrounded with a heavy
armor of bureaucratic enforcement. The wisdom of some of
these measures has been questioned, since they resulted in the
alienation of foreign capital and the forfeiture of foreign experts whose cooperation was needed to effect the economic
recovery. However, Vargas felt that the idea of nationalism was
the rallying point for the Estado Novo.

The Estado Novo was clothed in many of the trappings of the

fascist movement. Workers and employers were organized in syndicates. The syndicates were controlled by federations on the state and national level which spanned the entire economy. The federations were supposed to serve as a foundation for the political activities of the government, but, as in Italy, the corporative state remained a facade. It did, however, insure the Vargas regime the support of the working class, which felt that it was being cared for by "the father of the poor." Besides the benefits of social legislation which we have already noted, there was a modest housing program, and steps were taken to diversify the economy by building up a heavy industry. Brazil is rich in mineral resources, and it was Vargas who started the now famous steel plant at Volta Redonda.

A good deal has been written about Vargas's fascist inclination, but it seems more likely that he was an opportunist whose aim was the reconstruction of his country by any means that might come to hand. During the thirties, Vargas was quite willing to copy Germany's and Italy's vocabulary and even to enter into agreements with the Nazis. Brazil had long wished to be recognized as a great power and had withdrawn from the League of Nations when she was refused a permanent seat in 1926. The hostile front built up by the fascist dictators against the western democracies could serve a nation like Brazil as an ideological shield in her fight against foreign domination and economic colonialism. But conditions shifted as the Second World War approached; by 1939, trade with Germany was no longer possible.

The entrance of the United States into the war offered Vargas new opportunities. Brazil had traditionally been a friend of the United States, and there was little doubt as to where the sympathies of the people lay as the great struggle in Europe unfolded. The fall of France saddened them, and the English resistance was followed with admiration. Yet Vargas did not change course abruptly; he spoke in cryptic terms about virile people who must follow the lines of their aspirations, words which might be interpreted at will. But Vargas also realized that the war was ushering in a future which would not be guided in its economic, political, and social organizations by the antiquated formulas of the past.[20] In the end Brazil veered toward the Allied camp. It is hard to say whether Vargas vacillated between totalitarian and democratic allegiances or whether, cunning strategist that he was, he simply put a higher price on his cooperation. In any case, his nationalistic program notwithstanding, he was willing to make concessions to the United States, and in 1940 he permitted the installation of military bases for United States forces on Brazilian soil. Eventually these bases reached all the way from Amapá in the north through Belém, Natal, Recife and Bahia to Santa Cruz.

After Pearl Harbor, the inter-American security system was revitalized, and it was perhaps not accidental that a conference of foreign ministers met in Rio de Janeiro in 1942. Here Brazil openly sided with the forces of democracy. She declared war on Italy and Germany in August of 1942, and she was the only Latin American nation to send an expeditionary force overseas. Nor was this all. There were large German settlements in southern Brazil which were put through an enforced process of assimilation; German signs were removed from streets and stores, only Portuguese could be spoken in public, and the young men were drafted into the army, where they were given a thorough nationalistic indoctrination. The Japanese settlements received similar treatment. If today these acts appear insignificant, it is well to remember that at the time they curbed subversive activities by Nazi elements in Brazil. There can be no doubt about the popularity of these acts among the Brazilian people, who were proud of their nation's participation in the war.

It would seem ironic that this same participation should weaken the domestic regime of President Vargas. To the extent that the Allied forces advanced on their various battlefronts, the cry for a relaxation of the Brazilian dictatorship became stronger. And indeed it was an open contradiction to fight oppression abroad and cultivate it at home. Opposition to Vargas had been muzzled, but never completely silenced, and slowly its voice began to be heard. First to express dissent with the regime was a heterogeneous group that called itself the UDN, the National Democratic Union, which included in its ranks intellectuals, landholders, communists, and even some representatives from the military.[21]

Following the advice of his friends, Vargas began to relax his grip on the country. He permitted trade unions to elect their leaders and removed some of the restrictions which the Brazilian press had endured. He promised free election of the presidency for 1945 and assured the people that he would not run for this office. A general amnesty was declared and political prisoners were released. As the war drew to a close, Brazil's political life was once again in full swing.

A bewildering panorama began to unfold. The leader of the Communist Party, Luis Carlos Prestes, declared that he was backing Vargas and that the Communist Party would support the president until a new constitution had been drafted. No one is certain of the significance of this move or whether Prestes and Vargas had reached an agreement before Prestes had been released from prison, but the suspicions that surrounded this astonishing development did not strengthen Vargas's cause. Other parties appeared. There was the Social Democratic Party and the Brazilian Labor Party; both were well organized. Their names notwithstanding, they were composed of elements from the business world and the landholding class, but they also attracted a large number of officeholders, urban workers, and union leaders. The checkered composition of these parties reflects quite accurately the peculiar nature of Brazil's fifteen-year-old national revolution.

A year of political maneuvering followed, during which Vargas tried to hold on to power without openly breaking his promise for a presidential election. The crisis came to a head in October of 1945, when he appointed his brother as chief of the metropolitan police, a move which the army interpreted as a preparatory step toward a new *coup d'état*. The military considered itself pledged to the promise of a free election and answered the president's move by occupying strategic positions in Rio de Janeiro. Vargas resigned and returned to his estate in Rio Grande do Sul.

Elections were held in December of 1945 and brought General Dutra, the candidate of the Social Democratic Party, to power. But the party situation continued to be chaotic and ill defined. The Social Democratic Party held more than half the seats in the new constituent assembly, but the Liberal Democratic Union and the Brazilian Labor Party commanded a large portion of the electorate. The Communist Party was returned with fourteen seats. A unique feature of the elections for the constituent assembly was the election of the newly ousted Vargas to a seat in the senate.[22] In interpreting the returns one must, of course, beware of taking these figures at their face value. The electorate represented only a seventh of the population, the majority being illiterate and thus excluded from voting. And it is doubtful whether one can speak of a strong socialist movement that would compare with the communist parties that emerged in France and Italy after the war.

The assembly began its work on a new constitution, and this was completed by September of 1946. It attempted to preserve the most important achievements of the Vargas regime together with a return to parliamentary democracy. Strikes were made permissible and profit sharing was introduced. The president and vice-president were to hold office for six-year terms. The senate was to be composed of three senators from each state, and the chamber of deputies was to be made up of representatives elected on a population basis for four-year terms.

Elections were held in 1947 for governors and legislative assemblies of the states, and they confirmed the changes which had been made two years earlier. Most of the high-ranking posts were divided between the Social Democratic Party and the National Democratic Union. Dutra's cabinet represented both parties and relied on an alliance of both groups. It seemed as though an even balance between regional and sectional elements had been established.

This apparent stability was, however, transitory. The impact of Vargas and his ideas was by no means wiped out. Under him Brazil had undergone a "marvelous transition," and this is perhaps the proper moment to review his achievements in the perspective that has guided us throughout our study.

Our first observation would appear to be a negative one. In 1930 Brazil had been threatened with a serious breakdown of its national identity by the forces of regionalism. This menace, however, had been eliminated by the time that Vargas stepped down. The national government had been strengthened and had assumed responsibility for vast sections of the economy, for public education, for expanding commerce and industry. And all of this had been undertaken in the name and for the welfare of the nation.[23] The achievements of the Estado Novo are not limited to a single field, but cover many, if not all, aspects of the national life. We will address ourselves to a few of them.

As in many other Latin American countries, a middle sector had emerged in Brazil; it represented the bridge between the old landowning class and the dispossessed. The number of schools doubled between 1930 and 1945; enrollment increased even more. Teachers were still underpaid, but as their numbers grew their prestige increased. Vargas realized that industry and commerce could expand only if the people were able to master the elementary factors of a technological civilization. Employment would, in turn, be found in the rapidly growing urban centers, where a new stratum of consumers would help the merchant class. Since Brazil was lacking in foreign exchange for the importation of industrial goods and since such goods became increasingly scarce during the war, there was an incentive to produce such goods at home. Vargas's tariff policy was geared to the same purpose. Tariffs on raw material and on semi-finished products were reduced; those on finished goods were raised. These measures gave the nation a sense of purpose, economic in its immediate aim, but social and political in its consequences. Vargas's economic policy was widely accepted by those groups that were politically conscious, the military and the budding urban middle class. Gradually Brazilian output of manufactured goods rose to the level of its agriculture. This economic policy, as we have noted, was accompanied by restrictive measures designed to protect the Brazilians from exploitation and even from competition. Progressive nationalization had been one of the key measures written into the constitution of 1934. Besides the efforts to avoid foreign influence in the petroleum industry, Vargas began to buy out the foreign companies controlling the railroads and soon gained control of the transportation system, which was then put in the hands of the federal government.[24] The war provided ample excuse for ousting the Germans from the airlines, and as a result domestic aviation received a strong boost. The gigantic steel plant at Volta Redonda was another symbol of the country's growing pride in its economic potential.

But the economic emancipation of Brazil, though begun by Vargas, was not complete when he was driven from office in 1945. And as a matter of fact it could not reach completion under a dictatorship. Vargas had been obliged to play the rich against the poor and the poor against the rich, and he had been supported by both in his effort to get Brazil back into the running. But this conniving left some broad gaps in his program. The tax structure continued to favor the wealthy and to leave the burden to the low-income group. Only in this way could the moneyed classes be encouraged to invest in Brazilian enterprises, and, we may add, to be lured into support of the dictator. Likewise, speculation in urban real estate was in no way discouraged. Since heavy industry was the favored child of the Vargas regime, transportation and power development were neglected. The position of labor remained uncertain. No politician after Vargas could venture to ignore it altogether, but its influence vis-à-vis the older elements of society was ill defined. Finally, the ambitious economic policy with nationalistic aims had forced the country into heavy expenditures, which led to the proverbial inflationary spiral. Prices rose while the value of the cruzeiro fell. The new urban population, whether white- or blue-collar, clamored for better living conditions; these could be achieved only by higher wages, but higher wages jeopardized the stability of the fiscal system, and so on *ad infinitum*.[25]

Thus the heritage from the Vargas regime was, at best, ambiguous. He had saved the country from chaotic regionalism, but he left it plunged in the confusion of a multiparty system. As elsewhere the multiplicity of parties did not advance the course of orderly government. Brazilian party interests cut across economic interests and class structures and were largely influenced by personal factors, making analysis virtually impossible. "Nationalism and inflation recognize no class lines."[26]

Thus Vargas, as he departed from the political scene in 1945, could not claim that he had obtained national cohesion. Nor did he fare much better on his second try. Vargas's successor was a colorless general who represented the hostility felt by Brazilian society against dictatorial methods. Accordingly, the suffrage was liberalized to include members of both sexes over eighteen years of age, and attempts were made to prevent further centralization of power. But many of the tenets of the Vargas regime were reaffirmed; for instance, the obligation of the state to the masses, the promotion of industry, and the fostering of education. General Dutra was in reality a stopgap in the course of the national revolution. Vargas had bided his time during the Dutra regime, but as the new elections approached, he was much in evidence. The Partido Trabalhista, one of the three leading parties, nominated Vargas, and he was insured the support of the trade unions. The Communist Party, which had been banished in 1947, also backed him, and he was further supported by a large number of uncommitted delegates. He used his old campaign slogans—the cause of nationalism and his love for the poor—but both were accented more strongly. Brazilian nationalism was given a polemical thrust against the United States, and the poor were promised the aid of increased wages and a curb on inflation. Vargas was returned to the presidency with a strong mandate.

Vargas was still in possession of his nimble intelligence when he was restored to power, but conditions inside and outside Brazil had changed drastically during his absence. The armed forces, upon which he had once relied, were now committed to the cause of democracy. He turned, therefore, to the proletariat as the mainstay of his government; the father of the poor became a rabble rouser. Perhaps the aging Vargas had himself undergone a change.[27] He had never been over-scrupulous about the means he chose to keep himself in power, but what in former times may have seemed to be courage and deliberation now appeared to have turned into cynicism and ruthlessness. He used the trade union as his most powerful weapon to pressure the other sections of Brazilian society. It was said that he provoked strikes in order that he might step in and settle them and that he used violent and corrupt methods, which, becoming known, undermined his prestige. One of the enigmas of Vargas's second government was his appointment of João Goulart as minister of labor. Many thought that Goulart was Vargas's choice for his successor. In any case, he displayed all of Vargas's demagoguery before the army obliged him to resign.

Vargas persisted in his flag-waving policy and introduced a bill to make Brazilian oil an exclusively national enterprise. Petroleos Brasileiros (Petrobras) was established, to the great satisfaction of the majority of the nationalists. But the economic nationalism also had its drawbacks. Long-range plans for the development of the Brazilian economy which were to be undertaken with the assistance of the United States were canceled when the United States became increasingly disenchanted with Brazil's penchant for placing obstacles in the path of investment capital. A loan of half a billion dollars that should have helped to pay for the development of transportation facilities and electric power was canceled by the Eisenhower administration.[28] This setback did not seem to deter Vargas. He continued his social program, revised the minimum-wage law, and envisaged a wide project of land reform combined with some incentive to immigrants that would place new land under cultivation.

There is no need to detail here the incidents that brought about Vargas's downfall. Scandal loomed behind the facade, and again there were conflicts between the president and the armed forces. The army considered itself the guarantor of the constitution, and when it appeared that Vargas was determined to use strong-arm methods to silence the opposition, he was asked to resign.[29] It has been said that Vargas was strangely isolated, badly informed, possibly weary and bereft of faith in his own cause. He was disgusted with the "rivers of mud" that flowed through the presidential palace as the crisis rose to a climax, and on an August day in 1954 he ended his life by suicide. It was a melodramatic exit for a man over seventy, and many explanations have been offered for his act. His own comment is contained in his farewell letter: "I follow the destiny that is imposed upon me . . . I offer my life in the holocaust . . . I fought against the looting of Brazil and against the looting of the people . . . Serenely I take the first step on the road to eternity, and I leave life to enter history."[30]

It would seem clear that Brazilian nationalism and love for his people were the prime motives of Vargas's life even to his last moments. The country was caught up in emotions and erupted into violence. The communists, technically outlawed but in practiced tolerated, went into action without delay. They construed Vargas's farewell note as a blast against the United States. There were riots in Rio de Janeiro and Pôrto Alegre, the capital of Vargas's home state. But the succession to the presidency was orderly. The vice-president, Café Filho, took office and the army moved to prevent greater disturbances. Filho summoned members of many groups to make up his cabinet and embarked on a policy of conservative moderation. Elections were to take place in a year.

The elections of 1955 gave the presidency to Juscelino Kubitschek, the candidate of the Social Democratic Party; his running mate was João Goulart, former minister of labor under Vargas. Labor still represented the most vociferous political faction and had an easy victory over the more conservative parties of the Democratic National Union and the Christian Democratic Party. Kubitschek took office at the beginning of 1956.

A descendant of German and Portuguese ancestors, Juscelino Kubitschek represents the generation of Brazilians who had grown up in the Estado Novo and who had known poverty from childhood. Kubitschek put himself through preparatory and medical school by working as a telegraph operator. The medical profession did not hold him for long, and he entered politics in his home state of Minas Gerais. He was elected mayor of Belo Horizonte and got his first knowledge of the needs of Brazilian cities. In 1950, having joined the Vargas party, he became governor of Minas Gerais.

As president, Kubitschek was determined to follow Vargas's precepts, although with less rigidity. Transportation and electric power had been his slogan in Minas Gerais, and he did not change it when he became the country's chief executive. He wanted private enterprise to undertake the job, and promised to interfere only when private enterprise was either unwilling or unable to carry out the essentials of the operation. An industrial expansion of gigantic proportions was indicated. There were 6,200 miles of roads to be constructed; it was necessary to increase the electricity from 3 million kilowatts to 5 million. Heavy machinery was needed, as well as storehouses for food.

An ambitious program of this magnitude called for large capital outlay and caught Kubitschek on the horns of a dilemma. He would either have to increase the inflationary spiral that had plagued Brazil for more than twenty years, or attract foreign capital and thus provoke a xenophobic reaction. In the face of these hazards, Kubitschek topped his expansionist list with a still more extravagant plan—the construction of a new capital in the interior. We have mentioned the age-old tension between the coast and the interior in Brazilian history, the tension between *oceanismo* and *sertanejismo*. Kubitschek hoped that the rise of a new capital, far from the coast, would furnish great impetus to the colonization of the interior. "Enormous fertile lands," he said, "are as empty as the Sahara, while millions of Brazilians live in penury, clinging like crabs to the crowded shoreline." Eight months after his inauguration, the Brazilian congress passed a law that established the corporation which was to build the Nova Capital do Brasil: Brasília.

His enemies called him Pharaoh Juscelino, but the nation backed the mercurial president. And it became more and more apparent that the national revolution had transformed more than the social fabric; it had brought on a new generation of Brazilian architects, able to hold their own with such masters as Le Corbusier and Gropius. Lúcio Costa, Oscar Niemeyer, and da Silva Teles are a few of the names that come to mind when we speak of contemporary Brazilian architecture. They had already given proof of the new spirit in a number of buildings in Rio de Janeiro and in São Paulo. Their style was a combination of Le Corbusier, Miës van der Rohe, and ideas peculiar to their own tradition; they wished to express the national personality with techniques and materials native to their own country.[31] They were glad to join forces with Kubitschek on his master plan for a capital in "the heartland of the nation."

The new capital sprang up almost overnight. It was the purpose of the architects to create not only an *urbs* but a *civitas*, with the attributes of nobility, discipline, and proportion.[32] This is not the place to speak of the effort that went into the construction of Brasília, nor to describe the sculptural and decorative splendor that marked its completion. The new center caught the imagination of the nation—"Anyone who tries to stop it," said the president, "will be lynched by the people."[33] It is a monument to the national revolution that transformed a semicolonial country into a contemporary state.

But if Brasília is a monument to the nation's desire for dynamic unity, it is also a proof of its economic plight. It was accomplished at the cost of deficit spending which mortgaged the future of more important though perhaps less spectacular projects. The cruzeiro took a further plunge. National capital fled the country at an unprecedented rate, and the inflationary spiral speeded up. Nevertheless, regardless of the cost, Kubitschek's successor felt committed to finish the job.

Jânio Quadros came to power in the midst of Fidel Castro's switch to socialism, an important consideration in any discussion of Quadros's short tenure. It is probable that the president hoped to steer his country in the direction of a similar goal without using the same revolutionary methods. He was convinced that Brazil was a great power, or at least on her way to becoming one. He wanted to lead a revolution against graft and corruption, against social and economic backwardness, and he believed that the "nation's conscience" was already pregnant with this new spirit.[34] Some called him a savior; some called him a paranoiac, an autocrat, a dictator. Whatever he was, he was nobody's pawn.

Quadros came from the state of Mato Grosso and was born at the frontier of Brazil's western flank. Like Kubitschek he had been poor and had worked his way through the university. He entered politics in São Paulo as a member of the city council. He was called the mad Lincoln of Mato Grosso, but by 1950 he had made a name for himself as the champion of the little man. He too was in the Vargas tradition, playing a dangerous game with the communists, who thought they could use him while he maintained that he was using them. Yet he became mayor of São Paulo on a platform of "industry and honesty" and set about cleaning up the political machine. Less than two years later he was elected governor of the state. From the governor's mansion he followed the same course. He tripled São Paulo's network of highways and raised more than 1,700 miles of high-tension transmission lines. Three-fourths of all the new investment capital coming into Brazil was drawn to São Paulo. Few questioned that he was headed for the presidency. Though he seemed to be a political maverick, he proved to be a tireless and often brilliant campaigner. He had Vargas's concern for the poor and the same distrust of privilege and vested interests. Again and again he asserted, "I am no plutocrat."[35] He held a deep resentment against the contemporary civilization of North America, and did not hesitate to fraternize with Castro if only to prove that he was no stooge of the United States. He was elected to the presidency with the largest vote ever accorded a candidate for that office. In a multiparty system, he piled up a 48% majority.

He promised to "wield a broom" and to clean out corruption, to institute a program of austerity, to halt inflation, and to restore foreign confidence in the national economy. Inevitably he aroused the opposition of those who would be the target of his reforms: the tax dodgers, the landholders, and the speculators. Ultimately, however, it was his foreign policy that caused the greatest concern.

It was 1961, and the Bay of Pigs invasion had failed. Quadros thought that Brazil was in line to make her weight felt in the conflict between the Soviet Union and the United States. Like many another Latin American he hoped to build a third force that would act as a neutralizer. "A nation heretofore almost unknown," he wrote, "is prepared to bring to bear on the play of the world pressures the economic and human potential it represents."[36]

But though Brazil might have fancied the role of honest broker, Quadros was too erratic to carry out this ambitious design. While his intentions are understandable, they could not be achieved by hasty moves in all directions. He termed his policy "interested neutralism" and insisted that he stood for nonintervention and self-determination. But he also sent trade missions behind the Iron Curtain and advocated the admission of Red China to the United Nations. These moves clearly indicated that he wanted his country to be less dependent on the United States. Brazil needed markets, he said, both for its new industries and for its exploding population, and these could not be found within the western alliance. Material interests, he added, know no doctrine. Diplomatic relations with the Soviet Union were restored after a lapse of fourteen years, and President Tito was invited to visit Brazil. But suddenly the proud adventure of an independent foreign policy collapsed, not because of outside pressure, but because of troubles within the country.

Quadros's nationalistic policy failed for several reasons, but in general because Brazil was not ready to play the role he had envisaged and, at the same time, pursue economic and social reforms. The president had shown signs of increasing intolerance; the presidential palace was no longer open to the people; locks barred the doors and guards with machine guns protected the nation's leader. An observer said the atmosphere reminded him of Kafka's *Castle*. When Quadros's recommendations met with opposition, he threatened to take his case to the people. But the people were apathetic, and when he resigned they made no move to stop him. Bitterly disappointed, Quadros left office after a tenure of seven months.

The unexpected resignation left a temporary vacuum because of the absence of Quadros's constitutional successor, Vice-President João Goulart, then on a state visit to Red China.[37] It will be recalled that Goulart had been minister of labor under Vargas and was well known for his flirtation with the party line. The army seemed determined to prevent his installation as head of the state, but congress was unwilling to bow to the wishes of the military. Tension eased when, after a week of maneuvering, the constitution was amended by an "additional act" which left Goulart as head of the state, but placed the executive power in the hands of a cabinet, its majority drawn from congress. It was a swing toward the parliamentary system, British-style, but it did not solve the Brazilian problem. Instead, the country seemed to have fallen from the frying pan into the open fire. The new system of government was to be confirmed by plebiscite, and it was on this question that the new president and congress disagreed. Goulart asked for the full restoration of his executive power; congress was averse. National elections were held in October of 1962, but their results were inconclusive. They showed, however, a further drift to the left in Guanabara, Pernambuco, and Rio Grande do Sul. Here Brazilian nationalism once more took the United States as its main target and favored a policy not far distant from Cuba's. The focal point for a determined switch toward socialism was the impoverished northeast, where the situation of the peasants was alarming and where Cuban agitators attempted to organize a revolt.

It is difficult to say with any certainty whether Goulart would have welcomed closer ties with Castro. He did continue the policy of "independence" that Vargas and Quadros had pursued both in the United Nations and in the OAS. Brazilian spokesmen lamented Cuba's departure from the principles of representative democracy, but they persisted in their efforts to keep the island republic within the American system of security and solidarity. In the meantime, the country continued on its course of deficit spending and inflation, and the national currency took a further dive.[38] The money was needed to keep up with the steadily rising cost of living, to pay labor higher wages, and to pay the military and civilian employees of the government. Congress refused to increase the minimum wage, but authorized an end-of-the-year bonus to be paid to all salaried personnel.[39] There were ugly rumors of graft and corruption in high places involving the president and his brother-in-law, Leonel Brizola. Brizola was one of the most outspoken foes of the United States and, in 1962, had expropriated the National Telephone Company of Rio Grande do Sul, a subsidiary of International Telephone and Telegraph of New York. While clamoring for land reform, Brizola and Goulart had availed themselves of the opportunity to acquire a string of estates for themselves. Once more the army decided to step in. Goulart was ousted and fled to Montevideo, and a member of the army, Humberto Castelo Branco, became president. His term has been extended to 1966.

These various events would cause a great deal of confusion, were it not for the fact that many Brazilians consider the army to be the best guarantor of civilian government. Military morale is better than civilian morale, says one observer.[40] The Brazilian military has long considered itself an elite, capable of removing any government it believes inefficient or dangerous, but when order is restored it stands ready to return the direction of the state to the people. Recently the new government has revealed some of the shocking aspects of mismanagement under Goulart and has promised to stabilize the economy.

It would be incorrect to assume, however, that the latest turn of events will put an end to the national revolution, now in its fourth decade in Brazil. To begin with, the economic ills are more apparent than real, and it is easy to exaggerate the negative factors. Real production has been increasing at the rate of 7% per year in Brazil, while per capita production has been rising at 4% per year, and continues to outstrip population growth.[41] The market for consumer goods is steadily growing; new investments have been made to redeem the northeastern region, and São Paulo continues to expand its industrial power. These facts seem to prove that the national revolution has left an indelible mark on Brazil. Nationalism, once the concern of the elite, is now an emotion permeating all sectors of society. It has become institutionalized and has given the people a feeling of destiny. No group can be singled out as the sole representative of Brazilian nationalism, let alone one party. The political scene shows kaleidoscopic shifts and changes, but underneath there is a steady and increasing current toward unity. "The present preoccupation of the Brazilian mind with nationalism shows its desire to do away with the bovarysm of the past."[42] The illusion that the Brazilians are content to be mere cordial spectators of the great drama of humanity now unfolding will be dissipated. They are eager to drive ahead and to make Brazil a world power, even at the going price for world prestige.[43]

The Brazilian revolution may not yet have achieved the maturity it has reached in Mexico, but it has brought results that are both undeniable and ineradicable. Brazil has gained a feeling of identity and a sense of its own destiny. Brazil is an immense country, maritime as well as mediterranean, spread over an area almost entirely tropical, with a civilization that is both interregional and interracial, and Brazilian nationalism must affirm the plurality of races and the diversity of regions because the national reality encompasses them all. In its present phase Brazilian nationalism is focused on the social and economic reality of the country; it is an ideology that binds together all those who feel that the giant nation has not yet reached its potential. But as in Mexico and Bolivia, nationalism is a gravitational center for all constructive forces that point toward the future.[44]

CHAPTER IX

Enigmatic Argentina

Among the nations of Latin America, Argentina seemed to be the country least likely to experience the influence of revolutionary nationalism. Her constitutional development had been assured since 1853, and its progress had been accompanied by an economic prosperity without parallel in South America. However, this picture of stability and steady expansion was a thinly veiled disguise; social energies were fermenting which would eventually bring on an upheaval of unremitting aspect. The events have been reviewed many times, but the motivating forces have not been fully explored.

We have sketched the development of Argentina from its beginnings in 1810 to the turn of the nineteenth century. During these decades the nation was in a process of becoming, threatened by particularism and regionalism. Just as in Brazil, the men of the seaboard and the men of the interior had different interests and outlooks in political, economic, and cultural matters; anarchy or disruption seemed close at hand. But this menace was overcome, a balance was established, and Argentina appeared to be on her way to leadership in the Latin American world. Then began a second phase in the history of this perplexing state, lasting from 1890 to 1930. It was characterized by increasing cultural and economic nationalism, by xenophobia, and by a desire to assert influence in world affairs, especially those that concerned the western hemisphere.[1] In itself this attitude would not indicate revolutionary tendencies, but in Argentina, as in Brazil, the forces of nationalism became intertwined with the energies of the awakening urban masses.

The predominant philosophy of the young republic was democratic in politics, *laisser-faire* in economics, and Catholic in religious matters. It was dependent on western Europe for its culture. The reins of government had been held by an oligarchy, and, up to a point, this situation seemed to be in keeping with the national development.[2] The ruling group in no way interfered with the economic and technological evolution that swept the nation forward. Large amounts of investment capital had entered the country; technological skills had been acquired that supplied the republic with one of the best transport systems in Latin America, allowing for mobility within the country and for contacts with the United States and Europe. A truly national economy had come into being, depending on agricultural wealth in the first place, but allowing for the growth of industrial enterprises. Argentina became one of the most urbanized of the Latin American republics; 50% of her people lived in the cities. A large percentage of the urban population had immigrated from European countries. Argentina could boast of leadership in the field of education, and had a metropolitan press which commanded respect in many parts of the world. This was the era of "conservative liberalism," and the country flourished in its benign atmosphere; its watchword was "peace and administration."[3]

The oligarchy was not obliged to contend with organized opposition; it was faced only with a heterogeneous mass that had scarcely begun to visualize its aspirations. But by 1890 the picture had begun to alter. Opposition to the landholding aristocracy crystallized in two groups: the Radical Civic Union, known eventually as the Radical Party, and the Socialist Party of Argentina. For a time the oligarchy was able to ward off the radical offensive, mostly by fraudulent manipulations of the elections which robbed the opposition of many rightful votes. But by 1912 these machinations had become a national problem. Though himself a member of the oligarchy, President Roque Sáenz Peña pressed for electoral reforms, and on February 13, 1912, the Sáenz Peña Law was put into force.[4] Its success gave the Radical Party its triumph in 1916, and the party held the presidency for fourteen years, until 1930. This period marked the rise of the Argentinian middle class to a position of power and respectability. Throughout these years, the leader of the Radical Party, Hipólito Irigoyen, continued to be a controversial figure. Under him, presidential power was built up to a degree previously unknown in Argentinian history. Political patronage was used to buy support, and corruption continued. But the reform of the universities got under way, and this gave impulse to a more technological outlook in the institutes of higher learning. Some labor legislation was passed, though the basic philosophy of the Radical Party remained paternalistic, and Irigoyen was not above using the police to break up strikes. In international affairs he asserted Argentina's independence. When he entered the Casa Rosada, Argentina's White House, the First World War was in full swing, and the United States was preparing to enter the conflict. Irigoyen, refusing to be drawn into the carnage, declared, "Argentina cannot be dragged into a war by the United States, and the nation must take the place it deserves on the American continent."[5] His statement marked the beginning of a strong anti-American trend in Argentina.

Irigoyen entered the presidency in 1916, centenary of Argentina's declaration of independence. A new wave of patriotic feeling had been aroused, and it culminated in the appearance of a work of extremely nationalistic tendencies: Ricardo Rojas's *The Nationalist Restoration*.[6]

There had been literary nationalism in Argentina before the work of Ricardo Rojas. It was of liberal coloring, based on the great experience of the independence movement. Its assembled beliefs, going under the heading of the *doctrina de Mayo*, borrowed freely from the tenets of the French Revolution: liberty, equality, fraternity, and popular sovereignty.[7] To a large extent the *doctrina* was "an artificial creation based on imported ideas," and Argentinian writers have condemned it as such. Yet for almost a century it sufficed as the ideological foundation of Argentinian patriotism, mostly because it was a convenient frame of reference for the outstanding political figures that forged the nation's destiny: Mitre, Sarmiento, Avellaneda. The turn from patriotism to nationalism occurred only when the social and economic situation demanded a broader and more aggressive ideology.

Ricardo Rojas has been called a *visionario de la patria* (a visionary of the fatherland), and it is true that from the beginning he was bent on defining the essence of the *Argentinidad*. He was a prolific poet, philosopher, essayist, historian, and playwright, and even his choice of titles evidences his central ideal: *El profeta de la pampa, El santo de la espada, Poems of a New World,* etc. Eight volumes of his work are given over to the history of Argentine literature. He wrote about the gauchos and about colonialism, but his fundamental aim was not historical, but cultural and political. Rojas wanted to halt the influence of foreign models on the minds of his compatriots; he wanted to show that Argentina already possessed a literature of its own. Whereas Sarmiento had formulated the problems of the nineteenth century with the alternatives of civilization or barbarism, Rojas defines the issue of his age as exoticism or nationalism.[8] He thought of the native soil as lacerated and polluted by the excess of foreign ideas. He evoked the memory of the gaucho Martín Fierro and called Buenos Aires a tower of confusion wherein the old and austere virtues of the pampas had disappeared. It was the ancient conflict of the capital versus the provinces, reappearing now as a struggle between two conflicting ideologies. Argentina, so runs the argument, has two psychologies, one cosmopolitan, industrial, and materialistic, the other agricultural, contemplative, and idealistic. But the latter was in danger of being overpowered by the former, and it was the task of the poet-thinker to ward off this menace. Hence, Ricardo Rojas's *La restauración nacionalista!*

This nationalistic restoration demanded a new appraisal of the soil, of the race, of its language and its traditions. Rojas became the apostle of the fatherland and of Americanism, Latin-style. Echoes of his work may be heard not only in his own country, but even in Spain, where no less a person than Miguel de Unamuno praised its views.[9] The mystic of *Hispanidad* could well comprehend the mystic of *Argentinidad*. It was a new faith with quasi-religious qualities, a religion of the fatherland. This religion, it was urged, should be taught in the schools, which should be purged of the cosmopolitanism that had destroyed the old code of morals, neglected tradition, and corrupted the language. Rojas nationalism is cultural nationalism in much the same way that the nationalism of the Action Française was cultural in its beginnings. Yet it did not lack political implications. Rojas did not hesitate to ask for government control of education in order to restore the national spirit and to protect Argentina from foreign influence.[10] It was the theory underlying many a nationalism of romantic coloring: What is foreign is alien, and what is alien is bad and hence must be eliminated.

Rojas's purpose was not merely nostalgic and restorative. He wanted to free his land from foreign domination so that its native soul might find free and genuine expression. Thus it was natural that he followed the "Nationalist Restoration" with an aesthetic code, entitled *Eurindia* (1924). At the same time that Vasconcelos promulgated his idea of the "cosmic race" in Mexico, Rojas ventured to prophesy the birth of a new Latin art, emancipated from the tutelage of European forms and models and giving vent to the creative energies of race and landscape native to America. *Eurindia* is one more attempt to discover the traits that are common to all countries south of the Rio Grande, to point to a Latin American heritage which is neither European nor Yankee but combines the best of pre-Columbian characteristics with contemporary features. Many other Latin American writers have attempted to define this mysterious quality—Vasconcelos, Haya de la Torre, Rómulo Gallegos. It was a new mystique, the mystique of continental Americanism which moved so many intellectuals during the early twentieth century, and for which Eurindia is as good a name as any.[11]

Thus Rojas became the patron saint of Argentinian nationhood and of Latin America. There was an undercurrent of Christian symbolism in his thought that referred to the nation as crucified, tortured, and bleeding, but assured of its resurrection by the *restauración nationalista*.

If Rojas were an isolated visionary, he would hardly deserve a place in our studies, but his *obra* aroused an echo in many an Argentinian writer. There were Leopoldo Lugones, Carlos Ibarguren, and Manuel Gálvez, all of them working in one way or another to revitalize Argentina's nationality.[12] Some of them cherished far-flung schemes to bring about the galvanization of the body politic, which seemed to them exposed to serious threats from within. But all of them reflect a dichotomy in twentieth-century Argentina which no slogan of yesteryear could heal. Alberdi's *gobernar es poblar* (to rule is to populate) was replaced by "to rule is to Argentinize." Gálvez, who rephrased Alberdi in this manner, expressed most clearly a consciousness of two conflicting tendencies. The first, stated Gálvez, is conservative, traditionalist, and regressive; the second is liberal and progressive. "I believe that these two tendencies should be united," he said.[13] It might be said that the Argentinian national revolution took this as its goal—but failed to reach it.

There were abundant efforts in Argentina to understand what was then called *la realidad Argentina*, and these efforts were not confined to writers of nationalistic faith. To prove the point, it is sufficient to mention the names of Augustín Álvarez, Joaquín González, José Ingenieros, Alejandro Korn, and Martínez Estrada. But the intelligentsia failed to supply Argentina with any program for spiritual integration. The ills that afflicted the nation as a whole had not spared them either.[14]

Thus we are forced to return to a consideration of the political situation and the economic and social developments of the country. A glance at the Argentinian economy only adds to the perplexities of anyone attempting to solve the riddle of Argentina. Here, the national revolution was not the result of depression, overproduction, or unemployment, as had been the case in Brazil. Argentina had no difficulty in recovering from the economic dislocation brought on by the First World War, and after the war her prospects for continuous prosperity remained favorable. Her agricultural goods were in demand, and her industries, geared to the domestic consumer, showed remarkable growth. "Its working elements were the healthiest, the best fed, and the most literate in the area."[15] This comment, to be sure, applies more to the industrial workers of Buenos Aires and the coastal lands than it does to the workers of the interior, but it was generally agreed that there seemed to be no widespread discontent in Argentina before 1930. Although the Great Depression affected Argentina in various ways, it still cannot be said to have produced the same economic paralysis observable elsewhere. We must look further for the source of events that began in 1930.

The country had been ruled by Irigoyen and his Radical Party for fourteen years. A popular support of sorts existed, but it was neither strong nor organized. It has been said that Irigoyen's dictatorship was of the masses, but of disorganized masses.[16] His personal influence offended those who were opposed to a personality cult, and the more social-minded of the Radical Party were disappointed that the country was still lacking in labor legislation. In this manner Irigoyen brought about a fragmentation of the radical movement. The more conservative elements inclined toward allies further to the right; the more progressive were attracted toward the socialist camp.

In other issues too the Radical Party and Irigoyen fell short of national expectations. Although they advocated enfranchisement of the middle class and of labor, they had not thought it necessary to face up to the economic realities on which political power is based. They neglected the fact that a change in power structure will not last unless it is accompanied by an overhaul of the class structure. Irigoyen had continued the policy of free trade to which Argentina had traditionally adhered; in other words, he followed the economic policy of the oligarchy he had replaced. And he in no way attacked the system of large landholdings on which the influence of the oligarchy had been founded. Least of all did he wish to jeopardize the friendly relations between Argentina and the great financial powers of the postwar era, the United States and Great Britain. Such amicable relations secured the arrival of new capital, and it did not trouble Irigoyen that the same process led to a control of the national economy by non-Argentinian influences. He thought he had done enough when he defended Argentina's independent position in the field of foreign policy, making the republic the foremost champion of sovereign rights and of nonintervention in Latin American affairs from abroad.

A number of elements conspired to bring about the downfall of the Radical Party. When Irigoyen ran for election in 1928, he was seventy-six years old and painfully senile in his public appearances. The students of the University of Buenos Aires had lost faith in him, and they were an important factor in forming public opinion. The nation continued to depend for its survival on agricultural wealth, and those in control of this wealth believed once more that their hour had come.

The oligarchy was helped in its renewed bid for power by the support of the armed forces, whose outlook was definitely conservative. The army played a decisive role throughout Argentina's national revolution, to a greater degree than in Mexico, where the armed forces were eventually subdued, or in Brazil, where they acted as moderators.

Constitutional government in Argentina, instituted in 1853, came to an end in September of 1930 when Irigoyen was overthrown by a military coup led by General José Uriburu. At first there was little indication that the event was more than an incident; few people had any premonition of the consequences. But three months after the coup, Uriburu spoke out against the labor legislation introduced by Irigoyen, declaring that the

Sáenz Peña Law liberalizing the franchise was a pernicious piece of legislation.[17] He demanded a break with the constitutional tradition and an adoption of the fascist type of government then in power in Italy. It was the first indication that Argentina might try to follow the totalitarian model.

Once again, we must take care not to confuse surface events with underlying causes. The true meaning of the coup of 1930 lay in the fact that a conservative revolution had taken place which was designed to return the landholding aristocracy to power; the evocation of the corporative state was scarcely more than a veneer. Nevertheless, the floodgates to both fascist and Nazi propaganda were flung wide, and the character of the national revolution was thereby considerably altered. Since the oligarchy could supply few attractions for the masses, they devised the "Jewish peril" and the "red peril" in an attempt to disguise its own aims. The Uriburu government may be compared to the Papen government in Germany in 1932; both played the role of the doorman who opened the gates to a mightier force.

The oligarchy, long accustomed to look to the Old World for ideological support, was able to find in Italy and in Germany the props that would hide its class designs. Fascism in its Italian version had an appeal for the sons of the *estancieros* who had suffered during the Great Depression when prices for meat and wheat were falling on the world market; it attracted some of the intellectuals who interpreted the "new order" as a return to the old order of a simple and austere life when the spirit of the nation had not yet been undermined by international ideologies such as liberalism and communism; and it appealed to a part of the Argentinian clergy with its emphasis on authority and family. Last, but not least, both Italy and Germany opposed England and the United States, prime targets for economic nationalism in all Latin American countries.

But the strength of fascist influence in Argentina should not be overrated, at least not for the early years. The Radical Party was out, but by no means defunct. A strange compromise resulted, made up of radical, conservative, and nationalistic forces and known as the Concordancia. This combination held power under different presidents until 1943. Uriburu was replaced by Agustín P. Justo in 1932; Justo was followed by Roberto Ortiz in 1938. Argentina seemed to have returned to a parliamentary order, but again appearances were deceiving.

In reality, the conservatives prevailed and called the tune. Under the disguise of parliamentary rule, the press was censored and critics of the regime were exiled. Elections were fraudulent and were manipulated to favor the Concordancia. Immigration was restricted; eventually more persons left the country than entered it, a reversal of the policy that had prevailed for more than a hundred years. Economic policy likewise showed many restrictive features which, of course, could be explained by the exigencies of the world economy. Nevertheless, it is noteworthy that the most important commercial agreement to be signed in this period, the Roca-Runciman pact, favored the landholding aristocracy above the urban classes engaged in industrial production. The treaty, signed in 1933 for a three-year period, installed a rigid bilateral trade agreement between Great Britain and the Argentine. Great Britain pledged herself to purchase frozen beef at 1932 levels, while Argentina promised to spend the money from these purchases on British goods. In reality, it was a barter agreement that forced Argentina to abandon her policy of free trade.

While the immediate impact of the Roca-Runciman treaty was beneficial and led to a speedy recovery of the Argentinian economy, it neglected one aspect of the national situation which had long frustrated many Argentinians. British investors controlled about 60% of foreign investments in Argentina, and the Roca-Runciman treaty strengthened British influence rather than curb it.[18] Therefore, the nationalists objected to the treaty, saying that Argentina had been given "Dominion status." This criticism was partly justified; President Justo did little to hold foreign capital in check, whether it came from England, France, Belgium, or the United States. Whereas Vargas, in neighboring Brazil, took pains to impose punitive restrictions on the alienation of national resources, Argentina continued to be controlled by foreign investors, especially in the fields of transportation and public utilities. Moreover, the Argentinian customers of foreign companies gained little benefit from their forbearance; the service they received was far from their due. The resentment that followed was one of the most important elements in the rise of Perón.[19]

In other fields of the economy the regime of the Concordancia found itself forced to adopt state intervention where formerly a free economic flow had been enjoyed. Regulation and control of foreign exchange were established; national grain and national cotton boards were instituted; income tax reform was initiated; and many other unwelcome regulations were imposed. The result was a "restrained nationalism," which as yet did not make itself felt in the most important activities of the Argentinian economy.[20]

The nation had two choices: It could follow the example of Great Britain, France, or the United States, accepting a moderated socialism or a New Deal policy; or it could follow the path of fascism, German- or Italian-style. Fascism won the day. The reasons for this outcome are many. The crisis of the thirties coincided with the deaths of the old radical leaders who might have prevented such a turn. Irigoyen was dead; so was Alvear, and there was no one who could replace them in the public eye. In retrospect, the Concordancia seems like a government in transition, "still civilian, legal-minded, and frequently corrupt," but without sufficient foresight to recognize the danger of a militant fascism which loomed upon the horizon.[21]

In 1937 Roberto M. Ortiz was elected president of Argentina. He too came from the Radical Party, and he too seemed to represent both conservative and liberal forces. However, his running mate in the race for the presidency was a thoroughgoing conservative, Dr. Ramón S. Castillo, dean of the law school of the University of Buenos Aires, and it was Castillo who swayed the course of Argentina toward the far right. But we must beware of hindsight. Argentina's development might well have taken a different direction had it not been for the advent of the Second World War.

At the time Ortiz assumed the presidency, Hitler was moving rapidly from victory to victory. The Saar, Austria, and Czechoslovakia were the spoils of a policy in which cunning and brute force were inextricably mixed, and they aroused admiration from those who closed their eyes to the diabolic possibilities of his agenda. In Argentina, as elsewhere, there was a group of men and women who responded to the demoniac appeal of the Führer, feeling some link between him and the Rosas tradition of bygone days. The Nazis hastened to take advantage of the situation. In addition to the Argentinian admirers, there were more than a million Germans residing in the republic.[22] They were called *Volksdeutsche* in contradistinction to the *Reichsdeutsche* who were actually under the sovereign jurisdiction of the Reich. In 1937 the Deutscher Volksbund für Argentina was created to organize all Germans in the manner set up by the party. German schools were to be found in many parts of Argentina, and newspapers in Spanish or German began to spread the doctrine of the *Herrenvolk*. These activities did not pass unnoticed. The house of deputies appointed a committee for un-Argentine activities in 1940, and President Ortiz, faithful to his liberal convictions, attempted to block the fascist agitation.[23] But Ortiz was a sick man, and his resignation came on July 3, 1940, following by a few days Hitler's triumph over France. Many people in Argentina felt that the days of liberalism were over.

The ensuing vacuum could be filled only by a union of all sections of Argentinian society. Only a new force, a great movement, could pull the fragments of the body politic together. Had it not been for the international situation, socialism might well have carried the day. But the victorious German armies were sweeping the European continent, and the fascist sympathizers won out. Castillo became the chief executive in 1940, taking over vast powers, while the radicals and socialists were obliged to content themselves by castigating him through a policy of boycott and passive resistance.[24] Castillo, president by default, did not feel himself committed to a popular mandate and soon suspended the constitutional guarantees.

The domestic aspects of the Castillo regime, however, were immediately overshadowed by international problems. Officially, Argentina followed a policy of neutralism in the world conflict, trying to maintain business relations with both sides, but this proved to be no easy undertaking. Germany was cut off from the Argentinian commodities, as was most of Europe, and so long as the war lasted, there was little hope of finding a market for surplus wheat and surplus meat. However, it was now possible for Argentinian industry to replace European and American industrial goods in countries close to the Rio de la Plata—Uruguay, Paraguay, and Bolivia. There was discussion of the possibility of a customs union that would link these countries in a "Southern Union." This was not the first time that Argentinian nationalism had given evidence of imperialistic tendencies, but the Second World War gave new impetus to these ideas and also seemed to offer the circumstances wherein such ambitious plans might be realized.[25] The idea of a Southern Union around the Plata Basin quite naturally fired the imagination of the military, whose importance had increased as the war engulfed one continent after another. "Crisis was everywhere: war abroad, threats of Fascism and Nationalism at home."

Quite naturally, Castillo's policy of neutralism produced bitter reactions in Washington, and hints of retaliation and counter-pressure from the United States followed. All this was but fuel for the nationalistic passions which dominated the Argentinian scene.

The cry for a "greater Argentina" began to be heard, echoing distinctly the totalitarian slogans of Italy and Germany. Underlying this shift to the strong and aggressive national state, however, was a deep cleavage in the social structure which, the nationalists argued, could only be bridged by a new ideology. Liberalism in Argentina had been the product of commercial and industrial interests, as had been the case in most European countries; it had been the philosophy of the landholding bourgeoisie who had manipulated it to their own interest. Following the First World War, Argentina had entered the path of industrial capitalism, slow at first, but greatly accelerated after the Great Depression. A new bourgeoisie had arisen, mainly centered in Buenos Aires, and they were eager for power after having achieved wealth. Power would bring protective tariffs behind which the building industry, the flour mills, the breweries, could flourish unchecked. But this new industrial capitalism was not an enlightened capitalism; it had not yet come to consider labor as a partner in the production process. Thus the mass of industrial workers were forced to fend for themselves. It would not be fair to say that they were without a voice in Argentina. There was a well-organized socialist party which had shed the corroding influences of anarchosyndicalism and of communism, which sent senators and deputies to parliament, and which had an articulate newspaper. But its legislative performance was not impressive, and it could not boast of any significant victory in the fields of social security, unemployment insurance, medical care, or old-age pensions. As we have noted, such legislation, even though confined to paper, was, by 1940, standard in many Latin American countries. It follows that there was a large urban proletariat in Argentina which had not been incorporated into the body politic—sons and daughters of European immigrants for the most part, who felt that they had neither status nor protection and who constituted fair game for any demagogue who would promise them either.

It would seem preordained that the "infamous decade," begun in 1930 and continuing to function under the guise of a fraudulent democracy, should fall from power without resistance. It was overthrown by an army coup led by General Ramírez, and it fell "like a putrid fruit."[26] The seizure of power was accompanied by a bombastic manifesto in which the leaders of the uprising claimed that the days of the nation-state had passed and that the era of continents was at hand. Just as

Germany was uniting Europe, so would Argentina unify the nations of the Latin American world. "Our aim will be to be strong; stronger than all other nations united."[27] Civilians, the document asserted, will never understand the greatness of our ideal; we shall have to eliminate them from the government and give to them the only mission which corresponds to them: work and obedience.

The men who so arrogantly put an end to eighty years of constitutional government were a strange group. They went under the name of the GOU (Grupo de Oficiales Unidos), and at first used some front men like Ramírez, Rawson, and Farrell. The mastermind of the clique, however, was Colonel Juan Domingo Perón.

The GOU had come into existence after the coup of 1930, and it is said that by 1943 it embraced 60% of the active officers of the army. These men were disillusioned by the venality and corruption of the fraudulent democracy and advocated a system of military authoritarianism. They demanded Argentina for the Argentinians. But they also held opinions which were openly anti-Yankee and pro-Fascist, in the hope that they might offset the influence of the United States in the western hemisphere by uniting the countries of Iberic descent in a bloc of their own. "We already have Paraguay; we shall have Bolivia and Chile, and it will be easy for us to put pressure on Uruguay. The five united nations will draw in Brazil, because of its form of government and its great nuclei of Germans. The South American continent will be ours when Brazil falls . . . we turn our eyes . . . toward Germany . . . Our government will be an inflexible dictatorship, although at the beginning we will make the necessary concessions needed to put it on a solid basis."[28] In retrospect this proclamation reads like so much hot air, but we must bear in mind that in 1943 a pro-Nazi dictatorship in southern Latin America represented a serious threat.

The man who emerged rapidly as the leader of Argentinian totalitarianism was six years younger than Hitler. He was born on October 8, 1895, in the province of Buenos Aires. At sixteen he entered military school, and from then on, through his downfall, his exile, and his farcical return, he always thought of himself as a soldier. He had some of the traits of leadership, a strong belief in his own ability, a quick and cynical wit, the Latin gift of the word, and a powerful physique which he cultivated assiduously. He gained a reputation as an army ski instructor and was appointed military attaché in Santiago de Chile. From there he moved on to Rome, where he studied fascism at its fountainhead. He had been an admirer of German methods of schooling and discipline since his days in the military college, and he followed the triumph of the *Blitzkrieg* with ever increasing fascination. Those who knew the man were agreed that he was *muy guapo y muy macho* (very handsome and very male), qualities that have a strong mass appeal in Latin America. He was attracted to women and women were attracted to him. The sensuous streak in his nature was accompanied by a boastful and boisterous vanity. There is no doubt that he had a magnetic personality and that he was deeply convinced of his mission in life.[29] But his boundless ambition was not tempered by a skeptical appraisal of his own capacities; he never learned that politics is, after all, "the art of the possible." His facade was more impressive than the structure behind it. Like Mussolini, he was not a lion, but a "rabbit that roared."

Nevertheless, it would be idle to deny that he possessed considerable acumen; this was made evident during the years of his spectacular political ascent. From the ideological currents that were then sweeping Argentina, he decided upon the two that promised success: nationalism and socialism, that is, state socialism in its fascist form. His greatest feat, however, was the mobilization of the labor force as the tool of his personal goal. The pure genius of this move cannot be denied, even granting that he had Vargas and Hitler as guides.

Following the revolution of 1943, Perón was made secretary to the ministry of war and president of the national labor department. At the time the latter office seemed of less importance, since it did not carry ministerial status and did not provide its occupant with efficient machinery for dealing either with labor or management. Yet it was as president of the national labor department that opportunity for future power came into Perón's hands.

We do not know at what time Perón realized that the military coup had not been popular and that without mass appeal its failure was certain. In early 1944, however, he began to contact the leaders of the trade unions. The railroad workers and the commercial employees made up the most important unions; they represented a combination of white- and blue-collar workers, effective material for Perón's purposes. Progress was sluggish at first; the union leaders were not certain they could trust Perón and his clique. But the opportunist in Perón urged him ahead. The old labor department was converted into a secretariat, and Perón's labor policy became one of the hallmarks of the revolution. "The day we created the secretariat of labor and welfare," he said, "is for me the first day of our movement."[30]

Between 1944 and 1945 Perón established by decree a social security system that gave coverage to the greater part of the working force of Argentina. The Institute of Social Security, set up in 1945, included protection for white-collar workers, industrial workers, agricultural and maritime workers, and numerous other working groups. Other measures followed that endeared Perón to the working classes: low-cost housing, paid vacations, and a substantial increase in wages, well ahead of the rise in living costs. Labor leaders who did not cooperate were dismissed and shipped to concentration camps in Patagonia or the Chaco. However, it must not be assumed that labor was blind to its own advantages in its support of Perón. The benefits he had conferred on labor through the various measures he had put in force were fully recognized and created for the colonel a large labor following. "The workers," said Perón, "are determined to defend their conquests, and if they do, I shall defend them."

It is not difficult to understand Perón's rapid rise as champion of the revolution. By July 7, 1944, he held three important titles: minister of war, secretary of labor, and vice-president. With his customary aplomb, he declared that he prided himself on three titles only: soldier, Argentine worker, and patriot.[31]

His words summarized in a tidy way, not so much what he was, but the image he desired to project. His success still appears remarkable. If there were aspects of the national revolution that appealed to the urban masses, there were others that must have filled the nationalists with considerable apprehension. By 1944 the Allies had launched their invasion across the Channel, and the defeat of Hitler was merely a question of time. In Argentina, the opposition took full advantage of these developments; there were demonstrations for "constitution and liberty" in Buenos Aires; the cabinet itself seemed to be split, and even the army turned against Perón. He was detained, delivered to the navy, and confined on Martín García Island.

But Perón had an important advantage over his opponents: His aims were clear and he knew how to obtain them. He had no fear of the milling crowds in the streets of Buenos Aires; on the contrary, he was confident that he could bring them to his side. By means of a ruse, his request to be returned to the capital was granted. How he produced the October 17, 1945 "spontaneous demonstrations" that demanded his reinstatement has never been explained. But other totalitarians have succeeded in similar circumstances. Perón capitalized on the outburst of mass hysteria, and while "everybody shouted and nobody listened,"[32] he became the undisputed master of Argentina. After his coup, on October 17, the intramural rivalries and the international difficulties seemed to fade away in the glow of a national upsurge promoted by the working class and the youth of Buenos Aires, two groups that aspired "to play a role in that national hour . . . to defend what they thought were their vital interests."[33] Serious observers could not fail to be reminded of a day in January of 1933, when a palace intrigue brought Hitler to power, and the German people gave thanks that their prayers had been answered. Argentina, too, had found its leader.

If the events of October 17 had not cemented Perón's position as the potential leader of Argentinian authoritarianism, foreign opposition supplied the lack. The United States, especially, had good reason to feel hostile toward the military regime in Argentina, which had sympathized openly with the Axis powers as long as their victory seemed a possibility. With Hitler and Mussolini on the edge of total defeat, the Argentinian government experienced a "change of heart"; this hypocritical *volte face* was highly unconvincing. Its sole purpose was to avoid isolation in the postwar world and exclusion from the United Nations, then in process of organization.

The conference of Chapultepec, which met early in 1945, opened the road for Argentina's return to the fold of western hemispheric solidarity. The conference expressed its hope that Argentina would cooperate with the other American nations and identify itself with the common policy pursued by the latter, guiding its own policy until it achieved incorporation among the United Nations.[34] Argentina heeded the advice, and on March 27, 1945, she declared war on Germany and Japan. As a result of this tardy gesture, she was admitted into the United Nations, and the world was presented with at least the outward trappings of American solidarity.

It is uncertain whether the United States entertained any hope of strengthening the forces of democratic action in Argentina by refraining from punitive measures. It can be said, however, that the anti-Peronistas still had a good chance of wresting the power out of Perón's hands. Presidential elections were to be held in 1946, and a concerted effort by the democratic forces might well have stopped his bid for power. He was dubbed "the impossible candidate," since he had himself declared that his candidacy was "impossible." But Perón was no better than his word, and his word had never been worth a great deal. The opposition to Perón suffered from internal dissensions; it was made up of the former Radical Party, the Social Democratic Party, even the communists. Brought under one head by the situation, they called themselves the Unión Democrática. Although they were united in their hostility to Perón, they found it impossible to agree on one list for the senate and the house of deputies, thus inviting ticket-splitting and a weakening of their cause from the outset. Their candidate, Tamborini, had no qualities that could compare with Perón's personal magic, but he might have carried the election, had it not been for the heavy-handed intervention of Spruille Braden, former United States Ambassador to Argentina and currently Assistant Secretary of State. Twelve days before the elections, Mr. Braden considered the moment opportune for publishing a Blue Book on the Argentinian situation. A factual account of Argentina's wartime record was given, together with an account of her flirtation with the Axis powers. But the plan to influence the electors was ill conceived and recoiled upon its originators. Anyone familiar with Latin American psychology could have told Mr. Braden that the Blue Book would be interpreted as one more attempt by the *coloso del norte* to browbeat the Latin Americans into submission. It was denounced as open intervention in the domestic affairs of the sovereign republic, and it played directly into Perón's hands. Even Mr. Braden's friendly critics admit that the Blue Book was a major issue in the campaign, and those who are less well disposed toward the Assistant Secretary have called him the bull in the china shop. "Braden or Perón" became a campaign slogan from which only Perón could benefit.[35]

It is interesting to note the forces that carried Perón to victory. A new party had made its appearance, the Labor Party (Partido Laborista), founded in November, 1945. Its membership included the majority of the labor unions, and its leadership was held by two of the most influential union officials. Its program called for the nationalization of the railroads and the telephone and electric companies, and for the suppression of monopolies. In addition the Labor Party pledged itself to the preservation of those gains already made under the leadership of Perón. Reverberations of an older socialist ideology still persisted, inasmuch as the Labor Party promised "the scientific and cultural development" of the Argentinian nation, comparing itself with the British Labour Party, which had just scored its great postwar success. But the predominant note was that of class struggle against the big landowners and bankers.

Although Perón had some support from disappointed radicals, it was clear that his popular backing came from the urban proletariat of Buenos Aires. He also had the support of the government, which allowed and even encouraged the attacks against the opposition by political hoodlums. Perón tried everything in his effort to score a victory: A few weeks before the date of the elections, he ordered all employers to pay their employees a Christmas bonus amounting to 25% of their annual salary. The legality of this order was highly dubious, but its effect on the workers was electric. Thus it was not surprising that Perón, champion of Argentina in her fight against the United States and leader of the working classes, won the presidency with a huge margin. Like Hitler, he came to power through legitimate means, and he gained control of both houses of the parliament. Although the urban masses of Buenos Aires formed the bulk of his following, Perón had a respectable vote from the provinces. On February 24, 1946, he received a mandate that no one could question. The revolution of 1943 had been confirmed by plebiscite.

The Perón regime, if dated from 1946, covers a span of nine years. Characterized at first by spectacular advances, it ended in infamy and disaster. The "New Order" had more than a broad popular backing; some of the older institutions lent their support as well, especially the church, the army, and the police. These groups, says José Luis Romero, were the grid into whose openings Perón poured the cement of his proletariat support.[36] On such a foundation did Perón begin the erection of a political organization which would eventually be able to threaten the army with the force of the masses and to threaten the workers with military might. His game was not a new one; Mussolini had played it through to its end. But Perón's capitalization of the crude and chaotic exaltation of the masses added a new element to the history of fascism. As we have noted, his followers comprised elements of organized labor, but they also included the driftwood from the urban population, the *Lumpenproletariat,* given to rowdyism and violence. They went under the name of the *descamisados* (shirtless ones) and remind one of the *sans-culottes* of the French Revolution. They were prepared to follow their leader to the attack at any moment he saw fit to call them, whether it was against the landowners, the Jockey Club, or the urban oligarchy. Lacking experience in the methods of the plebiscite, the masses were easy victims of public oratory. The universities were under strict government control and the press was censored. The radio served as an effective instrument for inciting the populace. Against initial opposition from the union leaders, Perón succeeded in forging El Partido Único de la Revolución, called El Partido Peronista. It was not as well organized as the Nazi Party or the Blackshirts of Mussolini, nor even as well as Franco's Falange. Nevertheless, it managed to remain in power and to win elections year in and year out.

But the Peronistas acted only as a force that their leader might unleash at will to check whatever opposition his far-flung plans might encounter. Perón's comment was: "Como el séa, será la masa." (As he is, so will be the mass.)[37] It is more important, therefore, for us to understand something of Perón's ideas about the "New Order" he planned to erect. Perón has explained these ideas in a number of writings, some antedating his seizure of power, some written while he was head of state. Whether right or wrong, they do display a degree of consistency which can be summarized under the name of state socialism or state capitalism. Perón regretted the predominantly agrarian character of Argentina's economy. He complained that ". . . the economy of the country rested almost exclusively on the products of the earth, which were processed in a most inferior manner; later when these products had been transformed in foreign lands to the benefit of those economies, we acquired them again as manufactured goods . . . All that money left the country without benefiting our economy, our industries, or the working class whom it could have fed."[38] Perón extolls the virtues of the Argentinian worker who has shown himself the equal or even the superior of the foreign worker. In short, Perón was a devotee of the mystique of industrialization, which had enthralled so many Latin American politicians in this era. But combined with these ideas were others of an advanced socialistic order. In a speech delivered in 1947, he enumerated a long list of rights, among them the right to work, to receive a fair reward, to acquire skills, to demand worthy working conditions, to have a social security program, etc.[39]

Such sweeping reforms called for a complete overhaul of the constitution of 1853, which was still the foundation of Argentina's political life. Perón began with an attack on the supreme court, stating that the spirit of justice superseded judicial power. Judicial power, he asserted, did not speak in the same tongue used by the legislative and the executive branches of the government. Three of the justices and the attorney general were removed and their places filled with Peronistas. A purge of the lower courts followed. Once Perón was sure that the courts would follow his bidding, the revamping of the constitution became an easy matter. A convention, meeting in Buenos Aires in 1949, speedily carried out the wishes of the master.

The most important change was the removal of the obstacle to presidential reelection. The electoral college was likewise scrapped, allowing for a plebiscite election for both president and vice-president. The state received broad authorizations for control of the nation's economy. More significant still, all mineral and natural resources were declared the property of the nation (another imitation of the famous Article 27 of the Mexican constitution). The social charter, which we have noted previously, was incorporated into the constitution.

However, it must be pointed out that Perón did not eliminate the Basic Law of 1853, though he did make drastic emendations.[40] The one-party system, the formation of which has already been mentioned, became instrumental in muzzling the independent press, *La Nación* and *La Prensa*, once the pride of the Argentinians. The universities were also purged of most of their dissenting members.

Yet we would fail to do justice to the phenomenon that was Perón were we to take note of the regime's repressive measures only. It based its ruling prerogative on two principles: social justice and economic independence. We have already seen that a minimum of social justice had been infused into the body politic. Whether the economy could afford the expense of broad welfare programs was another matter.

The other half of Perón's program was by far the more significant. It had two complementary aspects. Economic independence meant first and foremost the emancipation of the national economy from foreign influences. And here the situation favored the dictator. Five years of war and devastation in Europe and Asia had helped the Argentinian economy to an amazing degree. Argentina had moved from the list of debtor nations into the column of creditor nations. Perón found himself with a gold and foreign exchange surplus of 1.6 billion dollars. The surplus was largely due to the high prices that Argentine foodstuffs commanded in the food shortage situation at the end of the war. Thus Perón was in a position to acquire control of the railroads, the interurban transport system, the airways, the communication facilities, and most of the utilities as well. He bought out the foreign investors, whether French, British, or American, with the surplus of hard cash that he had inherited from the previous regime. The process was called "repatriation" and was immensely popular with the Argentinians, who did not see that the national treasury would soon be exhausted and that the acquisition of various assets carried economic responsibilities and liabilities that would weigh heavily on the national economic expansion which Perón had envisaged.[41]

Yet, as we have seen, the process of nationalization was hemisphere-wide, even, one might say, worldwide. This was the result of the collapse of European finance capitalism after the Second World War, and as such, it was irrepressible and irreversible. It was Perón's good fortune that he could acquire the goods he coveted with gold and cash reserves, whereas other countries were obliged to make payments from the annual income of the national economy or resort to outright confiscation, as was the case in Indonesia and Cuba. Perón is not to be blamed for his line of conduct, only for the precipitate manner in which he proceeded.

Many of Perón's schemes were for show, as, for instance, the great expansion of the merchant marine. A crash program increased the tonnage from forty-five ships in 1939 to 386 in 1951. Tankers for the Yacimientos Petroliferos Fiscales, the government agency for the production and distribution of oil, were ordered to be constructed; luxury liners and cargo ships were commissioned, most of them to be built in foreign shipyards, thus putting an added burden on the gold reserves. To no one's surprise, they were christened *El Presidente Perón, Eva Perón, Juan Perón,* and so on.

Implied in such ambitious measures was a complete shift in the Argentinian economy from an agricultural and pastoral basis to an industrial one. And it was here that the Perón regime met its fate. On the occasion of the fourth anniversary of October 17, Perón enumerated the achievements of his campaign for economic independence: "We have nationalized the Central Bank and insurance; we have bought the railroads and their 17,000 adjoining properties; we have bought the telephones and all other means of transmission; we have bought the public services of gas, energy, transportation, and running water; we have bought the ports and the grain elevators; we have nationalized the sale of the country's agricultural production; we have paid the national debt; we have created a merchant fleet which is one of the world's most important; we have reequipped our industry, our transports, and our ports." He continued: "In less than three years we have bought all of these things worth more than 10 billion pesos, and have not only paid for them in cash, but have passed from being a debtor state to being one of the world's few creditor nations. . . . We have acquired all these things, but we have acquired much more—our independence, our dignity, our pride."[42] One might be in agreement with this proud stand, were it not for the high price of these accomplishments, a price far above Argentina's economic capabilities. The crash which ended the postwar boom proved that economic nationalism in Argentina had overreached itself.

As we have frequently stated, nationalism is a phenomenon that changes complexion and function according to its setting in time and place. This also holds true for the phenomenon of totalitarianism.[43] It is a twentieth-century occurrence, but it is rarely the same in any two countries. The combination of nationalism and totalitarianism, of which Perón is an outstanding example, shows certain very special aspects. Some salient features of totalitarian rule in other parts of the world apply to Perón's dictatorship: an official ideology designed to penetrate all sections of society; the mirage of a glorious future which would compensate for the trials and flaws of the present; the leadership principle and the attempt to control the life of the nation by a monolithic party; the use of terror by a secret police; the mobilization of public opinion by means of the radio, newsmedia, and television; control of the economy by the introduction of production plans covering a fairly extended period; and so on. On the other hand, there are characteristics of totalitarianism which Perón was never able to realize, notably the complete control of the armed forces and the complete subjugation of religious groups.[44]

The economic nationalism that urged a conversion of Argentina into an industrial country might have succeeded, if it had been held at a pace dictated by the existing economic situation both in Argentina and in the world at large. The industrialization of Argentina was without doubt a necessity; what was open to question, however, was the rate at which such a transformation should proceed and the amount of sacrifice which could be exacted from the various sectors of society. In prodding Argentina toward industrialization, Perón was inspired less by the country's needs than by chauvinistic pride. The idea of self-sufficiency has always appealed to the imagination of dictators, whether it was Stalin's "socialism in one country," or Hitler's idea of "autarky." Perón's two five-year plans, proclaimed with considerable fanfare in 1947 and 1953, were geared to national self-aggrandizement, a sentiment embodied in the person of Juan Domingo Perón.

Perón chose to disregard the warnings of impartial observers who maintained that the fundamental problem of economic development in Argentina, as in other Latin American countries, centered in the utilization of primary exports in a manner that would gradually reduce the country's dependence upon them.[45]

But any "gradual" process was repugnant to Perón, and he rushed into his program with more than deliberate speed. Articles 39 and 40 of the constitution of 1949 had introduced and legalized rigid controls of the economy. Not only did Perón wish to keep a tight rein on the means of exchange, but, following the example of Hitler, he wanted to acquire the needed industrial machinery by means of a barter system. In order to conclude such deals the agricultural producers were forced to accept ruinously low prices. As a result agricultural production declined.[46] Furthermore, the income from grain and livestock was drained off into other departments: Armaments were purchased (an unnecessary expense, since Argentina was under no threat of war) and public works were launched mainly for the purpose of increasing Argentina's weight in world affairs.

The high wages paid by the industries and the new social security system with its added benefits caused many a rural laborer to look for work in the cities. This occasioned a labor shortage on the farms which could have been compensated for only by the use of modern machinery. But there were no funds available for such machinery. From 1948 to 1952 production experienced a sharp drop. Argentina found herself in the throes of a depression, with serious shortages in meat and wheat, markets in which she had been one of the world's leading producers. Rationing was ordered for wheat, meat, and fuel. The depression soon affected other branches of the economy. Industrial production fell behind the quota assigned to it in the five-year plan; outworn machinery was not replaced, etc.

It would seem clear that the economic crisis was greatly aggravated by the social hatred and the class struggle deliberately promoted by Perón and the Peronistas. Perón himself had reason to oppose the oligarchy that had held the rule for so long in Argentina. He came from the "highly unstable Argentine middle class" with its multinational origins.[47] His great-grandfather, it is said, was Italian; his mother's family was of Spanish descent. The Peróns lived in the province of Buenos Aires and had no standing in the sophisticated capital. Nevertheless, Perón had entered the military academy, and if he had felt any aversion toward his social superiors, the feeling could hardly have been a consuming one. The situation is considerably different in regard to Perón's second wife, Evita Duarte. We would be glad to exclude the lady from the pages of this book, but the historian must stick to the facts even when he is obliged to ignore the admonition *de mortuis nihil nisi bonum.*

Evita Duarte was born out of wedlock in 1919, the daughter of a small provincial landowner. There can be little doubt that the social blemish of her birth left its mark on her. Years of ostracism and social isolation were followed by years of poverty and misery. From bitter experience, Evita knew that there were thousands of infants in Argentina who died simply because of lack of hygiene or care. She also knew that there were thousands who grew up without education and without a home.[48] Like so many others, she moved into the big city, perhaps because she could there better avoid the stigma of illegitimacy. She grew up to be a startlingly beautiful woman—blond, white-skinned, dark-eyed. Quite naturally she turned to the opportunities offered by show business—radio, the movies, the theater. Neither a success nor a failure, she managed to survive in some fashion during the years before she married Juan Perón. She met him at a party in 1943, and they were mutually attracted. She became his mistress, and in 1945 his wife. It is said that she played a leading role in the movement that brought Perón back

to Buenos Aires on October 17. In any case, Perón married her
four days later, and when he was elected president in 1946, she
became Argentina's First Lady. Her official name was María
Eva Duarte de Perón, but was known to the nation, and eventually the world, as Evita.

Her influence on Perón was enormous and notorious and soon
became a matter of public record. She was accorded an office
in the Casa Rosada, and arrived speedily at the knowledge that,
in the words of Lenin, power was lying in the streets; all one
had to do was to stoop and pick it up. Evita lost no time. In
Perón's secretariat of labor and welfare she found her opportunity and recognized at once the possibilities that were offered.

In Argentina, there had been men and women who had
spoken out on behalf of women's rights. But the timorous attempts that had been made by Rivadavía and others had been
smothered by the Hispanic Catholic tradition, which considered
woman as the proper object of man's affection but hardly his
equal in other matters. Women did not have the right to vote,
and only a few received an education beyond the secondary
level. However, at least one great party had made some effort
to assure women of a place in the political and cultural life of
the nation: the Socialist Party.

The revolution of 1943, of which Perón was a part, was at
first against the participation of women in public affairs. It is
idle to speculate on Perón's possible attitude in this issue had he
not fallen under the spell of Eva Duarte. But once her influence
had been established and institutionalized, he played the game
for everything that was in it.[49]

Evita's political career was charged with mixed emotions
which provided the fuel for a power drive ending only with her
death at the age of thirty-three. In all her writings and speeches it
is made evident that she was propelled not so much by her admiration for the charismatic leader who had chosen her as his companion as by her resentment against the socially privileged who
had caused her to suffer. She wanted revenge and she wanted
recognition, and the path to their acquisition lay in the satisfac-

tion of her awakened ambitions. Only in this way could she assuage the burning hatred she felt for those of legitimate birth and sheltered lives. To the public, she said, "I have seen that women have never had material or spiritual opportunities . . . and because I have known that women were a moral and spiritual resource of the world, I have placed myself at the side of all women of my country."[50]

She built up her own political organization, intervened freely in the appointment of high-ranking officials, and finally decided that she was not content to be merely the power behind the throne. In 1951 she ran for the vice-presidency. The attempt, though a failure, is revealing. As long as she lived, however, Eva Perón shaped the policies of the Perón regime. The bill granting woman suffrage, passed in 1947, was hailed as Eva Perón's "messianic message of emancipation."[51]

The mobilization of the women's vote for Perón was only one act of her "messianic mission." She undertook to become the leader of the downtrodden, the great army of underdogs. After all, she was herself a humble woman of the people; she had known hunger and humiliation. Her place would be with them. She became head of the social aid foundation, which was called the María Eva Duarte de Perón Foundation, drawing its funds from the national budget, but functioning as an independent agency, thus removing it from any control or any criticism that might be leveled against officers of the republic. This by no means prevented Evita from exercising pressure on private persons and corporations to provide ample funds for the social aid foundation. This organization soon rendered the private charitable institutions obsolete. It was just one more effort on Eva Perón's part to get even with the society which had snubbed her. That the foundation accomplished a great deal of good cannot be questioned. Evita had a soft spot for orphans and underprivileged children, and their well-being became one of the principal activities of the foundation. Hospitals and medical services were greatly improved, both in number and in the help they offered. And the First Lady made sure that the assistance rendered should no longer humiliate the receiver or reflect any separation of the classes. "As the word 'impossible' has disappeared from the language of Argentina . . . so the word 'charity' will disappear from the language of the world."[52]

It followed quite naturally that the image of Evita Perón was deeply etched in the hearts of all those who benefitted from her indefatigable activities. At parades and in mass meetings her picture was displayed along with Perón's, surrounded by flowers arranged in the shape of two hearts. She was the symbol of awakened womanhood in Argentina, a woman who easily caught the eye and the ear of the world. She added glamour to the drab world of politics and economics, and Latin Americans are famous for their adoration of the feminine mystique. If chivalry had died, it was resurrected in Buenos Aires.

But there was another element in the activities of Eva Perón that is more pertinent to our studies. Dictatorships of the totalitarian type contend that they unite the body politic above and beyond the class struggle. Since this line of reasoning is, more often than not, an ideological device used to justify state intervention in economic affairs, there must be found some social scapegoat whose subversive machinations threaten the welfare of the whole. In Nazi Germany, the Jews were used for this purpose. In Argentina there was the oligarchy that could be pictured as the enemy of the people and its great leader, Perón.

A certain amount of class antagonism was indeed inevitable in a state such as Perón envisaged, with its shift from agricultural to industrial wealth. But this antagonism was deliberately encouraged until it reached explosive proportions. Rumors were spread that the life of the president had been threatened, that attempts to poison him had been discovered. After due preparation by radio and news media, the *descamisados* were called together and informed about the sinister plans to deprive them of their leader, giving them to understand that such an event would also deprive them of all the benefits he had brought them. As was to be expected, the masses went wild and several instances of mob action took place, such as the burning of the

Jockey Club of Buenos Aires. All such outbursts were entirely "spontaneous"; the hearts of the people were simply burning with indignation!

Such procedures do not constitute an isolated phenomenon, but are a typical example of the methods used by totalitarianism to gain the support of the populace. Totalitarianism cannot exist without the continual infusion of mass emotion, and mass emotion leads to a state of psychological mobilization, a state of perpetual hysteria, which the manipulator of mass psychology can direct at will. The truth of this statement was demonstrated with great clarity in Argentina.

Perón was given a place beside the great founders of world religions, Christ, Mohammed, Buddha, Confucius. Peronismo was a holy doctrine, and any attack on it or deviation from it was counted as heresy. It was to be the religion of the twenty-first century. It would prevail in the world and the world would become Argentina's disciple. The history of this period sounds like records from a madhouse, and it differs but little from an account of Hitler's Third Reich, the state that was to "last for a thousand years." Perón was fully aware of the necessity for keeping the masses in this state of perpetual agitation. He gave suggestions for placing Peronismo on a permanent basis: "It will be necessary . . . to carry out the permanent task of indoctrinating the masses. If we are not capable of forming a mass that thinks in the same manner, has the same aim and acts in the same way, it would almost be better not to try; because when men think differently, then they fight. . . . According to the results of last November's elections, Peronismo has 70% of the population . . . we shall eventually be able to say 70% of all Argentinians are Peronistas, the rest barbarians."[53] What should be done about the barbarians? Well, one might attempt to persuade them, but if such efforts did not prevail, there was always "the revolver." Thus an open appeal was made to mass violence, and the Argentinian scene was soon characterized by the mobilization of violence, which seems to be the inevitable harvest of the mobilization of the masses. Shortly before her death, Evita

Perón addressed a crowd in Buenos Aires with these words: "There are traitors who in the darkness of night want to poison the body and soul of Perón who is the body and soul of the country. I pray to God not to let these fools lift their hands against Perón because, beware the day they do. I shall march with the women, with the workers, and with the shirtless ones, and no brick shall be left standing that is not a Peronista brick."

Though death brought an end to such violent threats, the cleavage in Argentinian society which resulted from constant menace and the play of one class against another widened perceptibly. Perón believed that the nation would forget about freedom while its attention was focused on imaginary enemies from within or from without. For years Argentina was to live in this state of emergency. But Perón and Peronismo fell victim to a dialectic of their own making, and a movement that had been hailed as the great unifying denominator ended by fragmenting the political will of the Argentinians; what was supposed to be the "general will" became Rousseau's "will of all," where private interests prevailed over the public good.

It is a paradox well worth pondering. When Perón proclaimed his famous "third position," a position independent from the great conflict that was tearing the world asunder, he seemed to have all the trump cards up his sleeve. He had risen to power after the fall of Hitler and Mussolini and should have known how to avoid their errors. He deftly sidestepped the stigma of fascism or Nazism by coining a new name for his movement. It was to be called *justicialismo*, or "the third position." As Mephistopheles says: "Do not give concepts overclose attention, for just where comprehension fails, a word steps promptly in as deputy."

Justicialismo is a curious blend of Hegel and Marx which hardly bears analysis. It made an attempt to amalgamate materialism and idealism, individualism and collectivism. Thus *justicialismo* has been defined as that doctrine whose objective is the happiness of man in human society achieved through the harmony of materialistic, idealistic, individualistic, and collectivist forces, each valued in a Christian way.[54] Or, it is a point of equilibrium, but then again, it is fluid and dynamic rather than static, etc. Quite obviously, it is an ideology invented for the sole purpose of filling the heads of the *descamisados* with just so much gibberish.

The vapid formulas of *justicialismo* could not bridge the gulf between the classes that Perón himself had widened, nor could it deal with the hard core of an economic crisis that was the result of the dictator's planless planning.

We have noted that Argentina found herself in a favorable position at the end of the Second World War. But her surplus of gold and foreign currency was soon spent. The agricultural recovery that took place throughout the world caused her foodstuffs to be in less demand; the hasty industrialization brought only chaotic results. By 1951, four years after Perón had taken over, the country was in the grip of a depression for which the country was in no way prepared. Since the government had assumed control over the nation's economy, it was the government's responsibility to cope with the problem.[55] Perón had identified economic nationalism with social revolution for the underprivileged, the *descamisados*. But the mounting expenses of the new welfare state, together with sinking revenues from agriculture and the increasing outlay for industrialization, produced an inflation such as Argentina had not seen in the twentieth century. The exchange value of the peso fell; prices rose and so did wages; exports fell while imports rose. It was the proverbial spiral, and it all but wiped out the achievements of Perón's innovations. One may still argue that the working class was better off in 1953 than it had been in the days before Perón, but the overall picture of Argentinian economy was not one of expansion or progress; rather it was one of confusion and regression.

The Perón regime might have collapsed earlier had Washington not come to its financial assistance. To avoid ruffling the tender sentiments of Argentinian nationalism, the loan was called a grant and was financially camouflaged in a manner that would spare Perón embarrassment.[56]

However, the irony of the situation was wasted on Perón. He maintained a brazen front which misled even sagacious observers. The New York *Times* predicted that he could not be overthrown so long as the opposition was in such complete disarray. Arthur Whitaker prophesied that Perón would complete his term as president and would pass the reins of government to one of his lieutenants.[57] Whitaker based his views on an appraisal that gave Perón the support of the two principal power groups: labor and the armed forces. Labor, indeed, did remain faithful to the president, but spiraling wages and increased fringe benefits were not accompanied with an expanding productivity, and Perón was eventually obliged to deny some of the demands of the *descamisados*. Gradually the country drifted toward economic bankruptcy. Nine million acres of farmland went out of production; money in circulation multiplied eightfold, while the cost of living rose sixfold. Although the industrial output had increased 63% between 1943 and 1955, the gross national output remained nearly stationary; graft and corruption in the ranks of the Peronistas was of epidemic proportions.

Perón must have known what was coming, because he tried to disentangle the state-controlled economy and to draw foreign capital into Argentina. Why he chose oil as the lure for foreign investment is a mystery. Oil production had fallen from 75% of the domestic needs to 35%. Even so, oil is, in most Latin American countries, the sacred cow of nationalism, and when Perón approached the Standard Oil Company of California with a plan to develop some 19,000 square miles of Patagonia, even the staunchest Peronistas grumbled.[58]

Whether it was these symptoms of discontent or the mobilization of violence looking for a new target or Perón's personal *hubris* that prompted his move against the Roman Catholic Church will never be clear. But his attack on the clergy was not only badly timed. It was devoid of aim.

The Catholic Church had been a state-supported institution

ever since 1853. Suddenly in 1954 Perón considered it necessary to expel certain high-ranking prelates, accusing them of "materialism and pride." For good measure, he also charged them with promoting "disorders and outrageous depredations" against the property and dignity of the nation. The church excommunicated Perón in June of 1955, and though the ban could not be published in Argentina, it was heard over the radio stations of neighboring countries. Reaction to the news was instantaneous. The naval forces rose against Perón on June 16 and were joined by some units of the air force. The army remained loyal to the dictator. Perón then called out the *descamisados,* and "mobilization by violence" was once more in full swing. By midnight Perón could announce that the uprising had been crushed. A more truthful statement would have been that the first act of the revolt had been unsuccessful.

The uprising had changed the atmosphere surrounding the president. The hopes of his enemies had been given new life, and it seemed as though Perón's own determination had been shaken. Rumors that he would resign spread through the capital. He showed his hesitation by dismissing two of the most outspoken foes of the Roman Catholic Church and went so far as to ask the opposition for "a truce in the political fight." The leader of the Radical Party, Frondizi, replied that there could be no peace until liberty had been restored.[59] Frondizi denounced Perón not only for his complete disregard for human rights and for the corruption of the masses by means of his welfare program, but also for his impending deal with the oil companies. The radicals were every bit as nationalistic as Perón and figured they could beat him at his own game. They were soon joined by other groups, the conservatives for one, but also by professional associations who disliked state control. The opposition made it clear that they considered Perón's fight with the Roman Catholic Church as a step toward empire, wherein the individual would be without defense against totalitarian power. It was a smoldering revolt with which the government found itself unable to cope.

Perón opened up the bag of tricks that previous Latin American dictators (including Bolívar) had used to their advantage. He offered to resign and become a simple Peronista, but this humble offer was directed to the Peronista Party and was read at a mass meeting. The outcome was predictable. After his offer had been rejected, Perón told the faithful that enemies of the regime would henceforward be lawful targets for the bullets of any true Argentinian. In other words, he removed the opposition from the protection of the state. If he had hoped to intimidate his enemies, he was soon to be disillusioned. The resistance to the dictator had reached such a pitch that the threat of civil war promised hope rather than disaster. Though a state of siege was declared in Buenos Aires and an enabling act rammed through congress, disaffection with the regime spread throughout the military, finally including the army. To confront the danger, Perón made a last-minute attempt to organize a militia from the rank and file of the *descamisados*. He should have been aware that professional soldiers do not care to fraternize with paramilitary political groups. On September 16, the army rose against Perón, attacking from the interior since most of the president's forces were concentrated in Buenos Aires. The navy soon joined the army, and almost overnight the revolt became a revolution. The navy controlled the Río de la Plata and threatened the city of Buenos Aires with bombardment. It was obvious that Perón had neither the material nor the moral forces to oppose such a danger. He capitulated, either to spare the nation a period of prolonged bloodshed, or to save his own skin. He was permitted to leave the country on a Paraguayan gunboat, evoking the sacred right of political asylum respected by most Latin American republics. The lion was only a rabbit after all, and from then on his fate belonged to the comic strip rather than to history.

Power passed into the hands of a military junta. However, as one of the new leaders pointed out, the aim of the revolution had not been to replace one dictatorship with another. "The revolution," he said, "is not one of a party, a church, an army, a faction . . . It is a liberating revolution which separated the diseased head of tyranny from the sane body of the nation."[60]

Unfortunately, the body of the nation was not entirely sane; in fact it was seriously sick, threatened as it was with political and social atomization and fragmentation. In the years that have followed the collapse of the Perón regime, Argentina has yet to find the coalition of political forces that could guarantee her a minimum of stability or the equilibrium on which to rebuild her society and her economy. It would not be fair to blame Perón for all of this instability; some of it, at least, is the inevitable result of the technological changes that have convulsed the entire world. Nevertheless, Perón and the Peronista movement must take the greater part of the guilt.

Before we try to assess the results of the nationalistic revolution in Argentina, something should be said about the re-emergence of constitutional government. The road to normalcy was long and arduous. Reconstruction was difficult and is by no means complete at the present date. Argentina's government during the last ten years could be called parliamentary democracy tempered by military dictatorship.

The aftermath of the Perón dictatorship brought forth a flood of revelations regarding the personal life of Perón which should have come close to destroying the myth of the heroic soldier battling to uplift his country. When attacked, he had capitulated; after Eva's death he took a teen-age mistress; his home revealed the taste of a man given to hedonistic enjoyment rather than to heroic action; and when the ignominious end came, he fled the country with a loot estimated, at least by his enemies, to be in the hundreds of millions of dollars. For some strange reason, the Peronistas were not dismayed, and sang a ditty to prove it:

> *Ladrón o no ladrón*
> *Queremos a Perón.*
>
> (Thief or not
> We want Perón.)

Peronismo had come to Argentina to stay, and we will have a few more words on the subject later.

The leadership of the military junta fell to General Aramburu, the elder statesman among the military and a man without personal ambition. The army wanted to set the country on the road to economic recovery and to give the political parties an opportunity to rebuild their machinery. They felt that a period of reconstruction, a breathing spell, was required before the country could expect a normally functioning government. Economic recovery seemed the easiest goal to achieve. The peso was devaluated, agriculture recovered some of the ground it had lost, and exports rose. An austerity program was instituted to curb the outflow of gold and foreign currency, but the proud nationalistic note of the Perón era was maintained and the offers of foreign investors were declined.

The political recovery was much slower and ran into more trouble. First there was the problem of de-Peronization, that is, the removal of Peronistas from the important positions they occupied in the army, the administration, at the diplomatic level, etc. The constitution was restored to the original 1853 version, and the megalomanic display of Perón's image was removed from the public gaze. The great newspaper *La Prensa* was restored to its original owner, and a date for elections was set (February 23, 1958). Aramburu declared that no member of the junta, including himself, should run for office. In the meantime, a constituent assembly, which was destined to curb the presidential power, was to be called together.[61]

The most difficult task was to resuscitate the domestic parties. There was constant danger that a counterrevolutionary movement might return Perón from exile. He had fled from the protection of the Paraguayan dictator to the haven of another dictator in Venezuela. From here he sent a stream of letters and propaganda by courier. But the threat from the man himself was less ominous than the perils of a neo-Peronismo movement. It was impossible to assess with any accuracy the mood of the populace. Of the old parties which Perón had trampled underfoot, at least five were still extant: the Radical Party, heir to the Irigoyen tradition, the socialists, the communists, and a Christian Democratic movement that had split into two groups.[62]

The radicals alone seemed to have any chance of gaining a compact following. Their leader, Arturo Frondizi, emerged as the voice of a disgruntled middle class and received his party's nomination for the presidency. His platform embraced economic and social reforms, slanted to attract the vote of the large mass of Peronistas. Frondizi supported statism, socialism, and nationalism in a lunatic mixture, hoping to outbid all competitors. The army became incensed and Aramburu was urged to cancel the election. But in Frondizi's campaign, Aramburu realized that a proof of restored freedom had been given to the country. "We think," he said, "that there must be a great national debate in which ideas can be freely expressed."

In 1958, Arturo Frondizi was elected to the presidency. The junta lived up to its promise to hand over power to an elected government. Yet the national revolution that had started in 1943 was far from over. The shadow of the exiled leader was still present; the military was still the guardian of constitutional liberties, and well prepared to assert its power when needed. Frondizi had won his office with the help of Peronistas, socialists, and communists.[63] It was obvious that he hoped to wean the million Peronistas away from Perón and to convert them into a stable front supporting the Radical Party. His was a policy of reintegration with the aim of healing old wounds, but, unfortunately, the economic measures he was obliged to adopt were not likely to draw the masses into the fold of a new democracy.

Frondizi's first concern was the stabilization of the economy, which was still swirling in the inflationary current. His program involved many unpopular measures: a further devaluation of the peso, the elimination of subsidies to domestic consumers, reduction of fiscal deficits, and most distasteful of all, a curb on wage increases. The results of these measures were inconclusive. The currency was stable during 1959 and 1960, only to weaken again in 1961. The balance of trade showed a deficit in 1960 and a much larger one in 1961. Prices continued to rise. It was impossible to balance the budget because the state-owned enterprises were operating at a loss. Among these were the railroads and the bus lines which had been nationalized under Perón. It became necessary to set up economy measures, which, in turn, threatened the precarious domestic peace. The labor force of many of the state-owned enterprises had swollen to such a degree that Frondizi planned the dismissal of 75,000 men in the railways alone. The union answered with strikes and work stoppages.

Officially the party of Perón had been outlawed, but in practice many Peronistas occupied important posts in the labor unions. Nationalism continued to be the rallying point for most Argentinians. Frondizi's attempt to attract foreign capital to the oil fields was highly unpopular with the communists, Peronistas, and nationalists alike, thus forcing Frondizi to rely heavily on the support of the military. This situation invited disaster, however, since a large sector of the military thought that Peronismo should be suppressed, with violence if necessary. Their spokesman was the commander in chief of the Argentinian army, Carlos Severo Toranzo Montero, and in the spring of 1960 he made the position of the army quite clear.

The events in Argentina which we have just recorded coincided with Fidel Castro's decision to join the communist bloc. The danger of some form of national Bolshevism thus became quite real to South Americans. Toranzo warned of the reappearance of the "exalted masses," which might bring Argentina into a position similar to Cuba's. But he reiterated his assurances that the armed forces were the best guardians of constitutional principles. "They will," he said, ". . . be a powerful force of dissuasion if either the government or other dissident elements take the wrong course."[64]

It was clear that Frondizi's popular support was rapidly thinning out. In 1958 he had controlled a large majority in the chamber of deputies; in 1960 it had been sharply reduced; and in 1962 he stood in danger of losing control of the parliament.

He had been very adroit in the business of surviving major and minor crises for four years, and it is possible that he had over-estimated his own cleverness. In any case, with new elections due in 1962, he convinced the military that now was the time to destroy the Perón myth for good by allowing his followers a place on the ballot. The elections proved his error. With eighty-six congressional seats and fourteen governorships at stake, the Peronistas won forty-four seats and nine provinces. To make matters worse, Frondizi's own party was badly split, allowing the Peronistas to emerge once more as the strongest group in Argentina. A number of legal maneuvers followed designed to prevent the Peronistas from taking office, but they could hardly save democracy in Argentina.

The country seemed to be in a peculiar mood. Even though the Peronistas staged a protest strike, they did not want a show-down. Perón himself, now sixty-six years old, appeared to be less eager than formerly to take advantage of his triumph, though he still promised to return "one day." Eventually the military took over and ousted Frondizi in a bloodless coup. Again, they promised that they were simply saving the constitution until such time as a free election would be possible.[65]

Contrary to the general expectation, Argentina elected a new president in 1963. Arturo Illia, a sixty-three year old country doctor, took office on October 12, 1963, and so far he has weathered the storms that have broken over the Casa Rosada. The armed forces have allowed Illia to remain in office as long as the Peronistas are kept in check. The Peronistas, likewise, with major strongholds still in the labor unions, have shown greater restraint than they did in the fifties.

Perhaps both factions felt that the country was not really with them and that Argentina favored reconciliation rather than the possibility of a renewed civil war. This, at least, was the tenor of Illia's inaugural address, wherein he attempted to draw support from the Christian Democrats by quoting from the encyclicals of the late Pope John.

And again nationalism was used to draw a fragmented country together and to bind the domestic wounds. Illia repudiated the contracts that Frondizi had signed with the foreign oil companies. This had been a campaign pledge, and Illia redeemed it almost immediately after he had taken office. There were about twelve such contracts, and the president declared that they had been concluded in violation of the existing laws. He alleged that the tax exemptions that had been granted to the oil companies were illegal and that they represented an encroachment on the rights of the Argentine National Oil Company, the Yacimientos Petroliferos Fiscales. The cancellation of the contracts was highly popular in Argentina, but led to tensions with the United States which have not yet been eased.[66]

Prices continued to rise, unemployment increased, and once more the Peronistas called for a return to state-controlled economy. Whether Perón really believed that the time had come for the fulfillment of his pledge to return one day, or whether the aging dictator simply wished to play the part of the redeemer once more, is hard to tell. But his attempt to enter Argentina was peremptorily denied at Rio de Janeiro, and he was returned to Spain. Very likely this was to be the last act of Perón's political life; the occurrence supplied a free libretto for a typically Latin American musical comedy. Argentina, assured of the cooperation of Brazil, Chile, and Uruguay, had shown that she had no desire to renew the fascist experiment. If nothing else, the events of the fall of 1964 strengthened Illia's middle-of-the-road policy, which lies between military coup from above and labor pressure from below.

It may be that the fate of Perón is now sealed. The abortive attempt to return the aging dictator to the Casa Rosada must have dealt a heavy blow to an already tarnished prestige. The man himself has now passed the point of no return, but this may not be true for the movement that bears his name. It may live on as neo-Peronismo, or it may christen itself under some other designation, but it would be foolhardy to ignore the indications that its influence is far from dead.

This brings us to the question of the prospects for nationalism in Argentina, together with an assessment of the national revolution. It is hard to imagine that *justicialismo*, or any other form of neofascism, will find a future in Argentina. On the other hand, the innovations that Perón brought to the nation, especially in the field of social legislation, will probably endure.

Latin American nationalism, it has been asserted, seeks "equality—and some one else to blame."[67] This attitude has been raised to the level of a major ideology, and, applied to Perón and his movement, it would mean that the mission of Peronismo was to draw Argentina into the nationalistic current —the most important trend in Latin American public life today. Statism, also, is part of this trend, since domestic industry in underdeveloped countries cannot survive without protection from foreign competition, and without the financial support of the state. Some form of security of the working classes, white- or blue-collar variety, is likewise essential.

But a question arises: was Perón's type of statism necessary? Would Argentina not have fared better if the social legislation he advanced had come by way of parliamentary democracy? Perón's answer to this would have been that the old society showed no sign that it was willing to come to grips with the problem of twentieth-century society; that Argentina was run by an oligarchy conscious only of its privileged position in a society rotten to the core and without any sense of the responsibility which has saved elites in other parts of the world; that the political parties were corrupt and utterly incapable of executing their public duties. The truth of these accusations may be granted. Yet Perón and Peronismo had not been able to change the situation. It had pitted class against class, social group against social group. Its ideology failed to amalgamate the Argentinians, to say nothing of the other countries where Perón hoped his ideas would take root. In the history of totalitarianism, Perón's movement was a sport, a marked variation from the norm. Fortunately, there is in Latin America no place for aggressive expansion as there was in Germany and Italy, and the continent was at least spared the experience of war waged for the sake of a greater Argentina.

But the dictatorship lasted, nonetheless, long enough to disrupt the party organizations, which were an erratic entity even before 1943, and to poison the channels of communication within the nation. If, as we have asserted, nationalism is a phenomenon that increases and strengthens the internal communications inside a given body politic, one must seriously doubt that Perón contributed substantially to the unification of his country. To be sure, foreign investors have been bought out, and the benefits of social legislation have been extended to millions. But these advantages seem to be outweighed by tremendous failures. Argentina did not have the economic maturity that could have made the nationalization of its communications and transport systems a success. The social security system has not been accompanied by an increase in national productivity; in fact, the very opposite is true. There is widespread distrust among the various sectors of society, to the point that the army has emerged as the guarantor of the constitution, and we observe the anomaly of military *coup d'états* becoming an established practice in the protection of democracy. In all fairness, it must be admitted that there is something in the Argentinian national character that responded to the flamboyant and irresponsible Perón, just as there was something in the Italian character that echoed the call of Mussolini.

Yet "national character" is not a fixed metaphysical substance; it may change, and it has changed under varying circumstances. From this viewpoint, Perón must be considered an unfortunate accident in the history of Argentinian nationhood. Compared with the Mexican revolution, the national revolution of Argentina is inconclusive and disconnected. And Perón, though he dreamed of greater heights than the position of dictator *in transitu,* has joined the long list of ephemeral and corrupt politicians and must be rated as a retarding rather than a constructive influence.

Whoever reads Perón's speeches and proclamations today

must smile at the exaggerated promises that remained unfulfilled. The Catholic corporate state founded on Hispanic tradition, the state above and beyond the principle of class struggle, a nation in full mobilization of its spiritual and material forces —these seem mere words. Perón's real bequest to the nation was a feeling of insecurity, a lack of confidence in its destiny, a confusion and equivocation within its basic political institutions. Argentina is far from being the leader of Hispanic America which Perón had announced as her future role.

CHAPTER X

The Cuban Revolution

C UBAN EVENTS have been in the limelight to such an extent during the last six years that nearly everyone considers himself fully informed about the situation. At first glance the Cuban revolution seems to be the left-wing counterpart of the right-wing Argentinian revolution we have just discussed. A national uprising occurs; the leader is a charismatic personality with great emotional appeal to the masses; the result is dictatorship and rule by violence. And the familiar features are there: nationalization of the economy and long-term planning; promises of a brilliant future which provide a cover for the shortcomings of the present; the perpetual mobilization of the masses, who are held in a state of hysteria to guarantee the revolution its permanent dynamics. Other parallels are not lacking. Here again is the conviction of a messianic mission, directed toward the other Latin American republics, the desire to establish a revolutionary center whose goal is the destruction once and for all of United States leadership in the western hemisphere.

The differences between the two revolutions are equally notable, and not merely because the Cuban revolution has turned communist while Perón's remained fascist. Cuba is a tight little island only ninety miles from the coast of Florida; its existence has long been overshadowed by the influence of its powerful neighbor. In 1958 its political, social, and economic conditions included revolutionary potentials that were lacking in Argentina. We include the Cuban story in our survey of nationalism in full recognition of the fact that the end is not yet in sight and that historical analysis of events in progress is a risky business.

Nearly everyone would agree that Cuba before Castro's revolution was one of the prime examples of economic imperialism.[1] Ever since the Latin American independence movement got underway, the United States has been concerned with the fate of the island. In 1823, John Quincy Adams said that Cuba would naturally gravitate toward the North American Union. Others stated the same opinion in even stronger terms and favored outright annexation. Although such plans were abandoned, the demand for open intervention on behalf of an "independent" Cuba grew stronger in proportion to the decline in Spanish power. By the mid-1880's Cuba had become an economic dependency of the United States while still a political dependency of Spain. A change in the political status was logical and took place in 1898. From the point of view of the United States the war with Spain was only one step in its imperialistic expansion. It is a different story if we turn to Cuba.

During the war many Americans favored the annexation of the island; others were definitely opposed to the idea. Under the circumstances a compromise was proposed and accepted granting legal independence to Cuba, but denying the republic the full substance of its sovereign rights.[2] The Platt Amendment, which was adopted by Congress in 1903 and written into the permanent treaty with Cuba, gave the United States authority to intervene in the policy of the island. In addition, Cuba became a subject of special interest to its great neighbor. In effect, Cuba was an economic colony and a political protectorate of the United States from 1902 to 1934. The United States used its prerogative to intervene in 1906, in 1917, and in 1920 for the purpose of maintaining law and order, but this display of authority prevented the development of a genuine political life in Cuba.

By the Reciprocity Treaty of 1902, Cuba became the happy hunting ground for dollar diplomacy then flourishing. Its effects were by no means detrimental to the Cuban economy. On the contrary, we may assert that the influx of American capital and technology were indispensable to the economic buildup of Cuba. This is particularly true of the sugarcane industry, but applies as well to railroad construction and the organization of the tobacco industry. Cuba also became the object of European capital investment, but it was only natural that the North Americans preserved their lead. Cuba followed the United States into the First World War, a step which further increased her dependency on her neighbor. The price of sugar was controlled during the war, but production increased so rapidly that by 1919 Cuba was producing 25% of the world's sugar. Most of the island's imports came from the United States, while at the same time the United States absorbed most of Cuba's exports.

The decade between 1919 and 1929 was characterized by the "dance of the millions." It was a time of illusionary prosperity which collapsed under the onslaught of the Great Depression, and Cuba is an excellent example of the folly that beset the world in those years. Sugar prices were decontrolled as soon as the war ended, and the large demands for this commodity throughout the world brought an unprecedented boom to the island. Overnight, Havana became a gaudy metropolis; its gambling tables and its cabarets became widely advertised tourist attractions. The businessman was suddenly in high esteem; banks were founded and then foundered. And all the while, Cuba was the outstanding example of the *monocultura* system, in spite of the fact that the great Cuban poet and patriot José Martí had warned his fellow citizens as early as 1883: "A people commits suicide the day on which it bases its existence on a single crop."[3] No one was surprised to see more and more Cuban property pass into American hands, thus increasing the hold that American banks and great corporations had on the Cuban economy. As in Argentina and Brazil, public utilities also came into American hands. The entire telephone system of the republic, the streetcars, the Havana docks, and at least two of the important railways of the country were controlled by United States interests.[4]

The situation was predictable and inevitable, but it was equally certain that one day the American economic preponderance would produce a hostile reaction. Cuban nationalism raised its head for the first time during the twenties. To be sure, there had been ardent patriotism in earlier days, witness José Martí and many others. But the nationalism which now came to the fore chose the United States as its target. The Cuban attitude as a whole, however, was ambiguous; the United States was admired and hated, aped and reviled at the same time.[5]

Domination by the United States provided the Cubans with a facile explanation for the corruption and graft rampant in their government. And it is true that during the terms of the five presidents who ruled Cuba from 1902 to 1933, Cuban politics were unstable and venal. The last of the five, President Gerardo Machado, displayed all of the vices and none of the virtues that a close relation with the United States might prefigure. His inner circle was rewarded with handsome incomes from government contracts and concessions, and Machado himself was not above pocketing a large share of the public revenue. Opposition grew; student riots forced the closing of the University of Havana; terror and counterterror mounted until the dictator finally fled to asylum in the nearby Bahamas.

Machado's flight took place a few months after Franklin D. Roosevelt had been sworn into the office of President of the United States. Roosevelt agreed to the abrogation of the Platt Amendment, thus ending formal political domination, but relations continued to be one-sided. In 1934 a quota for Cuban sugar was established by the United States for the purpose of protecting its own beet-sugar producers. Although Cuba received a high price for her sugar, it was, nevertheless, a unilateral arrangement set up by Washington.[6]

At the time, Cuba was mainly occupied with internal events. After a short period of parliamentary democracy, the island had turned to dictatorship. Fulgencio Batista, a one-time sergeant and army stenographer, emerged as the arbiter of the small country. For six years he ruled through puppet presidents, but in 1940 he took over the presidency in his own name. There can be little doubt that he did so with the blessing of the United States.

The war years, with their threat of Nazi subversion in the Caribbean, favored the dictator. The economy was stable and public order was maintained. In 1944, Batista allowed Dr. Grau San Martín to run for the presidency; in 1948, Prío Socarrás followed Grau San Martín. Neither man was able to check the growing corruption within the administration and in parliament. The venality of public officials had come to be a matter of common knowledge, and the general breakdown of the services they were supposed to render was all too obvious. It was thus an easy matter for Batista to stage a second coup in 1952. He was speedily awarded recognition by the United States and posed as the true enemy of communism, breaking relations with the Soviet Union and outlawing the communist party.

In spite of these measures, however, the communist apparatus remained intact, though forced to operate underground. If the United States was cognizant of the fact, they preferred to look the other way. Cooperation between the dictator and Washington remained friendly. He appeared to favor American business interests, and, in turn, was given military aid, supposedly against outside aggression (which was nonexistent), but actually used to maintain domestic tyranny. In the beginning, the Cuban Confederation of Workers had attempted to fight Batista, but finally came to terms with him when its legal status was recognized and economic benefits were promised. From the so-called democratic parties, of which there were two, Batista had little to fear. They had been discredited by their previous behavior, for one thing, and for another, Batista preserved the appearance of a democratic facade by holding elections in 1954 and 1958. Needless to relate, they confirmed the dictator as president.

On the economic scene, the country was replete with para-
doxes. On the one hand, Cuba was among the most advanced
of the Latin American nations. The per capita income was high;
more than half of the population lived in urban areas; many
held good jobs and were protected by their unions. A vigorous
middle class was developing, eager to play its part in the political life of the nation.[7] But on the other hand, 85% of Cuba's small
farmers rented their land, and 200,000 families had no land
whatever. Living conditions in both rural and urban areas were
substandard for the poor. Unemployment was endemic, and became epidemic in the months preceding the cutting of the sugarcane. Illiteracy was still high, though lower than in many Latin
American republics. The chasm between rich and poor was
made more apparent by the contrast between the rural districts
and the gaudy spectacle of the capital with night-club attractions, gambling casinos, and an air of luxury and free spending.[8]
Nevertheless, the Cuban revolution can hardly be explained in
Marxian terms, though these were very much in vogue among
the leaders of the Batista opposition.

Unrest germinated first among the middle class, especially in
student ranks. In Cuba, as elsewhere in Latin America, the
institutions of learning were the seeding grounds of demagogic
agitation.[9] Certain professors remained hostile to the sergeant-
dictator, and their opposition was a blend of two different
strains. One consisted of a rejection of "Plattismo," the economic
and political subordination of Cuba to the United States, which
was blamed for all the ills that beset the island's society. The
other was a vague and blurred kind of socialism that focused on
agrarian reform and was directed toward the peasant population. But such attitudes could be found in any number of Latin
American countries, whether or not a dictator was in command.
The distinctive character of the Cuban revolution must be attributed to the leadership of Fidel Castro; without him the
movement would either have fizzled out or would have taken
a different direction. The New York *Times* mentioned the name
of Castro for the first time on August 2, 1953.

Fidel Castro was born to a middle-class family in Oriente province in 1927. He had the traditional upbringing of a young man of his background: Catholic schooling at the Colegio de Dolores in Santiago de Cuba, and university training in Havana, where he enrolled in the school of law.[10] Even then he was known for his oratory and his penchant for conspiratorial affairs. He belonged to a group of students who planned an invasion of nearby Santo Domingo for the purpose of overthrowing the hated Trujillo dictatorship. This expedition was thwarted by the Cuban government. Another incident is more interesting, though still inconclusive as to Castro's involvement. When the famous uprising of April 1948 occurred in Bogotá (El Bogotazo), Castro was in the city.[11] He had been sent to the Colombian capital as a representative of the student body, which wished to carry out an "anti-imperialist" movement at the same time that the International Conference of American States was to meet there. It has been thought that Castro came under the spell of Jorge Eliécer Gaitán, the Colombian leader, and indeed this man did have a fascinating personality. It seems unlikely that Castro was then under communist influence, or that he had anything to do with the uprising that followed Gaitán's death. But there is no doubt that he was, even then, anti-imperialistic and anti-Yankee. The Cuban ambassador arranged for the young man's return to Cuba (Castro was then twenty-one years old), and he was allowed to finish his studies in Havana. He very soon joined the Partido del Pueblo Cubano, also known as the Orthodox, and became a candidate for the house of representatives. His election coincided with Batista's second coup. It was this event that launched Castro on his career as a putschist. But whatever the trigger, Castro would have become a public figure under any circumstances.

In July of 1953 Castro organized and led a suicidal attack by some 160 university students against Batista's barracks. The foray had no chance of success and was repulsed with ease by the Cuban army. Castro escaped arrest, but was later taken and brought to trial. He served as his own counsel, and in defense of his action made his famous speech "History will absolve me," which is as fundamental to an understanding of Fidelismo as Hitler's *Mein Kampf* is to an understanding of Nazism.

Any analysts of the speech must, of course, beware of reading later events into Castro's utterances. He proclaimed five laws that a new government would institute. Sovereignty would be returned to the people and the constitution of 1940 would be restored. Since there would be no properly invested authorities to impose sentence on those who had betrayed the people, it would be necessary for the revolutionary movement to take over all power, including the executive, legislative, and judicial branches of the government. Castro's speech was a clear statement of what Cuba could expect if the revolutionary movement were to triumph. Land was to be given to all tenants, share-croppers, and renters of land, but the owners were to be compensated. The workers would share in the profits of all enterprises, whether industrial, mercantile, or mining. All property that had been obtained through corrupt means was to be confiscated.[12]

The speech is important not only because of its revolutionary tenor, but also because it must be used as a basis for the much discussed question as to whether the revolution was later betrayed by Castro. It is certain that he had made promises to return to democratic government under the law, but it is equally certain that he anticipated a phase of transition during which constitutional guarantees would be suspended. From the outset there was a good deal of ambiguity in his program, and, very likely, in his thinking. It might be said that at this period of his career, Castro was a democrat with Marxist tendencies.

He received a harsh sentence, but was soon pardoned and allowed to leave for the United States. Some time later he moved to Mexico, where he gathered about him a small band of men who shared his determination to overthrow Batista. This group put themselves through a rigorous course in guerrilla warfare; neither arms nor funds were lacking. On November 25, 1956, a small yacht, the *Gamma*, conveyed some eighty men from Mexico to the shores of Cuba, where they expected to meet with members of the resistance movement within the island. However, the invasion was a failure, only thirteen men making it to the Sierra Maestra mountains. The Batista regime hastened to inform the world that the entire band of invaders, including Castro, had been killed, and it was only after four months that the truth was revealed. In February 1957, Herbert Matthews wrote three articles for the New York *Times*. His first sentence began, "Fidel Castro, the rebel leader of Cuba's youth, is alive and fighting hard and successfully in the rugged . . . Sierra Maestra."[13] Matthews's story contributed to Castro's success in more ways than one: not only was it a refutation of the Batista propaganda, but it presented Castro as a firm believer in liberty, democracy, and social justice. The image that Matthews evoked appealed to the idealism of the American people, and for a time, they were quite willing to accept this appraisal at face value. There is no doubt that Matthews helped Castro to win the revolution, because the *Times* articles accomplished a shift in public opinion both inside and outside Cuba that Castro himself could not have provoked. The Cuban communists, who had refused to cooperate with him because they considered him a putschist, changed direction. The middle class and the moderate socialists still working in the island were given new hope. A heavy ground swell of revolutionary discontent and sanguine expectation began to build up that was as important for Castro's final success as his military exploits, which, indeed, were on a small scale and, until 1958, were limited to the Sierra Maestra mountains.

Thus we come quite logically to the question: What kind of revolution had Castro hoped to set in motion? And to a second question: to whose cause was this revolution dedicated? A great deal of controversy over both questions has taken place between Castro's admirers and his detractors. This writer is inclined to agree with Theodore Draper's statement: ". . . the Cuban revolution was essentially a middle-class revolution that has been used to destroy the middle class."[14] The truth of Draper's words becomes evident when one studies the list of intellectuals who fought with Castro between 1956 and 1959, or notes the occupations of the men who served and are still serving in his government: lawyers, university professors, officers, engineers, and students.[15] These facts are of obvious significance for our study. It was among the revolutionary members of the middle class that the feeling of nationalism was strongest, a feeling composed of resentment against the United States, of domestic frustration and shame in regard to the corruption so prevalent throughout the country, of bitterness about the dependency on outside economic forces that were beyond Cuba's control. In 1957, an underground publication, called *Revolución*, summarized the program of the movement as follows: "The revolution is the struggle of the Cuban nation to achieve its historic aims and realize its complete integration. This integration consists in the complete unity of the following elements: political sovereignty, economic independence, and a particular or differentiated culture."[16] In other words, the Cuban revolution was a nationalistic-democratic revolution of Jacobin coloring that changed complexion after it obtained its victory.

During the two years spent by Castro and his followers in mountain fighting, some very typical features of the revolution were developed. There emerged the image of the guerrilla fighter, in army fatigues, black beard, and beret, which became the hallmark of the revolutionary. No insignia, such as Mussolini's fascists or Hitler's Nazis displayed so arrogantly, were adopted by revolutionary Cuba, but their garb and their appearance set them apart from the bourgeois world of corrupt politicians which they were intent on displacing. The old fighters of the Sierra Maestra formed the hard core of the revolutionary movement, and they looked askance at the civilian socialists and communists who contented themselves with undermining the Batista regime by sabotage or strikes. This circumstance accounts for certain contradictory, even schizophrenic features of the Cuban affair, which became more evident as time passed.

During the long months in the Sierra Maestra, Fidel Castro

rose to be the undisputed leader of the movement. He was, and is, as much demagogue as idealist, as much adventurer as revolutionary, as much anarchist as disciplined socialist, if such a bundle of contradictions can exist.[17] He and his followers were young, and they had had no time to prepare themselves for the grim and arduous tasks they were to undertake. They had no experience in government or organization; they had little formal schooling. It followed that they were unwilling to commit themselves to any doctrine or system of politics and were eager to embrace impromptu solutions for pressing problems no matter what the price. What Che Guevara (until recently Castro's chief lieutenant and later Cuba's minister of industry) wrote about them in 1960 was quite true: "The principal actors of this revolution had no coherent theoretical criteria."[18]

The story of Castro's triumph has been told many times, and we will, therefore, limit ourselves to a bare outline. At the time of his landing in Cuba in 1956, Castro's force had been so small that he could with difficulty hold his own. In March of 1957, he obtained help from the underground movement in Santiago de Cuba, which sent him some sixty men and a supply of weapons stolen from the American base at Guantanamo. Eventually, the Castroites made contacts with the poor peasantry in their immediate neighborhood and from them managed to get their food and bits of valuable information. But Batista occupied an apparently invincible position: he had money, a well-equipped army, and a specially created secret police force, the "tigers," which attempted to break the revolution by terroristic methods. Against them, Castro could employ only the hit-and-run tactics of guerrilla warfare and hope that the resistance movement in the cities might turn the struggle in his favor.[19] In the process, the moderate position of those who had hoped for a return to democracy was polarized and pulverized, a fact which goes a long way in explaining the final radical nature of the Cuban revolution.[20]

During 1958 the movement gained ground. Bombs were planted in Havana, policemen were killed, and the rebels extended their control from a foothold in the mountains, deep into eastern Cuba. Large sums of money were put at Castro's disposal. Some of it came from neighboring Latin American countries; from the United States there were collections amounting to $25,000 a month. But a part of the money that Castro received came from the Communist Party inside Cuba. Castro's early relations with the Communist Party in Cuba are still virtually unknown, but there is sufficient evidence that party functionaries visited Castro in his mountain hideout and that they supplied him with funds.

Perhaps of greater importance than the financial support given Castro by the communists was the agreement on a common strategy. By the fall of 1958 a unity of sorts between Castro's middle-class revolution and the labor unions had been achieved—"in the defense of common objectives." If these objectives had ever been defined, they would certainly not have included specific points of domestic or international politics. Their aim was to destroy the Batista regime, and success was closer than anyone could have predicted.

Toward the end of 1958, the revolution began to move westward, and at the beginning of 1959 the war was won. Batista fled to Santo Domingo and his army surrendered to the rebels. With Batista's own tanks and armored cars, the revolution rolled into Havana. Castro became the idol, the *líder máximo,* praised in verse and song. He appeared on street corners and balconies, speaking for two or three hours to the multitudes, still to all appearances the visionary warrior who had promised to purify Cuba. "I want to go back to Sierra Maestra and build roads and hospitals and a school city for 20,000 children. We must have teachers—a heroine in every classroom." He promised land to the poor squatters in the mountains. The army would be a people's army, built up around the *barbudos,* the bearded ones.[21] But Castro had other promises to keep. In 1953 he had said that those who had betrayed the people would be punished, and the revolution lost no time in carrying out this commitment. Although the constitution of 1940 had abolished capital punishment, the firing squads began their awesome task. The first to fall were the "tigers," the torturers and mass murderers of the dictatorship. But the fury of revenge gathered momentum, and the victorious rebels soon adopted the roles of judge and jury. Hundreds were put to death without trial, and world opinion, which had earlier welcomed Castro, began to cool toward the revolutionary leader, who apparently regarded the bloodshed and violence of his followers with little perturbation. We have given orders, he said, to shoot every last one of these murderers, and if we have to oppose world opinion to carry out justice, we are ready to do it. With Castro's rise to power, a note of defiance crept into his speeches: "If the Americans do not like what is happening, they can send the Marines; then there will be 200,-000 gringoes dead. We will make trenches in the streets."

Castro picked up the tools of dictatorship where Batista had dropped them, and increased his power by popular support. Nationalism and love of freedom had been the fuel that had driven the revolution to victory. The year 1959 saw Castro at the crossroads, and a great number of factors conspired to propel him toward the path he finally chose.

The records leave no doubt that Castro had promised a different revolution from the one that was finally put into operation. He had given a formal pledge that free elections would be held and an additional assurance that all individual rights guaranteed by the constitution would be upheld. The path of dictators has often been paved with such promises. Castro had likewise denied that nationalization would be desirable for Cuba, condemning it as a "cumbersome instrument." Quite rightly he predicted that it would hamper progress toward the main goal: industrialization.[22] But here again Castro reversed himself. There has been much speculation as to why the revolution changed course, whether it could have avoided the shift, and who the prime instigators of the turning might have been. Much of this speculation seems fruitless, especially the question of Castro's "betrayal" of the revolution; this holds interest only for those who put their faith in his promises and now feel betrayed themselves.

What Castro wanted for himself and for his movement above all else was political power, and he did not conceal that this was his prime goal. This does not mean that the Castro revolution lacks a social content and a social direction. Quite obviously such is not the case. But what we have here is a socialism *sui generis,* or to be more specific, it is the national socialism of a typical Latin American stamp which we have made an effort to comprehend throughout these studies. Here it is in its most radical form. From the point of view of socialism, Castro's revolution may appear to be one more revolt against colonialism or imperialism, and the parallels to Asian and African situations may be striking. But in the framework of hemispheric history Castro's revolution takes on a different meaning.[23] From this viewpoint, it stands out as the most radical attempt yet to be made for the solution of the social and economic problems which had poisoned the life of Cuba. Theodore Draper has spoken of the Cuban Variant, and it has become increasingly apparent that there is now a Cuban socialism just as there is an Arab socialism or an Indonesian socialism. The historian and the social scientist, interested in comprehending a phenomenon, are well advised to shy away from the easy generalization (whether applauding or condemning makes little difference) and turn their efforts to a study of the peculiarities of the case. In regard to Cuba, this means that a genuine revolution has taken place and is taking place, regardless of whether or not it is the one Castro promised. Likewise the question of whether this revolution is a peasant revolution or one designed to benefit the industrial proletariat is of small import in making a general assessment. This is a social revolution, which feels free to shift emphasis from one sector of society to another, which may be trying to do too much too quickly, but which defies Marxian or capitalist orthodoxy alike.[24] Thus, in 1959, Castro could say, ". . . ours is not a Communist revolution; ours is, I admit, a radical revolution— probably the most radical in Cuban history."[25] Yet a year later he and his followers could call themselves Marxist-Leninists. They were "pragmatic revolutionaries," who by the dynamics of the revolutionary events they had precipitated and by their own impatience became allies of communism rather than communists.

Again, it was due to a number of elements that the most radical faction of the Cuban movement came to the top. The reforms which Castro initiated provoked hostility inside Cuba from the middle class; finding themselves under a continual threat, they preferred emigration to submission. As many as 300,000 people have left the island, a figure that represents 5% of the total population. There was also a certain puritanism in Castro's revolution, a sweeping dismissal of the gaudy and corrupt life that had made pre-Castro Cuba a paradise of leisurely vice; this same puritanism now fostered the zealot and the fanatic. But above all, Castro's agrarian as well as his industrial policies led of necessity to clashes between the new regime and the United States. During the early days of the Cuban upheaval, the United States watched with bewilderment as the property of its citizens was expropriated and confiscated; finally this feeling turned to anger, though an impotent anger, and scant consolation was to be found in the fact that Cuban nationals fared no better.

All of these factors contributed to produce an atmosphere in Cuba wherein the old slogan of the Popular Front became appropriate: *No hay enemigos a la izquierda* (There are no enemies to the left). Jean-Paul Sartre, who visited Cuba in 1960, saw clearly that Castro needed Yankee imperialism in order to keep the revolutionary flame burning; if the Yankees had not existed, Castro would have been obliged to invent them.

Some observers have tried to explain Cuba's turn toward communism by saying that there had been in reality two revolutions in Cuba. One reached for social reforms by democratic means; the other was "a haphazard, totalitarian operation, run in mobocratic fashion, complete with government by marathon television spectaculars, by artificial crises, organized hysteria, calculated bloodletting, and deliberate vulgarization."[27] Even admitting the existence of two revolutions, it would still be true that by 1959 the totalitarian operation had won the upper hand.

We will not discuss the question, so frequently aired in the United States, as to whether our inept and bungling policy forced Castro's hand and drove him into the arms of the Soviet Union, which were, indeed, wide open for a friendly embrace. To be sure, the Eisenhower administration had little understanding for a revolutionary mystique, Cuban-style. From 1952 to 1960 the Department of State had adopted an attitude of unsalutary neglect toward the entire Latin American world, which made it doubly difficult for the United States to anticipate or to give much attention to affairs within the island. Yet it is ridiculous to blame the Department of State for the deterioration of relations between the two countries. Castro provoked the United States beyond all endurance. We gladly concede, what we have asserted throughout this study, that the trend toward nationalization was irrepressible in Latin America, as it was throughout the world, and that Cuba's economy cried out for a change in this direction. But there never was any sincere attempt on Castro's part to fulfill his promise that the owners of utilities, mines, cattle ranches, and sugar mills would be compensated. Other governments, such as Venezuela or Chile, have shown that the road to nationalization may take a profitable course through negotiated settlements. But Castro was not willing to wait. He was tired of United States interference, and in 1959 he declared that it was time for Cuba to "solve its own problems."

A number of minor issues between the two countries aggravated the situation: the United States gave asylum to the Cuban refugees, and certain leaders even advised training them as guerrillas for use in a future invasion; in addition, there was an arms embargo against Castro. Obviously, these problems had only nuisance value; the main problems were economic. Some Cuban officials, especially Che Guevara, began in 1959 to deride the sugar quota as a means of imperialistic exploitation. It was said to be a form of blackmail designed to secure Cuba's good behavior toward the United States. The Eisenhower administration seemed to lend credence to this argument by first reducing and then cutting out the sugar quota in 1960. As relations between the United States and Cuba worsened, a deep penetration by avowed communists was taking place in Cuba. The governmental structure underwent a rapid change. The moderates were forced out and were replaced by members, or former members, of the party on which Castro depended to keep the revolution afloat.[28] Communists and Fidelistas were headed for a United Front.

Khrushchev rattled his missiles and gave assurances that the Soviet Union would never allow any military intervention by the United States. But of greater importance was the wholehearted economic aid offered by the Russians. They promised to buy more sugar, a commodity on which the entire Cuban economy depended; they also promised to sell crude oil to Cuba and in general to replace American industrial goods, on which Cuba had relied, with goods from the Soviet Union. In addition to the trade agreements, the first of which was signed in February of 1960, the Russians promised a credit of 100 million dollars for industrialization. In 1961 Red China also got into the act and agreed to buy sugar and grant an interest-free loan of 60 million dollars.[29]

A look at the map shows that Cuba's adherence to the communist bloc violates all geographic laws. The total reorientation of Cuba's trade caused inordinate confusion and plunged the country into chaos. Orders that had been processed under United States brand names and catalog numbers had now to be made months ahead of time under unfamiliar specifications and then dispatched to the other side of the world. Still worse, Havana lacked warehouses to store goods from thousands of miles distant.[30] The docks were soon jammed with cargo, while machines stood idle for want of necessary tools. Inevitably, agriculture suffered. The sugar production dropped far below the level it had held before Castro had come to power. Food became scarce and had to be rationed; fresh fruit was imported to this tropical island from Bulgaria! The worker's paradise had become the housewife's nightmare. But to Castro and his friends it still seemed worth the price. It is difficult to understand how Castro could have been blind to the fact that he had thrown off the old fetters only to replace them with freshly forged chains.

Had Castro been a more seasoned politician, he would have hesitated before leaping from the frying pan into the fire, but for the Cuban revolutionary the alluring opportunity to singe his adversary in the process could not be withstood. The short-term advantages of his somersault were obvious. He solved his immediate economic problem without surrendering to the demands of the United States for "prompt, adequate, and effective compensation" for confiscated property. But he did not realize that he would inevitably become the prisoner of the economic barter system of the communist bloc. American experts were replaced by Russian and East German "technicians" who were engaged to steer the country's passage into industrialization. Yet the long-term perspectives were anything but promising. Castro could have foreseen that the United States, which had never tolerated hostile neighbors, would not assent to a communist outpost ninety miles from her frontiers. What might be a clear advantage for the Kremlin could only be a handicap for a young socialist state trying to rebuild its economy on a diversified basis. But there had always been a streak of the megalomaniac in Castro's makeup, and he may have believed the flattering words addressed to him in Moscow.

From this point on we will be obliged to separate the international events that affected Cuba from the domestic policy pursued by Castro, though they are concurrent and correlative.

From 1960 on there existed a state of undeclared war between the United States and Cuba. The United States used the rather cumbersome machinery of the OAS to obtain a condemnation of Castro, and Castro countered by calling for revolution on a hemispheric scale. His hopes for such an enterprise must have been high at that time and go a long way toward explaining some of his daring. His eyes were set on Brazil and Venezuela, Bolivia and Colombia, and there is no denying that his broad-

casts and his emissaries found sympathetic ears in many sections
of Latin America. Anti-Yankeeism will always strike a passion-
ate chord in Latin American hearts, even if it is not enough of
an inducement to join the ranks of the revolutionists. Fidelismo
became an ideology that was echoed in many places; there were
even those who proclaimed that Castro was the greatest *caudillo* that Latin America had produced since Bolívar.[31]

One cannot overlook the fact that the revolutionary trend in
Cuba tended to soften the United States toward the demands of
the other Latin American nations for economic assistance; Latin
America had long before called for a "Marshall Plan." Castro's
Cuba was, at the very least, a frightening example of what might
happen if the plea of the Latin American countries went un-
heeded. It was thus to the advantage of the various republics
to keep Castro in power, if only to prod the *coloso del norte*
toward more generous action. In 1961, President Kennedy announced the Alliance for Progress as the Latin American program for the United States. Unfortunately, this was not all that
the United States intended to do to check Castro's plans.

Since 1960, the Central Intelligence Agency had been preparing blueprints for an invasion of the island; the case was referred to as the "disposal problem." The CIA conceived of an
invasion of Cuba by an army of refugees, specially trained for
the purpose and with active support from American forces.[32]
How much support, however, was still the question. President
Kennedy let it be known that he did not wish to commit American forces to the adventure openly, a decision which all but
doomed the invasion before it started. There was a great deal of
indecision among the members of the President's inner council;
few of his advisers had any knowledge of the Latin American
temper; few were skilled in military planning. As the date for
the invasion approached, the United States saw fit to publish a
White Paper on Cuba, thus providing Castro with fair warning,
if, indeed, he stood in need of it. Rightly or wrongly, Castro had
always predicted that the United States would attempt to overthrow him by force, and he was prepared for the onslaught. He

had Russian and Czech weapons at his command, together with a large militia for the defense of the island and the preservation of the revolution.

Castro repulsed the invasion with little difficulty, taking many of the invaders prisoner and releasing them later for appreciable ransoms. Before setting them free, Castro had them paraded through the streets of Havana before TV cameras for five consecutive nights. He took great pleasure in telling his enemies where they had erred, though even a lay intelligence could locate the mistakes with ease. The Cuban disaster was one of those rare events in history, "a perfect failure."[33] Needless to say, it strengthened Castro's position immensely both at home and abroad. The United States had not enjoyed much popularity since the close of World War II, and the open attempt to force her will on a recalcitrant neighbor could only add fuel to the bitter criticism that was launched against her in many parts of the world. Latin America particularly has lived in constant fear of intervention by the United States, a fear that seemed to be more than substantiated by the events of April 1961.

However severe the blow of the frustrated invasion may have been to the prestige of the United States, its effect was soon erased by the situation it produced among her opponents. The facile triumph that Khrushchev and Castro had scored went to their heads, and, throwing caution to the winds, they conceived a scheme to further humiliate the enemy. Who hatched up the idea of installing missile sites on the island of Cuba is not yet known, nor is it at all clear what the communist leaders hoped to accomplish by this measure. Did they think that the United States would yield to pressure on her immediate frontiers and give up certain of its own missile bases on European or Asian soil? Did they think they might bluff their way to a further victory? Or did they go so far as to contemplate a nuclear war, which, if initiated in the western hemisphere, might bring them an early advantage? These questions cannot be answered with the information now at hand.[34] But so much is certain: If Cuba agreed to have missile sites on her soil, it must have been with the full knowledge that she might bear the brunt of an immediate counterstrike from the United States which would obliterate the island within a few hours. If it was a policy, it was a suicidal one. Castro was offering his country as the sacrificial lamb on the altar of world revolution.

As a result of Cuba's overconfident move, the United States announced that no missile sites, whether Cuban or Russian, would be tolerated at any point so near her coast. A blockade was thrown around Cuba with orders to intercept any ship that was suspected of carrying material or technicians engaged in this venture. After brief hesitation Khrushchev abandoned his ill-conceived project and agreed to remove the missiles from Cuba. The United States maintained its blockade and air reconnaissance until any immediate danger of military threat from Cuba was eliminated.

Castro's role in the crisis must have been highly unpleasant. He was forced to accept the fact that the Soviet Union had no intention of risking a major war for the sake of an ally who could provide no appreciable assistance, and who, in any case, meant little in the Soviet Union's design for power. Castro's only success was his refusal to allow international inspection of his island, but he did not dare challenge the reconnaissance flights of the United States, which were as efficient as any inspection might have been. As a further indignity, Castro was obliged to swallow whatever anger he may have felt, since he continued to be totally dependent on Russia for the sale of his sugar. As far as can be seen, the missile crisis also ended his role as the future deliverer of Latin America from capitalist exploitation. The Latin American nations followed the last act of the Cuban adventure with dismay and unmitigated fear, realizing that Castro might have easily dragged the entire hemisphere into a global conflict. The OAS voted on October 23, 1962, for the withdrawal of all offensive weapons from Cuban soil, and went so far as to recommend military measures to stop the flow of material into Cuba.[35]

An economic embargo against the island had been in effect

since 1962. In 1964 the United States succeeded in convincing most of the Latin American nations to break diplomatic relations with Cuba. At the time these words are being written, Mexico alone has refused to fall in line, and Cuba's isolation in the western hemisphere is well-nigh complete. Her attempts to undermine democratic governments in Venezuela and in Colombia have met with failure, as have her efforts to produce a lasting rift between Panama and the United States. All these factors without doubt decreased Castro's value as an ally of the communist bloc. Since October of 1962, Cuba has lost much of its strategic importance as one of the potential trouble spots of the world. It has been overshadowed by the Congo and Vietnam. This does not mean that a new flareup may not occur. Even less does it indicate that Castro's own position or the fate of his revolution is in any immediate danger. We must therefore try to assess the changes that Castro's revolution has produced in Cuba.

It is clear that Castro has wrought a social revolution that will have lasting effects, if only in a negative way. The old middle class, which in percentage was one of the largest in Latin America, has been eliminated. We have spoken of the mass exodus of refugees to the United States and other parts of Latin America. Castro may have watched their flight with mixed emotions. Although they deprived the island of professional and technical skills, they also lowered the menace of counterrevolutionary moves from within. Obviously, the revolution is creating its own class system, as revolution has done the world over. A new revolutionary elite is taking over, and this brings us to the question of the organization of the revolutionary movement after 1960. We have noted that Communist Party functionaries began to penetrate Castro's following shortly after his ascent to power. This did not take place without resistance from some of Castro's own friends, such as Huber Matos, but this opposition was speedily crushed. The next target for the Communist takeover was the unions. Thanks to a personal intervention by Castro himself, all the unions were brought under party control. Hence-

forth all pretense was dropped, and communism was openly recognized as the political faith of the island. The president and the
high-ranking officers of the cabinet were drawn from the party
roster, or were men who had left the party for tactical reasons
only. These matters were not settled without considerable fric-
tion, however; the men of Castro's original following were not
always in agreement with the men of whom the communist party
approved. Eventually a new directorate emerged, the ORI (Integrated Revolutionary Organizations), in which the hard-core
Castroites had a majority of three out of five, while the Communists had to be content with a two-to-three minority. Castro
remained the *líder máximo,* to be succeeded by his brother
Raul in case anything happened to him.[36]

It is difficult, if not impossible, to make any clear assessment
of affairs inside Cuba. For the time being at least, the political apparatus was in Castro's hands. An editorial in *Pravda* approved of
his organization of the ORI, which meant that the party leaders
in Moscow were in no hurry to precipitate a complete takeover
by its members. In all probability it was "an unsentimental and
unresolved alliance between Castro and the party." It cannot be
said that Castro had become the prisoner of the party; neither
can it be maintained that he was free to proceed as he wished,
since the Russian investment in Cuban economy was rapidly
rising.

Let us then consider the economic changes introduced by
Castro. In the beginning, they were an attempt to destroy the
bases of the opposition and to bring to an end the American influence on Cuban economy. They were confiscatory in character
and were in operation until 1961. Private wealth was seized in
the cities, while large sections of the rural properties were taken
over by collective farms or state farms. Castro, who had no economic training whatever, simply followed the Marxian blueprint
of industrialization plus socialization of agriculture—and reaped
the disastrous harvest. After his break with the United States,
Russian experts were brought to Cuba, and a four-year plan
was introduced.[37]

Since the United States no longer bought from Cuba and had imposed an embargo on all trade with the island, the Soviet bloc had to fill the gap. But the plans to diversify agriculture and to develop new industries were complete failures. Even Castro's most fanatic followers finally realized that it was ridiculous to produce articles at home which could be had for a lower price in the world market. Likewise the diversification of agriculture did not get off the ground, and in the attempt to get it moving much of the sugar production was dislocated and disorganized. The sugar had been pledged by Castro to the Soviet bloc in payment for the imports on which he depended. Facts and figures are not needed in support of these statements, since Castro and Guevara have admitted their truth. In August of 1963, Castro publicly denounced the economic policy of the revolution as "disoriented" and announced a return to agriculture as Cuba's most important source of national wealth. He still had the support of the Soviet leaders, who signed a new trade agreement for a six-year period. Castro benefited from the Sino-Russian split, in which he sided with Khrushchev rather than Mao Tse-tung, but he had to accept a low price for his sugar (six cents per pound), which profits the Russians rather than the Cubans.

In 1965, the island is still in a state of upheaval. Most observers agree that its cities have taken on a shabby appearance, that electric power failures are common, that water is in short supply, and that the traffic in Havana looks like a "moving junkyard."[38] Some Cubans live better than they did before Castro's advent, but the majority of the population cannot boast the same fortune. Food is rationed, and consumer goods are in short supply. The country is suffocated under yards of red tape that hampers the simplest economic activities. There are serious labor problems, especially in the sugar industry. As of 1964, the government was trying to find 25,000 volunteers to help in harvesting the sugar crop.

Obviously, this is not the complete picture. Castro has been successful in his campaigns for public health and sanitation;

sickness and death rates have been appreciably lowered. But here, too, the revolution becomes entangled in its own web. Many doctors have left the country, and the supply of hard cash is not sufficient to meet the purchase price of medicines. Many years will pass before this void can be filled.

In the meantime Castro sets his hopes on the new generation now coming of age in the Cuban schools and universities. The idea is common to all totalitarian regimes: let the old generation die out, and school the young to adopt the new society. Scholarships are available for the youth of all ages, running into many thousands each year. Communist indoctrination is part of the education, and both the Soviet Union and Cuba are set up as the shining examples of revolutionary idealism. The effects of the educational system are considerable. "The minds of most young people seem to be closed: fanatically in Castroism and against the United States—even against their parents. They don't remember what it is like to live well—or what freedom really means."[39] The young form Castro's greatest asset, providing he is able to wait for today's children to become tomorrow's adults. There are certain other symptoms that seem to prove that the regime may be more durable than its enemies promise. The militia that was so much in evidence after the invasion of 1961 is not quite so ubiquitous today, and the Cuban peso, officially at par with the dollar, has risen from ten cents on the black market to twenty.

There is a certain irony in the fact that Cuba is experimenting with the crude formula of Stalin's socialism at a time when the Soviet Union is turning to "Libermanism" and the use of the profit motive. Cooperative farms or state farms will probably have as little success in Cuba as they did in Russia. Admittedly, the landless peasant or the sharecropper has a better life today than he had before 1959, since he is kept on a year-round salary by the Cuban government. But for the small farmers, the new regime marks a heavy disadvantage, since they have been incorporated into the state farm system, or, if allowed to keep their land, they must now sell their produce at low prices fixed by the state.[40] The question is frequently asked if Castro's Cuba is a state of workers and peasants. As of today the answer is no. Cuba could be called a dictatorship for the proletariat, but not by the proletariat. And this brings us to another question: Will Castro's Cuba survive? First-hand knowledge of the situation within the island is difficult to come by, and the hazards of prediction based on the volcanic ground of Latin American procedures are well-known. However, a number of observations may be in order.

An overthrow of Castro could only come from the forces that are now in control, *i.e.*, the communists or the hard-core Castroites. Neither gives promise for a return to democratic government, western-style. The middle class has been decimated to the point that it no longer counts as a factor in the political future of Cuba. There is no independent army, as there is in Argentina, Brazil, and even Bolivia, which might set itself up as a policy maker. Following the pattern of most dictatorships, Castro and his followers know how to secure their power by the elimination of possible successors. These factors leave the Cuban people, and the world, with the dismal perspective of an indefinite survival for socialist Cuba.

Of course, no one can tell what might happen if another great international crisis should occur. In the case of a general war, the United States would lose no time in destroying a communist beachhead in the western hemisphere. For Castro, there would be the dubious satisfaction of going down under a worldwide holocaust for the sake of the socialist revolution in which he believed. Or does he so believe? Is Castro at heart a convinced socialist? Does he not, instead, make use of communism as a tool in his daring scheme—as, indeed, the communists doubtless used him? Castro's revolution would not have been possible except for the climate of the cold war and the chance of setting the great powers against each other. Nasser has played this game of international blackmail with consummate skill, as has Sukarno. Both, however, are in a better geographical position than Cuba; both have great natural resources; both can use China against the Soviet Union, and the Soviet Union against the United States. Castro's choice is more limited; China, with neither navy nor mercantile fleet, would be unable to come to his assistance.

As Castro assesses his chances, it would seem that he has no fear for the survival of the revolution. He may admit that the revolution has not yet reached maturity, but he believes time will take care of this.[41] Only occasionally does a rumble issue from Cuba indicative of some resentment which Castro may harbor against the party.

On January 2, 1965, Castro declared, "We are a people with the right to speak with our own thought and voice . . . what every Marxist party should do in each concrete situation cannot be told by anyone from anywhere. If any party would try to do this with us, it would meet a determined and decided rejection . . . It is clear that each country has concrete conditions under which each revolution developed." And he added with some anger, ". . . if some persons have doubts about whose head we are using, we must clearly answer that we do not need to ask anyone to lend us his brains."[42] Such outbursts should, very likely, not be overrated, especially when they come from a man like Castro, but they do reveal that he chafes under his dependency on the Soviet Union just as he resented his dependency on the United States. "Technical advisers" can be quite as annoying as managers or bank presidents. The gist of this is that true independence is impossible either way, and if national independence was Castro's goal, he could have had more for less.

There are some lessons to be drawn from the Cuban experience. More than any other occurrence between 1945 and 1965, it pointed to the social and economic ills in Latin America that jeopardize any stable government. The people are held in a state of unrest between despair and great expectation in which any remedy may be tried, right-wing totalitarianism or left-wing revolution. The social and economic problems likewise tend to prolong the reliance on the *caudillo* system; Castro is as much a *caudillo* as was Perón. From our vantage point, we may say that the Cuban revolution started as a democratic and nationalistic uprising against dictatorship and foreign exploitation and ended as a socialist revolution of uncertain future.

In Cuba's case the nationalistic passion did not act as a catalyst, nor was it strong enough to restrain the leaders of the revolution from selling their birthright for communist support. Whether Cuba's experience will have a sobering effect on other Latin American countries, spurring the democratic and Christian forces toward more determined action, remains to be seen. There are some indications that such a process is going on. One thing, however, is certain: Cuba will never be the same. No one but a fool could dream of a return to the bad old days.

CHAPTER XI

Conclusion

Now that we have come to the end of our studies, it would seem that some assessment of our findings is in order. Our undertaking has admittedly been an ambitious one. We have been confronted with an enormous segment of the contemporary world, and our efforts to bring it into focus have been hampered by the bewildering changes which mark the day-to-day life of Latin America. Added to the political instability which has been characteristic of the continent for the past 150 years are the present social and economic shifts, making generalizations still more precarious. The favorite sport of the political commentator, that of jumping to conclusions, must be avoided, but we should never have embarked on these studies if we had not hoped to provide some prefigurement of the future.

We are in agreement with J. J. Johnson's recent statement that "the most important single phenomenon in Latin America is the rapid growth of nationalism."[1] We have noted the development of this nationalism from its timid beginnings in the nineteenth century, when it was a patriotism of regional coloring, to the time when it became a cultural and aristocratic nationalism which in our century turned into a popular and revolutionary nationalism, actually the Latin American version of national socialism. This nationalism fulfilled a function for which the seventeen republics of the hemisphere had long been waiting: that of giving them the necessary minimum of political and social cohesion without which no body politic can survive. We have observed the obstacles lying in the path of such developments, a major one being the Iberic heritage with its aristocratic, semi-feudal outlook on life, its resistance to manual labor and technological progress, its stress on military virtues, all imposed in Latin America on a society composed of heterogeneous racial layers.

Political independence was won, but it did not bring stability with it. The continent was torn between conflicting ideologies borrowed from Europe and the United States. From the ensuing turmoil only one institution reaped a benefit: rule by *caudillo*. The contact with western capitalism and the industrial revolution only added to the already existing difficulties. It entailed economic dependence first on the more advanced nations of western Europe and later on the United States. Political colonialism was replaced by economic colonialism. Thus nationalism developed along two lines in Latin America, one domestic, the other international, both interrelated and interacting.

On the domestic level, we have seen how nationalism became the rallying point in the revolutions that occurred in Mexico, Brazil, Bolivia, and Argentina; but it is also a factor in those republics where there was no prolonged national revolution, *i.e.*, in Chile, Colombia, Venezuela, and Peru. The results in these latter states are still inconclusive.

Colombia seems the most retarded of the four countries listed above. When the liberal rule drew to a close in 1946, the conservatives made a return, but a vicious civil war which took thousands of lives plunged the country into anarchy. From this state of affairs emerged, predictably, the military strongman, Rojas Pinilla. When he was ousted in 1957, the feuding parties concluded a truce aiming at national pacification.[2]

The truce was designed to remain in effect for sixteen years, during which period a unique arrangement of bipartisanship was to be installed. The two parties were to alternate in the office of chief executive, thus warding off the recurrence of civil war. Each party, however, was pledged to preserve its ideological and organizational unity during this interim. The National Front made out fairly well under the first president, the able Alberto Lleras Camargo, who claimed that *el frente nacional* was to be a long and glorious chapter in the history of Colombia.[3] But when the conservatives took over in 1962, the country veered from its steady course. There were some, like Alfonso López Michelsen, who argued that the National Front should be supported by the establishment of a one-party system after the model of Mexico.[4] Much could be said in favor of this line of reasoning, except that in Colombia no group or class would have backed such a party. The country was fragmented and began to look once more to authoritarian solutions, among which the return of the discredited dictator, Rojas Pinilla, seemed a possibility. The causes of this interior discord are not easily ascertained. No doubt, personalities have played their role. The conservative president, Guillermo León Valencia, has not proved the equal of Lleras Camargo. Strikes, banditry, and stagnation of the economy have undermined confidence in the government. Coffee remains the main source of foreign exchange, but it is no longer able to furnish the economy with sufficient reserves to pay for growing imports. The Colombian peso is now worth only a fraction of its value at the end of the Second World War. Capital is leaving the country at an alarming rate, as are the inhabitants—at least the rich, who appear to be seized with panic at the thought of another civil war.[5] Colombia, therefore, presents us with a case in which the energies of nationalism have failed to overcome the centrifugal tendencies that have threatened the Latin American people for so long.

It is too early to make any prediction about the fate of Peru. President Fernando Belaúnde Terry is engaged in a vast reform program gleaned mainly from Haya de la Torre. Belaúnde talks of an "Indian renaissance" and has promised more food, better jobs, and new roads, schools, hospitals, and industries. He too has brandished the banner of nationalism in a dispute with an American oil company, International Oil, an affiliate of Standard Oil of New Jersey. But retarding influences have always been strong in Peru, and we have yet to see whether Belaúnde can keep the military in check and convince the ruling oligarchy that concession to reform may be the better part of valor.[6]

Venezuela and Chile offer much more promising prospects. The changes that have occurred and continue to occur in both countries have a broad backing from groups on all levels who are convinced of the necessity of a peaceful revolution in all Latin American countries. As one of the leading intellectuals of Costa Rica has expressed it: *"Yo entiendo la revolución como un cambio necessário, inevitable, en las estructuras económicas y sociales de nuestros paises con miras a garantizar el bien-estar de los pueblos."* ("I consider revolution to be a necessary and inevitable change in the economic and social structures of our countries with the purpose of guaranteeing the well-being of the people").[7] The necessity of revolution is recognized by most; the only question is who will carry it out and what kind of revolution will it be. The national revolution of Venezuela is much more perplexing than the other Latin American revolutions since Venezuela appeared to be the most unlikely country for a successful experiment of this kind.

Venezuela had been the paradise of military *caudillos*. Until 1958 there had been a long and inglorious line of this type of ruler, rarely interrupted by any attempt to give the country some semblance of constitutional government. But Venezuela had also become one of the foremost producers of oil, and by the time that the tyrant of the Andes, Juan Vicente Gómez, had died in 1935, the petroleum industry was firmly entrenched in the country, providing it with its main source of income. It is no exaggeration to say that the entire country depended on oil in one form or another and that this dependence gave rise to social changes of revolutionary proportions. The rural population began to leave their farms and flock to the oil fields or to the cities, especially to Caracas, where wages were higher and living conditions more attractive. The capital embraced one-fifth of the total population of Venezuela by 1958.[8] Some progress toward an enlightened policy of social reform was made in the period from 1943 to 1945. A social security system was introduced and a public housing program got under way. But the gulf between those who benefited from the oil boom and those who lived on the crumbs falling from the tables of the rich was fantastically wide. The "black gold" was the foremost interest among both rich and poor, and the latter began to hate the foreign oil companies with a fury that was no less violent because it seemed condemned to impotence. When this writer reminded a friend in Caracas of the benefits that his country had been receiving in hygiene and wealth from the great American corporations, he received this answer: "Sure! For every mosquito they kill, they get an oil well." Inevitably, oil became the principal issue in the revolutionary propaganda that came to the fore in 1945.

A group of intellectuals and officers calling itself Acción Democrática overthrew the government in 1945. It first ruled by junta, headed by Rómulo Betancourt, and later installed a constitutional president, the novelist Rómulo Gallegos, of international fame. But Acción Democrática lost power to another dictator, Pérez Jiménez, who maintained himself in power until 1957. It was then that Acción Democrática was once more returned to power by popular mandate. Betancourt assumed the presidency in 1959.

Betancourt had been in politics since 1928, when he and some of his fellow students attempted to oust Juan Vicente Gómez. After spending two years in the dungeons of his intended victim, Betancourt was allowed to go into exile, and in Costa Rica he joined the Communist Party. He refused to embrace the creed of world revolution, however, and eventually severed his allegiance to the party. His experience, though brief, was not without advantage; Betancourt came to know the aims as well as the techniques used by the party to sway underdeveloped countries, and his conviction of the necessity for economic and social reform in Venezuela was thereby deepened. He wanted to include in his party all the "nonparasitic classes of the population," those who would fight for democracy, social justice, and economic redemption.[9] He first tried to introduce some measure of reform when he headed the revolutionary junta of 1945. Again forced into exile, moving to Washington, Havana, Costa Rica, Puerto Rico, he had ample time to consider the mistakes that had been committed during his first attempts.

At his election to the presidency in 1959, he not only had the support of his own party, but that of the Social Christian Party (Copei) as well. This fact marked a significant development in that it augured cooperation between the forces committed to social democracy and those committed to the social teachings of Christianity. Furthermore, he had the backing of the Republican Democratic Union, a group to the left of Acción Democrática. Betancourt knew that he would need all the support he could muster if he hoped to complete the job he had started in 1945. He was quite willing to concede that his first effort at reform had been riddled with mistakes. He had overrun the country like a bulldozer, signing hundreds of decrees, disregarding the sensitivities of minorities, adopting an arrogant and intolerant attitude toward those who advised him to proceed at a more cautious pace. By 1959 he had also become aware of the great importance of the armed forces in Venezuela. They had dominated the country's history for so many years that it was essential not to challenge them, to keep them content—but powerless.

Just as in Brazil, Mexico, and Argentina, the national revolution had to attack on a broad front: agrarian reform, industrialization, education, housing, welfare and public health. More than half of the population was still illiterate; the large landowners, representing only 2% of the nation, controlled three-fourths of all farmland in production. In a country the size of Texas, much of the important staples, such as wheat, corn, rice, and even meat and eggs, had to be imported from abroad. The country begged for immigration to fill the vast empty spaces and to bring to its industry much-needed skills and technicians, but living and working conditions in Venezuela offered little to attract even the venturesome immigrant.

Betancourt assessed the difficulties realistically when he turned his attention to the plow and the man behind the plow. There was no need for further revolutionary upheaval, which could only serve to profit his enemies to the right or to the left. He even used nationalistic slogans sparingly, since they might create hostility against foreign capital, and Betancourt was determined to keep relations of friendship and understanding with the United States.

There can be no doubt, however, that his aims were revolutionary and nationalistic, even though his means and his procedures were peaceful and temperate. The execution of the revolutionary program was designed and drawn up by an office for coordination and planning, which in 1960 came forth with a four-year plan. It embraced everything from highway construction to heavy industry, and its primary motive was nationalistic, *i.e.*, the country's basic industries should be controlled and managed by Venezuelan nationals. In his New Year's message of 1960, Betancourt proclaimed his goal with candor: "There is going forward a structural change in the national economy," he said, "and we are beginning to break our dependence on foreign production."

The oil industry naturally became the focal point for the contemplated changes. In 1960 Venezuela still depended on the United States to buy 44% of her oil exports; in the same year she imported from the United States 63% of all goods purchased abroad. In order to correct this situation, Betancourt considered changes which he himself described as of a "revolutionary nature."[10] He had studied the oil problem for years and he had gone on record that he would not expropriate or cancel existing concessions; but he had also declared that no new concessions would be granted. This allowed for an interim period of thirty-three years during which all the existing concessions would expire. In the meantime a national agency for the production, transport, and sale of petroleum was to become operative, and a tanker fleet was to be constructed which would allow Venezuela to market oil with profit in the world market. For the time being, royalties received by the government from foreign concessionaires were raised to 65%. Even so, the oil companies seemed able to continue their operations in Venezuela with satisfactory results. The very fact that all this could be achieved without threats on the part of the government and counterthreats of reprisals from the United States reveals what a consummate politician Betancourt had become.

Again it should be pointed out that such procedures would not have been possible without the examples set by Mexico, Brazil, and even Bolivia. And we must also bear in mind that at the time Betancourt assumed the presidency, many other countries, such as Iran, Egypt, and Indonesia, had demonstrated what can be achieved by intrepid nationalism in a world where the two superpowers compete with each other for the support of the unaligned nations. Venezuela, however, remained firmly committed to the western cause; in fact Betancourt's government came as close to being the model for the Alliance for Progress as any republic in the western hemisphere. President Kennedy welcomed the efforts of the Acción Democrática in December of 1961 when he said: ". . . we will be partners in building a better life for our people."

The many-faceted activities of the Betancourt regime—in agriculture, education, heavy industry, and consumer goods—though significant in themselves, need not delay us here. They are in the nature of long-term investments in the future of Venezuela, and can be judged only by their results.

Venezuela had, of course, additional reasons for staying close to the international line that was being followed by Washington. Betancourt had come under heavy attack from the right as well as the left, and had to contend with enemies from within and from without. Rafael Trujillo looked with fear upon a democratic government in such close proximity to his own fief and went so far as to hire assassins to remove Betancourt from the scene. Betancourt escaped with only minor injuries, but the attempt revealed that reactionary forces were only biding their time. From another quarter, Fidel Castro observed Betancourt with a jaundiced eye and dispatched arms and guerrilla fighters to harass and, if possible, to topple his rival. In 1960 he was successful in dividing Acción Democrática; a group calling itself Movimiento de Izquierda Revolucionaria was established which advocated insurrection or civil war should the opportunity present itself.[11] An underground operation for the National Liberation initiated sabotage tactics on a large scale. Bombs were thrown, United States officials were kidnapped, factories were set on fire, with the clear intention of intimidating the electorate and discrediting the democratic process. Betancourt's term expired in 1964, and it was for this date that the communists or Fidelistas saved their heaviest onslaught. But the year 1963 was not favorable to dictatorship in Venezuela, whether it came from the right or the left. Trujillo had fallen in 1961 by the same weapon he had so frequently found useful himself, and Castro's revolution had lost much of its glamor, having become the victim of all manner of economic entanglements. The National Liberation Front did not give up their efforts, however, and pressed on to the very end in their attempt to prevent the holding of elections.

According to law all Venezuelans over eighteen years of age were obliged to vote, and vote they did. The candidate of the Acción Democrática, Raúl Leoni, a labor lawyer, triumphed with almost a million votes cast in his favor. The leader of the Christian Socialists, Rafael Caldera, received about 20% of all votes, thus affirming once more that democratic-socialist forces were in control. Betancourt had been the first constitutionally elected president in Venezuela to complete his term and to pass the office on to a lawfully chosen successor. An unprecedented 86% of the voters had gone to the ballot box, thus confirming their faith in Venezuela's nascent democracy.[12]

After one year in office Leoni has proved his ability. However, it would be rash to dismiss the possibility of further attempts by the military to seize power or by the Communists to undermine the regime. They have taken to guerrilla activities in Venezuela as well as in Colombia and Peru, concentrating for the most part in the country districts. Such action, emulating Castro's stand in the Sierra Maestra, is not likely to succeed, but has, of course, a nuisance value and may hamper land reform, which today is indispensable to any democratic government in Latin America.

Recent events in Chile follow a significant parallel to the developments in Venezuela. In Venezuela it was the Acción Democrática which triumphed; in Chile it was the Democrácia-Cristiana. This was the first resounding victory for a movement apparently destined to play a large role in bringing social and political reforms to Latin America. Strange though it may seem, this particular combination in political effort had never before materialized in the western hemisphere. Given the almost total adherence of Latin America's population to the Christian faith in its Roman Catholic frame, one might well have expected the church to exercise a profound influence on the political and ideological development of the continent. But such had not been the case. In its majority the clergy represented an element of conservatism, one might say of reaction, in most of the Latin America countries; together with the army, they favored the preservation of the *status quo*. The background for this attitude is to be found in the history of the church and its subservience to the state in colonial times, but also in the fact that liberalism in Hispanic America was hostile to the established church, thus driving the clergy into the conservative camp. The social ideas of Leo XIII had found little or no echo in Latin America.[13] On the other hand, liberalism did not threaten the church with extinction, as does communism. Before the Second World War, the menace of communism had rarely been felt in Latin America, but with the emergence of the communist bloc as a world power, the situation altered. Even so, it would seem that the church had been tardy in adjusting doctrine and practice to the danger. She was also dilatory in recognizing the national and social revolutions which have been almost continuous in one or another of the Latin American republics since 1910, as the irrepressible movement that they undoubtedly were —a spontaneous occurrence which might be delayed or deviated, but in the end could not be suppressed.[14]

The answer to such a dilemma would appear to be obvious: the formation of Christian-democratic parties. Such groups had emerged in Europe at the end of the Second World War in Germany, France, and Italy and had contributed greatly to the political firmness of these countries in opposing communism. In Latin America, however, the rise of a Christian-Democratic movement came late, though there are, to be sure, some cases of its appearance in a few republics, such as Venezuela and Chile. Similar organizations in Argentina and Brazil have not yet made much headway.

The tenets of Democrácia-Cristiana are not essentially different from those of Acción Democrática. *Un cambio revolucionario* (a revolutionary change) is advocated which, its supporters hope, will bring a rapid and profound transformation in Latin American society.[15] It recognizes the imminence of revolution and admits the alternatives to be faced: *"O hacemos una revolución pacífica, constructiva y cristiana, o los pueblos serán para su daño, arrastrados a una revolución violenta, materialista y destructora"* ("We will either have a peaceful, constructive and Christian revolution, or the people will be swept toward a violent, materialistic, and destructive revolution").[16]

Chile was confronted with exactly this alternative in 1964. The country had enjoyed a long and peaceful history, in which dictatorships had been the exception rather than the rule. The old parties, conservatives, liberals, and socialists, seemed, however, firmly entrenched when the Christian Democratic party appeared on the political scene. In the presidential election of September 1964, the candidate of the new party, Eduardo Frei, ran against a socialist, Salvador Allende, who had the backing of the communist party. Frei won with a clear majority of 57.4% of all the votes. Seven months later, elections for the Chilean parliament confirmed this amazing turn of public opinion. The Christian Democrats gained an absolute majority in the house of deputies and increased their number in the senate by thirteen seats. Thus Frei is now in a position to carry out his reform program; he has proved that the Christian-Democratic movement is supported by a Chilean majority; communism has been rejected, and the old parties which were unwilling or unable to deal with Chile's problems have been reduced to silence.[17]

Frei has recently given an account of his faith in the Christian-Democratic movement.[18] He insists that, whatever their difficulties, the Latin American people have a western Christian tradition and that they have had a persistent sense of freedom even under the most obnoxious of tyrannies. He also notes that in all Latin American countries there is a university-trained stratum able to become an active and leading element. Moreover, there is now a middle class of about 20% of the population to act as a stabilizing factor in society. But Frei warns that these positive elements can be of value only to the extent that they are stimulated to solve Latin America's problems. His program may be summarized as "revolution with freedom" as opposed to "revolution with dictatorship."[19]

Translated into specifically Chilean terms, Frei's projections would include land reform for the landless peasants, a public housing program that would eliminate the slums in Santiago de Chile, and, still more important, the nationalization of public utilities and the mineral wealth on which Chile has depended for so long. His plans also include a reform of the administrative structure which has hampered rather than guided Chilean life. Says Frei: "Old and inefficient social organizations that paralyze the economic system must be replaced, but only through administrative and institutional reforms that will permit authentic participation of the people in civic life."[20]

Frei's plan for the nationalization of Chile's mineral wealth looks forward to orderly procedures. The government plans to buy into a friendly partnership with the three great American corporations that produced 545,000 tons of ore in 1963, representing 80% of Chile's foreign exchange. The arrangement announced by Frei foresees the purchase of stock from the North American companies up to 50% of the total, to be paid for in installments over a period of twenty years. But it also outlines a heavy capital outlay by both the Chilean government and the American corporations for the purpose of ensuring an increased productivity in the years to come. The equipment from such investments will enter Chile tax-free. Some of the copper will be refined in Chile, and Frei expects to increase Chile's earnings in foreign currency by selling the copper in the world market. He is aware that such a gradual nationalization places a responsibility on the community. "This policy," he declares, "represents a true challenge to the Chilean community. It puts our national conscience face to face with the destiny of our principal industry." As a first step, Frei nationalized the telephone company, an affiliate of International Telephone and Telegraph, applying much the same pattern that will be followed in the mining industry.[21] Here again, as in Venezuela, we will have to wait for results, but indications are promising. If Christian Democracy can make further conquests and establish itself in other countries, in Peru or Argentina, for instance, it would seem the logical escape from the cul-de-sac where so many Latin parliamentary groups find themselves. It would be a solution which could command the support of the clergy, in addition to having a strong appeal for the middle class, plus a large percentage of the women's vote in many countries. However, Latin America has turned a deaf ear to many logical solutions, and no one can make a safe prediction in regard to the future of Christian democracy in the southern hemisphere.

In the international field, Christian democracy advocates integration on the regional level, with a Latin American parliament and a Latin American court of justice.[22] This leads us logically to the other problem posed by the rise of nationalism in Latin America: its international aspects. Once more we must assert that nationalism in these regions is neither an artificial nor an accidental phenomenon, but the result of the transformation of those republics from within and world conditions that must be faced from without. The older forms of patriotism and of cultural nationalism have, as we stated, been superseded by a popular nationalism, but this nationalism does not negate them; it retains them. In other words the new nationalism of the sixties is at the same time patriotically conscious of its cultural heritage and inflamed by the passions characteristic of mass movements. The Iberic-American world could not have avoided this phase of its development; only through its adherence to the tenets of Mexicanism, *Argentinidad*, Brazilian destiny, Chileanism, etc., could these countries have hoped to overcome the handicaps of semicolonialism that had delayed their evolution in the contemporary world. This is even more true for those nations whose fate it had been to endure the rule of the *caudillo*, as in Peru, Bolivia, and Venezuela. Democratic government may not necessarily be the answer to their problems, but popular awakening and popular participation are indispensable if they are to be rescued from the doldrums of 150 years of public apathy. This is particularly true of the small Central American republics, which are endeavoring to maintain themselves in a world where technological advances demand the scope of large and productive countries.

The six Central American republics have a total population smaller than California or New York.[23] Living standards are low, and most of the countries have been afflicted by the ills frequently listed in these pages. But whatever the size or condition of his homeland, there is hardly a man who would be willing to surrender his nation's sovereignty or its inviolability without violent protest. In Guatemala, President Juan José Arévalo (1945–1950) attempted to introduce into his own country some of the innovations of the Mexican revolution.[24] Under his successor, Jacobo Arbenz Guzmán, his policy was continued, but with a definite veering to the left. It became a focal point for communist agitation, leading to a barely camouflaged intervention on the part of the United States and to a return of the military rule which is still in effect.[25] Arévalo has not abandoned hope of being returned to the presidency. In 1963 he once more outlined his program in a document called *A Letter to the People of Guatemala*.[26] He says, in part: "We are nationalists in theory and practice. We want to rule Guatemala without anybody daring to give us advice from the outside. Ours is a defensive and sentimental nationalism, not a narrow, closed and aggressive one. We do not share the opinion of those who think nationalism is a bad word. . . . Our nationalism is a brotherly nationalism which operates on the basis of dignity." Although he denounced John Foster Dulles with some violence, he expressed a good deal of sympathy for Roosevelt and John Kennedy.

A similar attitude can be found in many of the Central American republics. Their most democratic and most articulate spokesman has been the Costa Rícan José Figueres, a leading figure in the domestic politics of his country and a man of hemispheric vision. Figueres, who was his country's president from 1953 to 1958, was fully conscious of the basic political, economic, and cultural deficiencies of the Latin American world, and while in office he made great efforts to overcome them in his own nation. His position is akin to Betancourt's, whose friend he is, and also to that of Luis Muñoz Marín, governor of Puerto Rico. He avoided foreign investments, which he called a form of "economic occupation" capable only of increasing the very grievances about which the Latin American nations so loudly complained.[27] Though conscious of the role the Latin Americans are called upon to play, he cannot be accused of hostility to the United States. Nevertheless, this man delivered a candid, straightforward and forceful accusation against the United States in the wake of Mr. Nixon's ill-fated tour through South America.

Let us quote some parts of his Washington speech: "As a citizen of the hemisphere, as a man who has dedicated his public life to the cultivation of inter-American understanding, as a student who knows and esteems the United States . . . I deplore the fact that the people of Latin America, as represented by a handful of overexcited Venezuelans, should have spit at a worthy functionary who represents the greatest nation of our times . . . people cannot spit at a foreign policy, which is what they wanted to do. But when they have run out of other ways of making themselves understood, their only remaining course is to spit." The tone of his discourse alters as he turns to another subject, directing his remarks to the United States in general: "If you are talking about exercising human dignity toward the Russians, why is it so difficult to talk about the dignity of man when speaking of the Dominican Republic? Which is intervention and which is nonintervention? [Figueres referred to the excesses of the Trujillo regime.] . . . We Latin Americans are tired of pointing out these mistakes, especially the lack of interest in the prices of our products . . . We are not asking for handouts . . . We have inherited all the defects of the Spanish character, but also some of its virtues. Our poverty does not lessen our pride. We have our dignity."[28] And there is no doubt that Figueres spoke for all the rest of the Central American republics, who may respect the might of their northern neighbor, but who have not given up their pride in their own countries.

From what we have said in the preceding pages, it should be clear that South America's basic problem in international relations lies to the north. And the principal issue emerging from the new nationalism is, therefore, the finding of a satisfactory basis for harmonious coexistence throughout the hemisphere. This problem has no easy solution, nor will any single method suffice, since the needs of the Latin American countries vary so tremendously. Moreover, the importance of hemispheric policy changes depending on whether it is viewed from Washington, Buenos Aires, La Paz, or Brasília.

The responsibilities with which the United States found itself burdened at the end of the Second World War led to an overemphasis on European and Asiatic issues, to which the African troubles were added in 1960. Latin America, which had been the spoiled child of the western world during the war, was given little or no attention. This writer, together with many others familiar with hemispheric problems, gave warning of the inevitable consequences of a policy obsessed with fear of communism, and valuing the Latin American nations only according to their potential as allies in the fight against the great international conspiracy. Apparently it did not occur to Mr. Dulles that his policy was an open invitation to the communist bloc to capitalize on his neglect, in spite of the fact that communist theorists had long viewed Latin America as the ideal terrain for the advancement of their dominion. Latin America is the soft underbelly of the American dragon, even though the army and the church may oppose communism.

Cuba opened the eyes of Washington's credulous strategists, who had taken the goodwill of 200 million people for granted. The Alliance for Progress was a tardy answer to the sudden breakthrough of communism in the western hemisphere. Its advance has been slow and apathetic. Obviously the Alliance for Progress is no panacea, nor does any panacea exist. National growth is a slow process, especially when it is complicated by racial differences, historic habits ingrained through hundreds of years, and the crosscurrents of world events that will spare Latin America no more than they will spare any other continent.

In the wake of the Cuban disaster of 1961, a flood of books appeared whose aim was to find a way out of the impasse.[29] One author lists seventeen suggestions which, in his opinion, would help to solve the manifold ills of the Latin American countries, though he admits that none is an infallible cure.[30] We will concern ourselves with this subject only insofar as it concerns the topic of this book.

The policy of the United States toward Latin America can not be guided by any other criterion than that which regulates all international relations, the criterion of enlightened self-interest. The great task of all foreign policy consists not only of defining the interests of a power in any given situation, but of implementing them, that is, adjusting its self-interests to the

self-interests of other countries, either by persuasion or, in the
last resort, by whatever means it commands. Most observers
of the hemispheric scene would agree that the nations of the
Americas have a common destiny, just as they have a common
heritage. The inhabitants of the two continents, whether of
Anglo-Saxon or of Iberic descent, are still closer to one another
than they are to the Afro-Asian nations. This is true even for
racial minorities, such as the Negroes in the United States or
the Indians in the Andean countries. Their fate is inextricably
woven into the fabric of our western civilization.[31] Consequently the future of Latin America will not be to throw its
lot in with the communist bloc. Geographic circumstances are
the most powerful argument against any determined leaning
toward such an orientation. Trade with the communist countries can, of course, exist and will probably increase, barring a
sudden deterioration of international relations, but it will always
remain exposed to the danger of American blockade. In case of
war, needless to say, the entire hemisphere would be at the
mercy of the military power of the United States.[32] It is folly to
think that any of the republics could survive under the umbrella
of neutrality.

For the same reasons, the Latin American nations will have
a hard time trying to occupy a "third position," a position of
unalignment in the great struggle that dominates the twentieth
century. Perón tried to occupy this position and failed, Quadros
tried and failed. The geographic and economic currents will
speak with a louder voice than any desire for self-assertion,
however tempting such a position may appear to Latin American politicians. Mexico is the only nation which has followed
an independent line in regard to Cuba, but even Mexico has not
opposed the policy of the United States. However, if the power
of the United States is to remain a constant in hemispheric relations, it does not follow that the twenty American republics will
form a solid bloc, or, on the other hand, that the United States
could ignore hostility and Yankee-phobia with impunity—on
the contrary. Thus we return to our original search for measures

that may strengthen a feeling of harmony and solidarity in the Americas.

Again, there seem to be no solutions to this phase of the Latin American problem that may be applied *en bloc* to the entire hemisphere. One oft-repeated complaint of the Latin American countries concerns what they consider a low and unfair price for their products. They object to the importation of industrial goods bought from the United States at constantly rising prices, while the commodities they export are exposed to violent oscillations. They have demanded that the price of sugar, tin, coffee, copper, lead, etc., be stabilized by a program that would put a floor under the commodity market, in the same manner that American farm products are supported. But there can be no certainty that such a stabilization would succeed. In the first place, it is highly unlikely that Congress would look with favor on such a measure. Secondly, the United States would necessarily have a voice in the quantity of raw material or foodstuffs that any Latin American country would be permitted to produce, a situation that very few of these countries would be inclined to accept, since it would run counter to the tenets of nationalism and sovereignty which they are so eager to obtain and to defend. In the third place, the commodity market has undergone and is undergoing great changes resulting from the liberation of the African nations, which, in many instances, specialize in the same products as the Latin American nations. Anticolonialism, obviously, cuts two ways. It is doubtful that the United States would sacrifice its trade with the emergent African or Asian nations for the benefit of the Latin Americans. Nor would a price stabilization or a quota system be more than an artificial device to avoid the competition and fluctuation of world market prices.

The perspectives for a more intimate collaboration between the democratic regimes in Latin America and the United States merits some skepticism. Certainly the type of democratic government represented by Betancourt and Frei will be more to the liking of the United States. In Milton Eisenhower's felicitous phrase, there should be "a handshake for dictators and an *abrazo* for democratically elected rulers."[33] But the case of Cuba is ample proof that even a dictator may command a large popular following. Pronunciámentos and *caudillo* rule are too deeply ingrained in Latin American history to be summarily excised by fatherly advice. Populism of the Fidelista or Peronista coloring can be as troublesome and unpredictable as any military strongman. Furthermore, the role of the army in Latin American policy has undergone a functional transformation with the rise of the new middle sector on the one hand and the constant menace of leftist revolutionary upheavals on the other.[34] There is no denying that in Brazil, Argentina, and Bolivia the army has stepped in to avoid economic chaos and to prevent constitutional paralysis. These interventions have been constructive rather than repressive, even though they may run counter to traditions of liberalism. If the United States lent active support to the governments which are freely elected, giving them aid in their struggles against sedition and guerrilla activities within their territories, it would find itself once more in the position of intervening in the domestic affairs of a sister republic, and would very likely reap the same criticism and abuse she has received during the years of gunboat diplomacy. Foreign policy cannot be run as a seminar in civic education or self-government.

The Alliance for Progress, as we have said, has yet to show the results so hopefully envisaged by its authors; some critics in Latin America have remarked that it resembles an attempt to cure cancer with aspirin tablets. Whether the total amount of aid earmarked for Latin America should be increased or whether a new list of priorities should be drawn up is a moot question. Public opinion in the United States has of late (1965) favored an increase in aid to Latin America. But even more extensive aid and improved programs will hardly prevent the abuses from which the Alliance for Progress has suffered, *i.e.*, misdirected efforts, mismanagement, corruption, and dishonesty. The main difficulty lies in the lack of an efficient civil service in Latin American countries and the absence of managerial and technical personnel necessary for the implementation of reform programs of such magnitude. On the other hand, if North American personnel were to be employed in any other capacity than an advisory one, it would be met with open or silent opposition that would soon reach the point of sabotage. Parkinson's law, that "work expands according to the time available," is confirmed every day in Latin American offices; they have "raised the historical art of avoiding work to new heights of sophistication."[35] Inertia combined with xenophobia is a powerful deterrent to any reform. In this respect, nationalism is a weapon *de doble fila:* you can't have your leisure and your economic progress too.

There is, of course, the field of education, in which the United States can give assistance. More doctors and pharmacists are needed, and technicians of all kinds and descriptions; illiteracy must be wiped out or at least reduced. Mexico has shown what can be accomplished by determined efforts, and as we have noted, Castro has made education the principal tool of indoctrination. But such innovations imply a long and determined program and will succeed only where the people have the expectancy of a better life for which they are willing to make the sacrifices that all education demands. American educators who come to Latin America are not likely to make much progress with their students unless they arrive at their destinations with a thorough knowledge of the *milieu* in which they will be living, and are besides gifted with tact and *politesse du coeur.* The same holds true for the Peace Corps and all enterprises of goodwill.

Apart from the problems of language and psychological rapport, there still remains a much more important issue: what type of education is most practical and most acceptable to a world so rich in cultural varieties? Surely this question can be answered only by the Latin American people themselves, and it is a fair assumption that their choice will not be the technological, materialistic education prevalent in the United States. We should not try to make them over in our image; if we do we are bound to fail. The Latin American people are more likely to look to Europe rather than to the United States for ideological orientation, but the whole problem involves not merely philosophical directives, but a sustained effort on all levels of education. No one should expect miracles or short-term results; any progress along these lines will of necessity be slow and arduous.[36]

But in the meantime the process of industrialization, which is considered by many to be the remedy for countries who have lived too long from their natural riches, will be stifled. Industrialization is under way in many republics, but it is still far behind other nations, and the growing populations in all Latin American countries hold the economic gains within small percentages. The Latin American nations have frequently blamed the lack of investment capital for their tardy development and have besought American investors, either public or private, to come to their aid. But here, too, they are caught in the snare of an economic nationalism which would accept foreign capital only to resent it at a later date.

Admittedly the entire question is heavily burdened with complexities, and the view from one side of the fence bears little resemblance to the view from the other. The North American industrialists point to certain achievements in engineering and the erection of industrial plants, and measure capital investment on the profit basis, *i.e.*, at the rate of returns derived from it. The Latin Americans, however, see only the drain of foreign exchange in their countries because of profits, interest obligations, and repayment of capital.[37] The question of capital investments in Latin America is further complicated by the constant threat of nationalization which, as in the case of Cuba, may turn into outright confiscation. If to all this is added the ever existing danger of devaluation by inflation, it is not hard to understand why the North American investors expect a return from 40% to 50%, while the Latin Americans consider such returns as exploitation and a return to colonialism. Both sides are right.[38]

The desire of the Latin Americans to exercise control over their basic industries is wholly justified and has been advanced to such a degree during the last five decades that it would be foolish to expect any reversal of the trend. In the eyes of many Latin American economists and statesmen the solution lies in government control or ownership of old and new industries. They prefer this solution because it would allow foreign investments to take the form of loans "with no strings attached." It should be obvious, however, that such loans carry an even greater risk of forfeiture.

The answer, at least a partial answer, may be found in joint ownership or economic partnership between American enterprises and Latin American corporations. Some attempts in this direction have been made by Sears, Roebuck, Ford, General Motors, Kaiser, and others, but there is still a long way to go. Thus, though nationalism in Latin America may be more evident on the economic scene than anywhere else, it cannot prevail without reservation, since it runs counter to the economic needs of the countries which demand industrialization to raise the standard of living and to meet the overall expectations of their citizenry. Here too, Latin America pays the price of centuries of stagnation; she did not experience the continuous revolutionary economic movements which brought Europe and the United States to preeminence.[39] Progress will be slow and will advance by trial and error. No Marshall Plan for Latin America can change this picture, which, after all, is a reflection of the entire social fabric.

There has been some hope that the Latin American countries may be able to achieve by cooperative effort what they find beyond their powers as individual states. There is sound reasoning behind such an argument, since many of the Latin American countries are either too small or too underpopulated to flourish on their own; only Mexico, Argentina, and Brazil would seem large enough to organize their economies on a strictly national basis. They may also have learned certain lessons from the European development of the Common Market and the Outer

Seven. There is now in existence a Central American Common Market, which has eliminated trade barriers between the member countries and has standardized external tariffs for many commodities.

In addition there exists the Latin American Free Trade Area, which includes the republics of Argentina, Brazil, Chile, Colombia, Ecuador, Mexico, Panama, Peru, and Uruguay. Venezuela and Bolivia are expected to join. Such a development is not a negation of the trend toward nationalism, but rather its fulfillment. It is based on the continental nationalism of which we have spoken and will integrate the individual republics as nations. Whether it will be able to overcome the deeply ingrained habits of mercantilistic and neomercantilistic thinking among Latin Americans is a question for the future to answer.[40] First results have been promising, but in these matters the test of time is of the essence. In theory one could argue that an economic, political, and juridical integration of the Latin American countries has been a hoped-for consummation ever since Simón Bolívar raised his voice. Yet centrifugal forces in the hemisphere have so long prevailed that it would be incautious to speak of such moves as the solutions of the future. Whatever the fate of the actions in favor of greater integration, they will not negate the nationalism of today, but only supersede it. Just as the European nations will be integrated as nations and not simply as members of a European union, so will the Latin American republics become elements of a greater whole when and if the time is ripe. It does not appear that the time has yet arrived, however, in view of the vast number of problems on the national level which are still unsolved.

In the meantime nationalism will flourish, and industrialism is more than likely to stimulate its growth.[41] Nationalism will remain the rallying point for all elements of society that wish to participate in the forward thrust of the country to which they belong. This has become very clear in Mexico, Brazil, Uruguay, Chile, and Costa Rica, and it will be confirmed, we would judge, in the other countries as time goes on. It is the only ideology that blankets contemporary Latin America. The continent has developed no other common ideology during its history, and the faith that nationalism inspires will act as a binding element to keep the many mystiques, that fill the land, in operation—Indianism, industrialism, anticolonialism, anti-imperialism, etc. Nationalism can and has attracted the labor groups, just as it exercises its spell over the middle sector, and it may thus help to overcome class antagonism and even class struggle. This is, of course, the true aim of any national socialism, and it would be an irony of history should the racially mixed countries of Latin America succeed in realizing this goal. Nationalism might also provide leadership and create institutions to channel the tremendous social changes that shake the world. Mexico has taken the lead here, as she has done in so many fields. But one should not expect that such institutions will fulfill all the commandments of orthodox Anglo-Saxon democracy.

These are optimistic predictions, and there can be no assurance that they will be fulfilled. Nationalism could well be used as the vehicle in which *caudillo* rule returned to power, as has happened in Argentina and in Cuba; it could be and has been employed to increase the revolutionary ferment in Bolivia and in Cuba; and it could be abused by communist interests to initiate "wars of liberation" against real or imaginary foes. It might rekindle the tendency toward strong paternalistic government, so deeply rooted in the Spanish tradition, thus weakening the tender sprouts of self-government and self-reliance on the local level wherever they may be found.

Continents and civilizations do not shift their characters overnight, and it is only prudent to expect some of the old ills to survive, though they may be disguised in the twentieth century. But whatever the future of Latin American nationalism, it will always preserve its appeal to one chord in the human heart that is particularly dear to the Latin American: its appeal to the value of human dignity. These are words that reverberate in the public utterances of Latin American statesmen and writers, and in many instances they are used in close connection with nationalistic ideas; they awake the one emotion that links the highest and the lowest members of society. Only through nationalism will the masses, whose silence has been maintained over centuries, finally achieve personality and integrity. They are the "voiceless ones," as Theodore Moscoso has named them, and they believe their hour approaches.

Nationalism in Latin America is a constructive and positive ingredient as long as it does not overshoot its mark, allowing pride to become arrogance, or *soberbia,* as the Spanish say. Latin America must learn to treasure another pride, the pride which claims only that which is one's own, and which finds its glory in the *dignidad humana.* Nationalism in the southern hemisphere must be considered a positive and indispensable force wherever it contributes to the growth of the body politic in which it makes its appearance. It becomes corruptive when it takes a position of exclusiveness in which it can no longer universalize its aims.

The immediate goals of Latin American nationalism may be political and economic, but its expectations are human, and therein lies its value.

Notes

CHAPTER I: *Introduction*

[1] Hans Kohn, *The Idea of Nationalism,* New York, 1944, p. 3; Kohn, *Nationalism, Its Meaning and History,* New York, 1955.

[2] Carlton J. Hayes, *Essays on Nationalism,* New York, 1926, p. 6, p. 26, Hayes, *The Historical Evolution of Modern Nationalism,* New York, 1931.

[3] Karl W. Deutsch, *Nationalism and Social Communication,* New York, 1953, p. 3.

[4] Ernest Renan, *Qu'est-ce qu'une nation?,* Paris, 1882, p. 27.

[5] John Stuart Mill, *Representative Government,* Oxford, 1946, p. 291.

[6] Friedrich Meinecke, *Weltbürgertum und Nationalstaat,* Munich, 1908, p. 2.

[7] Quoted by Deutsch, *op. cit.,* p. 13; see also E. H. Carr, *Nationalism and After,* New York, 1945.

[8] Deutsch, *op. cit.,* p. 12.

[9] *Ibid.,* pp. 60–61.

[10] *Ibid.,* pp. 62–63.

[11] Kohn, *The Idea of Nationalism,* p. 13.

[12] Leonard Krieger, "Horizons of History," *Am. Hist. Rev.,* Vol. LXIII, No. 1, p. 71.

[13] When the author began his study, few books on nationalism in Latin America had appeared in English. Since then a number of valuable essays have come to his attention: Arthur P. Whitaker, *Nationalism in Latin America,* Gainesville, Fla., 1962; John J. Johnson, "The New Latin American Nationalism," *Yale Review,* Winter 1965. The author presented a paper on the same subject at the conference held by the International Society for the History of Ideas in Mexico City, Nov. 1962.

He is indebted to the other members of the congress for a lively discussion and criticism of his concepts.

[14] Karl Jaspers, *Vom Ursprung und Sinn der Geschichte*, Frankfurt, 1957, p. 37.

[15] Gerhard Masur, *Prophets of Yesterday*, New York, 1961, p. 3; William H. McNeill, *The Rise of the West*, Chicago, 1963; Wilcomb E. Washburn, "The Meaning of Discovery in the Fifteenth and Sixteenth Century," *Am. Hist. Rev.*, Vol. LXVIII, No. 1, p. 1.

[16] Donald Marquand Dozer, *Latin America*, New York, 1962, p. 27; Richard Konnetzke, *Süd- und Mittelamerika*, Frankfurt, 1965, p. 27; Silvio Zavala, *Filosofía de la Conquista*, Mexico, 1947.

[17] Ramón Menéndez Pidal, *La España del Cid*, Buenos Aires, 1939.

[18] Salvador de Madariaga, *Spain*, New York, 1960, p. 24.

[19] Quoted by Dozer, *op. cit.*, p. 28; see also Manuel García Morente, *Idea de la Hispanidad*, Madrid, 1947; and the still useful study by Alfred Rühl, *Vom Wirtschaftsgeist in Spanien*, Leipzig, 1928.

[20] Silvio Zavala, *La encomienda indiana*, Madrid, 1935; Lesley Byrd Simpson, *The Encomienda in New Spain*, Berkeley, Cal., 1950; Magnus Mörner, "Das Verbot für die Encomenderos unter ihren eigenen Indianern zu leben," *Jahrbuch für Latein Amerika*, No. 1, 1964, p. 187. For the whole problem see also the many publications by Lewis Hanke on Las Casas, especially his *The Spanish Struggle for Justice in the Conquest of America*, Philadelphia, 1949.

[21] C. H. Haring, *The Spanish Empire in America*, New York, 1963, pp. 241–243; an older, still useful book is E. G. Bourne, *Spain in America*, New York, 1962.

[22] Konnetzke, *op. cit.*, pp. 86–108; Angel Rosenblat, *La población indigena y el mestizaje en America*, Buenos Aires, 1954, 2 vols.; Pal Kelemen, *Baroque and Rococo in Latin America*, New York, 1951, p. 21.

[23] Haring, *op. cit.*, pp. 166–193; Konnetzke, *op. cit.*, p. 220 ff.; E. Benz, "Weltgeschichte, Kirchengeschichte und Missionsgeschichte," *Historische Zeitschrift*, Vol. CLXXIII, 1952, pp. 1–22. For the influence of the Inquisition see the numerous works by José Toribio Medina about the proceedings of the tribunal in different parts of Latin America.

[24] Alfonso García Gallo, *Los origenes de la administración territorial de las Indias*, Madrid, 1944; R. B. Merriman, *The Rise of the Spanish Empire in the Old World and in the New*, New York, 1918–1934, 4 vols.

[25] Haring, *Trade and Navigation Between Spain and the Indies*, Cambridge, Mass., 1918; Earl J. Hamilton, *American Treasure and the Price Revolution in Spain*, Cambridge, Mass., 1934; Vera Lee Brown, "Anglo-Spanish Relations in the Closing Years of the Colonial Era," *Hispanic American Historical Rev.*, Vol. V, pp. 327–483.

[26] J. M. Ots Capdequi, *Instituciones sociales de la America Española durante el periodo colonial*, La Plata, 1934, p. 136 ff.; Constantino Bayle, *Los cabildos seculares en la America Española*, Madrid, 1952; Konnetzke, *op. cit.*, p. 138.

[27] Haring, *op. cit.*, p. 161.

28 Ernst Cassirer, *The Philosophy of the Enlightenment,* Boston, 1955, p. 3; Paul Hazard, *European Thought in the Eighteenth Century,* London, 1954.

29 Arthur P. Whitaker, ed., *Latin America and the Enlightenment,* 2d ed., Ithaca, N.Y., 1961; John Tate Lanning, *The Eighteenth Century in the University of San Carlos de Guatemala,* Ithaca, N.Y., 1956, pp. 342–356.

30 Whitaker, *op. cit.,* p. 7.

31 Roland D. Hussey, "Traces of French Enlightenment in Colonial Hispanic America," in Whitaker, ed., *op. cit.,* p. 27 *ff.;* see also Madariaga, *The Fall of the Spanish Empire,* New York, 1948.

32 William S. Robertson, *Francisco de Miranda,* Chapel Hill, N.C., 1929, 2 vols.; Joseph F. Thorning, *Miranda,* Gainesville, Fla., 1952.

33 Raymond E. Christ, "Why move a capital?" *Americas,* Vol. 15, No. 8, p. 14.

34 Gilberto Freyre, *The Masters and the Slaves,* tr. by Samuel Putnam, New York, 1946.

35 Gerhard Masur, *Simón Bolívar,* Albuquerque, 1948, p. 82; see also Richard M. Morse, "Toward a Theory of Spanish American Government," *Journal of the History of Ideas,* Vol. XV, No. 1, Jan. 1954, p. 78 *ff.*

CHAPTER II: *The Independence Movement*

1 Quoted by Ricardo Levene, *Las ideas históricas de Mitre,* Buenos Aires, 1948, pp. 85–86, tr. by the author.

2 Bolívar to Santa Cruz, October 26, 1826, quoted by Masur, *Simón Bolívar,* p. 32; for San Martín see J. C. Metford, *San Martín,* New York, 1950, p. 31.

3 Vicente Lecuna, ed., *Cartas del Libertador,* 12 vols., Caracas, 1929–1959, Vol. II, p. 186.

4 Arthur P. Whitaker, "Nationalism and Social Change in Latin America," mimeographed copy of paper given at the conference held by the International Society for the History of Ideas in Mexico City, Nov. 1962.

5 Charles C. Griffin, *Los Temas Sociales y Económicos en la Epoca de la Independencia,* Caracas, 1962, pp. 31–52; Griffin, "Economic and Social Aspects of the Era of Spanish American Independence," *Hispanic American Historical Rev.,* Vol. XXIX, 1949, pp. 170–187; Miron Burgin, *Economic Aspects of Argentine Federalism, 1820–1852,* Cambridge, Mass., 1946.

6 Griffin, *Los Temas Sociales,* p. 50.

7 K. H. Silvert, "Nationalism in Latin America," *The Annals of the American Academy of Political and Social Science,* March 1961, p. 3.

8 James R. Scobie, *Argentina, a City and a Nation,* New York, 1964, p. 101; John F. Cady, *Foreign Interventions in the Río de la Plata, 1830–1850,* Philadelphia and London, 1929; John Street, *Artigas and the Emancipation of Uruguay,* Cambridge, 1959.

CHAPTER III: *The Road to Nationhood*

1 Dozer, *Latin America*, p. 222.
2 Quoted by H. E. Davis, "Juan Bautista Alberdi," *Journal of Inter-American Studies*, Vol. IV, No. 1, 1962, p. 61.
3 Whitaker, "Nationalism and Social Change," p. 6.
4 Hans Kohn, *American Nationalism*, New York, 1961, p. 112.
5 *Ibid.*
6 Luis Monguío, "Nationalism and Social Discontent as Reflected in Spanish American Literature," *The Annals of the American Academy of Political and Social Science*, March 1961, pp. 66–67.
7 Lucas Alamán, *Historia de Mejico*, Mexico City, 1849–1852, 5 vols.; Henry Bamford Parkes, *A History of Mexico*, New York, 1938; E. Gruening, *Mexico and Its Heritage*, New York, 1940; H. F. Cline, *Mexico and the United States*, Cambridge, Mass., 1953; Ralph Roeder, *Juárez and His Mexico*, New York, 1947, 2 vols. This is, of course, only a very small selection from the large body of literature on Mexico and the War of the Reform.
8 Egon Conti, *Maximilian and Charlotte*, Eng. tr., New York, 1928, 2 vols.; Charles C. Griffin, *The National Period in the History of the New World*, Mexico City, 1961, p. 90 *ff.*; Walter V. Scholes, *Mexican Politics during the Juárez Regime*, Columbia, Mo., 1957.
9 Daniel Cosio Villegas, *Historia Moderna de Mexico*, Mexico City and Buenos Aires, 1955–1963, 5 vols.; Carleton Beals, *Porfirio Díaz*, Philadelphia, 1932; for a very interesting view by a socialist historian from East Germany see Friedrich Katz, *Deutschland, Díaz und die Mexikanische Revolution*, Berlin, 1964.
10 Lewis Hanke, *Mexico and the Caribbean*, New York, 1959, p. 72.
11 John J. Johnson, *The Military and Society in Latin America*, Stanford, 1964, p. 4.
12 L. F. Hill, ed., *Brazil*, Berkeley, Cal., 1947; Gilberto Freyre, *Brazil, an Interpretation*, New York, 1945; T. L. Smith and Alexander Merchant, eds., *Brazil, Portrait of Half a Continent*, New York, 1951; Mary W. Williams, *Dom Pedro the Magnanimous*, Chapel Hill, 1937; Gilberto Freyre, *Masters and Slaves*.
13 C. H. Haring, *Empire in Brazil*, Cambridge, Mass., 1958, p. 100.
14 John J. Johnson, *Political Change in Latin America*, Stanford, 1958, p. 153.
15 Sylvio Romero, *Historia de literatura brasileira*, quoted by Lewis Hanke, *South America*, New York, 1959, pp. 78–79.
16 José Luis Romero, *A History of Argentine Political Thought*, tr. by Thomas F. McGann, Stanford, 1963, p. 129 *ff.*; W. Rex Crawford, *A Century of Latin-American Thought*, 2d ed., Cambridge, Mass., 1963, pp. 12–51.
17 Romero, *op. cit.*, p. 131.

18 *Ibid.,* p. 147; Crawford, *op. cit.,* p. 18 *ff.* Sarmiento's famous *Facundo, o civilización y barbarie en las pampas argentinas,* 1845, was translated by Mrs. Horace Mann as *Life in the Argentine Republic in the Days of the Tyrants,* New York, 1961.

19 Scobie, *Argentina, a City and a Nation,* pp. 112–135; see also Scobie, *La consolidación de la nación argentina, 1852–1862,* Buenos Aires, 1964.

20 José Hernandez, *The Gaucho, Martín Fierro,* Eng. tr. by Walter Owen, New York, 1936; see also Madeline W. Nichols, *The Gaucho,* Durham, 1942.

21 Quoted by Hanke, *op. cit.,* p. 153.

22 Romero, *op. cit.,* pp. 167 *ff.*

23 José Ortega y Gasset, *Obras,* 3d ed., Madrid, 1943, 2 vols., Vol. I, pp. 659–670.

24 Robert Frost, *Poems,* New York, 1946, p. 399.

25 Ricardo Donoso, *Desarrollo político y social de Chile,* Santiago de Chile, 1942; Gilbert J. Butler, *Chile, An Outline of Its Geography;* Luis Galdames, *A History of Chile,* Eng. tr., Chapel Hill, 1941.

26 George M. McBride, *Chile, Land and Society,* New York, 1936; Gene Ellis Martin, *La división de la tierra en Chile Central,* Santiago, 1960.

27 McBride, *op. cit.,* p. 14.

28 Arturo Alessandri, *Recuerdos de Gobierno,* Santiago, 1952; Robert J. Alexander, *Prophets of the Revolution,* New York, 1963, pp. 53–74.

29 John Street, *Artigas,* Cambridge, England, 1960.

30 Russell H. Fitzgibbon, "Uruguay," in Frederic Pike, ed., *Freedom and Reform in Latin America,* Chap. XI, Notre Dame University Press, 1959; Fitzgibbon, *Uruguay, Portrait of a Democracy,* New Brunswick, 1954; George Pendle, *Uruguay,* London, 1952; Simon G. Hanson, *Utopia in Uruguay,* New York, 1938.

31 Leonard Krieger, "The Idea of the Welfare State in Europe and America," mimeographed copy of paper given at the conference held by the International Society for the History of Ideas in Mexico City, Nov. 1962.

32 Alexander, *op. cit.,* pp. 9–31; Fitzgibbon, *Uruguay, passim;* A. zum Felde, *Evolución Histórica del Uruguay,* Montevideo, 1945.

33 *Uruguay and the United Nations,* prepared under the auspices of the Uruguayan Institute of International Law, New York, 1958; *Pan American Union,* Bulletin, Vol. LXXIII, pp. 596–608.

34 James L. Busey, *Notes on Costa Rican Democracy,* Boulder, Colo., 1962, pp. 77–78.

35 Jaime Jaramillo Uribe, *El pensamiento colombiano en el siglo XIX,* Bogotá, 1964, especially the chapter on "Rafael Núñez y el Neoliberalismo," pp. 288–306.

36 Quoted by Hanke, *op. cit.,* p. 157.

37 Johnson, *op. cit.,* p. 36; see also George S. Wise, *Caudillo, a Portrait of Antonio Guzmán Blanco,* New York, 1951.

CHAPTER IV: *Latin America and World Economy*

1 Sanford A. Mosk, *Industrial Revolution in Mexico*, Berkeley, Cal., 1950; Mosk, "An Economist's Point of View," in W. W. Pierson, ed., *Pathology of Democracy, a Symposium; The Am. Pol. Science Rev.*, March 1950, p. 129 *ff.*; Simon G. Hanson, *Economic Development in Latin America*, Washington, 1951; Albert A. Hirschman, ed., *Latin American Issues*, New York, 1961.

2 Mosk, "An Economist's Point of View," p. 132.

3 *Ibid.*

4 George M. McBride, *The Agrarian Indian Communities of Highland Bolivia*, New York, 1921.

5 Stewart Watt, *Henry Meiggs, Yankee Pizarro*, Durham, 1946; George Whyte, *Industry in Latin America*, New York, 1945.

6 Thomas Rourke, *Gómez, Tyrant of the Andes*, New York, 1936, pp. 163–176; Edwin Lieuwen, *Petroleum in Venezuela*, Berkeley, Cal., 1954.

7 This is a reference to the abortive British invasion of 1806–1807. The quotation is from José Luis Romero, *A History of Argentine Political Thought*, p. 193.

8 Mark J. van Aken, *Panhispanismo*, Berkeley, Cal., 1959.

9 José Enrique Rodó, *Ariel*, Montevideo, 1926, Eng. tr. by F. J. Stimson, Boston, 1922; W. Rex Crawford, *A Century of Latin American Thought*, Chapter IV.

10 Masur, *Simón Bolívar*, pp. 579–594. The significance of Bolívar's project is a matter of controversy: at times he proclaimed his lofty international aims with great sincerity; at other times he spoke of them in a cynical vein as a political device of expediency to defend the independence movement against the Holy Alliance or other possible forms of encroachment. See also Arthur P. Whitaker, *The Western Hemisphere Idea*, Ithaca, 1954, pp. 41 *ff.*

11 Whitaker, "Nationalism and Social Change," p. 8.

12 Gaston Baquero, "Spain, Unamuno, and Hispanic America," *The Americas*, June 1964, p. 14.

13 Whitaker, *The Western Hemisphere Idea*, pp. 86–107.

14 Thomas Walsh, ed., *Hispanic Anthology*, New York, 1920, pp. 597–598.

15 Johnson, *Political Change in Latin America*, p. 38; Richard Morse, *From Community to Metropolis*, Gainesville, Fla., 1958; Herbert Wilhelmy, *Südamerika im Spiegel seiner Städte*, Hamburg, 1952.

16 Johnson, *op. cit.*, p. 40; Johnson, "The New Latin America and the United States," *The Pacific Spectator*, Vol. IX, No. 3, 1955; see also Sanford A. Mosk, "Latin America and the World Economy, 1850–1914," *Inter-American Economic Affairs*, Vol. II, No. 3, 1948, pp. 52 *ff.*; Lucio Mendieta y Nuñez, *Las clases sociales*, Mexico, 1947; Gustavo Adolfo Otero, *Sociologia y nacionalismo en Hispano America*, Quito, 1947.

CHAPTER V: *The Mexican Revolution*

1 The basic work for Mexico under Díaz is now Daniel Cosio Villegas, *Historia Moderna de Mexico*, Mexico City and Buenos Aires, 1955–1963, 5 vols.; see also Katz, *Deutschland, Díaz und die Mexikanische Revolution;* Parkes, *A History of Mexico;* E. A. Molina, *Los grandes problemas nacionales*, Mexico, 1909.

2 Howard F. Cline, *The United States and Mexico;* Charles C. Cumberland, *Mexican Revolution: Genesis under Madero*, Austin, 1952; Stanley Ross, *Francisco Madero*, New York, 1955; Daniel Cosio Villegas, *Change in Latin America*, Lincoln, Neb., 1961, p. 26.

3 Parkes, *op. cit.*, pp. 317–326.

4 Frank Tannenbaum, *Peace by Revolution*, New York, 1933, p. 33; for the highly complicated land problem see George M. McBride, *The Land System of Mexico*, New York, 1923; Nathan Whetten, *Rural Mexico*, Chicago, 1948; Eyler N. Simpson, *The Ejido, Mexico's Way Out*, Chapel Hill, 1937.

5 Quoted in Whetten, *op. cit.*, pp. 122–123.

6 Anita Brenner, "A Critic's View," in *Atlantic Monthly*, special supplement on *Mexico Today*, March 1964, p. 132; Brenner, *The Wind That Swept Mexico*, New York, 1943.

7 Eugen Weber, *Action Française: Royalism and Reaction in Twentieth-Century France*, Stanford, 1962; Carlton J. Hayes, *Historical Evolution of Modern Nationalism*, New York, 1930, pp. 184 ff.

8 Tannenbaum, *op. cit.*, p. 235.

9 Isidoro Fabela, "Mexico Looks to the North," in *Mexico Today*, p. 96. William W. Pierson and Frederico Gill, *Governments of Latin America*, New York, 1957, pp. 184–185.

10 Whetten, *op. cit.*, p. 122.

11 Fabela, *op. cit.*, p. 96.

12 Fred Rippy, José Vasconcelos, and Guy Stevens, eds., *Mexico*, Chicago, 1928, p. 138.

13 Whetten, *op. cit.*, passim; Clarence Senior, *Land Reform and Democracy*, Gainesville, Fla., 1958.

14 José Vasconcelos, *La Raza Cósmica: Misión de la Raza Ibero-americana*, Paris; Vasconcelos, *Ulises criollo*, Mexico City, 1937–1946. Crawford, *A Century of Latin American Thought*, has a fine chapter on Vasconcelos. Crawford has also translated and condensed Vasconcelos's autobiography. Hubert Herring and Herbert Weinstock, *Renascent Mexico*, New York, 1935; Martin R. Stabb, "Indigenism and Racism in Mexican Thought, 1857–1911," *Journal of Inter-American Studies*, Oct. 1959, pp. 405–423.

15 Bertram D. Wolfe, *Diego Rivera*, New York, 1963; Lawrence E. Schmeckebier, *Modern Mexican Art*, Minneapolis, 1939; Virginia Stewart, *Contemporary Mexican Artists*, Stanford, 1951.

16 Alfred Neumeyer, *Die Kunst in unserer Zeit*, Stuttgart, 1961, p. 92.

17 Herring and Weinstock, *Renascent Mexico*, p. 85.
18 Joaquín Gutiérrez, "Music in Transition," in *Mexico Today*, p. 112.
19 Sonja Karsen, *Jaime Torres Bodet*, Skidmore, N.Y., 1963, p. 12.
20 Johnson, *Political Change in Latin America*, p. 135.
21 *Ibid.*, p. 136.
22 Nathaniel and Sylvia Weyl, *The Reconquest of Mexico*, New York, 1939 (strongly biased); Frank Tannenbaum, *The Struggle for Peace and Bread*, New York, 1951 (sympathetic but more objective); Robert J. Alexander, *Prophets of the Revolution*, pp. 31 ff.; W. Townsend, *Lázaro Cárdenas*, Ann Arbor, 1952; Dozer, *Latin America*, pp. 507 ff., uses the term "national socialism" to define the prevailing tendencies in the Latin American revolutions.
23 Quoted by Dozer, *op. cit.*, pp. 516–517; for the oil problem see J. Richard Powell, *The Mexican Petroleum Industry*, Berkeley, Cal., 1956.
24 Lyle C. Brown, "Mexican Church-State Relations, 1923–1940," *A Journal of Church and State*, Vol. VI, No. 2, 1964, p. 221.
25 Weyl, *op. cit.*, pp. 307–308.
26 Howard F. Cline, "Mexico: A Matured Latin American Revolution, 1910–1960," *The Annals*, March 1961, p. 84; Cline, *Mexico: Revolution to Evolution*, London, 1961.
27 Johnson, *The Military and Society in Latin America*, pp. 157–158.
28 Quoted by Gladys Delmas, "Mexico from the South," *Mexico Today*, p. 94.
29 For the 1964 presidential election see *Hispanic American Report*, Vol. XVI, No. 12, p. 1133.
30 Cline, "A Matured Revolution," p. 87.
31 Delmas, *op. cit.*, p. 92.
32 Frank Brandenburg, *The Development of Latin American Private Enterprise*, Washington, 1964; Brandenburg, *The Making of Modern Mexico*, Englewood Cliffs, N.J., 1964.
33 Cline, *Mexico: Revolution to Evolution*, p. 116.
34 Stanley R. Ross, "Mexico: Cool Revolution and Cold War," *Current History*, Feb. 1963, p. 91.
35 *Time Magazine*, July 3, 1964, p. 22.
36 New York *Times*, financial page, Aug. 9, 1964; Robert R. Scott, *Mexican Government in Transition*, Urbana, Ill., 1959; Leopoldo Zea, *El occidente y la conciencia de Mexico*, Mexico City, 1953; Jesus Silva Herzog, *Un ensayo sobre la revolución mexicana*, Mexico City, 1946.

CHAPTER VI: *The Andean Countries: Indian Renaissance*

1 Arthur P. Whitaker, *The United States and Northern South America*, Cambridge, Mass., 1947; F. Tannenbaum, "Agrarismo Indianismo, y Nacionalismo," *Hispanic American Historical Review*, Vol. XXIII, 1943, pp. 394 ff.

2 Edmund S. Urbanski, "The Development of Andean America," *Current History*, Feb. 1962, p. 96.

3 Harry Kantor, *The Ideology and Program of the Peruvian Aprista Movement*, Berkeley, Cal., 1954, p. 7; Crawford, *A Century of Latin American Thought*, Chapter VI; Alexander, *Prophets of the Revolution*, pp. 75 *ff.;* Alexander, "The Latin American Aprista Parties," *Political Quarterly*, Vol. XX, No. 3, 1949, pp. 236 *ff.*

4 Lima, 1928; see also Crawford, *op. cit.*, p. 182.

5 Kantor, *op. cit.*, pp. 12, 22.

6 *Ibid.*, p. 40: "*40 preguntas y 40 respuestas sobre el partido Aprista Peruano*," a kind of catechism for the Aprista movement.

7 See the article by the Peruvian historian Luis Alberto Sánchez, "A New Interpretation of the History of America," *Hispanic American Historical Rev.*, Vol. XXIII, Aug. 1943, p. 441.

8 Gabriel Rene Moreno, *Bolivia y Argentina*, Santiago de Chile, 1901, quoted in Lewis Hanke, *South America*, p. 134.

9 Guillermo Francovich, *El pensamiento boliviano en el siglo XX*, Mexico, 1956, pp. 29 *ff.;* Hanke, *op. cit.*, p. 135.

10 Kantor, *op. cit.*, p. 63.

11 Luis Monguío, "Nationalism and Social Discontent in Spanish American Literature," *The Annals*, March 1961, p. 70; Emilio Uzcategui, "Ecuadorian Novels and Novelists," *Americas*, May 1964, p. 29.

12 Monguío, *op. cit.*, p. 71.

13 In conversations with the author.

14 Kantor, *op. cit.*, p. 52.

15 John and Mavis Biesanz, *The People of Panama*, New York, 1955; Gerstle Mack, *The Land Divided*, New York, 1944; Edwin Lieuwen, *Arms and Politics in Latin America*, New York, 1960, p. 90; an older book still of interest is André Siegfried, *Suez and Panama*, New York, 1940.

16 Norman Padelford, *The Panama Canal in Peace and War*, New York, 1942, pp. 63, 66.

17 Donald W. Beatty, "Middle Class Government in Chile," *Current History*, Feb. 1962, p. 112; see also John J. Johnson, "Whither the Latin American Middle Sector," *Virginia Quarterly*, Autumn 1961.

18 To the best of my knowledge there is no treatment of this important subject matter.

CHAPTER VII: *The Bolivian National Revolution*

1 David H. Zook, *The Conduct of the Chaco War*, New York, 1960, p. 31.

2 *Ibid.*, p. 26.

3 Francovich, *El pensamiento boliviano en el siglo XX*, p. 83: ". . . el nacionalismo comenzó a manifestarse en el país hacia 1928."

4 Alcides Arguedas, *Pueblo Enfermo*, Barcelona, 1909. The book produced considerable interest, both in Spain and in Latin America, and went into many editions.

5 Richard W. Patch, "Bolivia: The Restrained Revolution," *The Annals*, March 1961, pp. 123 *ff*. Further bibliography in Charles W. Arnade, "Bolivia's Social Revolution," *Journal of Inter-American Studies*, July 1959, pp. 341 *ff*.

6 Harold Osborne, *Bolivia, a Land Divided*, London, 1955.

7 Francovich, *op. cit.*, pp. 98–99.

8 Patch, *op. cit.*, p. 124.

9 Anita Brenner, "A View of Mexico's Political Life and Influences," *The Caribbean*, Gainesville, Fla., 1956, pp. 291–292.

10 Robert J. Alexander, *The Bolivian National Revolution*, New Brunswick, 1958, p. 46. Mr. Alexander is frankly partisan in his evaluation of the Bolivian revolution. He belittles the Nazi influences on the MNR and is too optimistic in his appraisal of the accomplishments of the revolution. For the Nazi influences see Francovich, *op. cit.*, p. 83.

11 *Report of the United Nations Technical Assistance Mission to Bolivia*, New York, 1951.

12 Carter Goodrich, *The Economic Transformation of Bolivia*, Ithaca, 1955.

13 Richard Konnetzke, "Mittel- und Südamerika," *Weltgeschichte der Gegenwart*, Bern and Munich, 1963, Vol. I, p. 468.

14 Alexander, *op. cit.*, p. 119.

15 *Ibid.*, p. 59.

16 *Ibid.*, pp. 57, 85 *ff*.

17 *The Andean Program*, International Labour Organization, Geneva, 1958.

18 Quoted by Alexander, *op. cit.*, p. 67.

19 See the article by Günther Kahle, "Die Diktatur des Dr. Francias und ihre Bedeutung für die Entwicklung des Paraguayischen Nationalbewusstseins," *Jahrbuch für Latein Amerika*, No. 1, 1964, pp. 238 *ff*

20 Alexander, *op. cit.*, p. 127.

21 *Ibid.*, pp. 146–147.

22 Patch, *op. cit.*, p. 131.

23 New York *Times*, Aug. 23, 1964.

24 As does Alexander, *op. cit.*, p. 271.

25 Patch, *op. cit.*, p. 127.

26 Anne Geyer Georgie, "Belaúnde Breaks with the Past," *San Francisco Chronicle*, July 21, 1964; *Time* Magazine, March 12, 1965; Olive Holmes, "Army Challenge in Latin America," *Foreign Policy Report*, Dec. 1, 1949, pp. 166 *ff*.

CHAPTER VIII: *The National Revolution in Brazil*

1 Hubert Herring, *A History of Latin America*, New York, 1955, p. 707; Charles Wagley, *An Introduction to Brazil*, New York, 1963; Gilberto Freyre, *New World in the Tropics*, New York, 1959; Fernando de Azevedo, *Brazilian Culture*, New York, 1950.

2 Eng. tr. by Samuel Putnam, Chicago, 1944, titled *Rebellion in the Backlands;* see also J. Cruz Costa, "Nationalism and the Evolution of Brazilian Thought in the Twentieth Century," mimeographed copy of paper given at the International Congress for the History of Ideas in Mexico City, Nov. 1962, p. 5.

3 Gilberto Freyre, "Which is the Real Brazil?" *Americas,* April 1964, p. 10.

4 Herring, *op. cit.,* p. 713.

5 Cruz Costa, *op. cit.,* p. 7.

6 *Brazil,* British Survey, London, 1948; Nelson Werneck Sodré, *Orientacaõ do pensamento Brasilerio,* Rio de Janeiro, 1958.

7 J. Cruz Costa, *op. cit.,* p. 10.

8 A good biography of Vargas is still lacking. However, there are several studies covering the most important aspects of the Vargas era: Karl Loewenstein, *Brazil under Vargas,* New York, 1942; *Brazil,* Lawrence Hill, ed., Berkeley, Cal., 1947; Alexander, *Prophets of the Revolution,* p. 219; George Pendle, "Perón and Vargas," *Fortnightly Review,* CLXXVI, 1951, pp. 723 ff.

9 Quoted by T. Lynn Smith, *Brazil, People and Institutions,* Baton Rouge, 1963, pp. 10–11.

10 Alexander, *op. cit.,* p. 222.

11 Harvey Walker, "The Vargas Regime," in L. Hill, ed., *Brazil,* p. 110.

12 *Ibid.,* p. 112.

13 Loewenstein, *op. cit.,* p. 46; Smith, *op. cit.,* p. 561.

14 The analysis of the constitution in Loewenstein, *op. cit.,* pp. 56–58, 206–208; A. F. Macdonald, "Brazil—The New State," *Latin American Governments,* New York, 1949.

15 Loewenstein, *op. cit.,* p. 210. There is an interesting parallel to the Brazilian legislation in Colombia's "ten-twenty-thirty" law which stipulated that in large enterprises, whether foreign or domestic, aliens could not constitute more than 10% of the wage workers or 20% of the salaried employees, and that no more than 30% of total salaries could be paid to non-Colombians. See Johnson, "The New Latin American Nationalism," *Yale Review,* Winter 1965, p. 193.

16 Smith, *op. cit.,* pp. 597, 599, 601.

17 Alexander, *op. cit.,* p. 224.

18 Loewenstein, *op. cit.,* pp. 342–344; Alexander, *op. cit.,* p. 229.

19 Loewenstein, *op. cit.,* p. 206.

20 Herring, *op. cit.,* p. 726.

21 Alexander, *op. cit.,* p. 231.

22 *Brazil,* British Survey, pp. 10–11.

23 Johnson, *Political Change in Latin America,* pp. 163 ff.

24 *Ibid.,* p. 164.

25 *Ibid.,* p. 166.

26 *Ibid.,* p. 172.

27 Alfonso Arinos de Melo Franco, "The Tide of Government," in *Atlantic Monthly*, special supplement on *Brazil Today*, Feb. 1956, p. 152.
28 *Time* Magazine, Sept. 1, 1952; C. H. Haring, "Vargas Returns in Brazil," *Foreign Affairs*, Vol. XXIX, No. 2, 1951, pp. 308 *ff*.
29 Melo Franco, *op. cit.*, p. 156.
30 The letter is quoted in Alexander, *op. cit.*, pp. 240–241.
31 Lucio Costa, "Testimony of a Carioca Architect," *Brazil Today*, pp. 138–139.
32 Osvaldo Orico, *Brazil, Capital Brasília*, Rio de Janeiro, 1958; Alfred Neumeyer, *Die Kunst in unserer Zeit*, p. 32.
33 *Time* Magazine, April 25, 1960, p. 37.
34 John J. Johnson, "Politics and Economics in Brazil," *Current History*, Feb. 1962, p. 93.
35 *Ibid.*, p. 89.
36 Jânio Quadros, "Brazil's New Foreign Policy," *Foreign Affairs*, Vol. XXXX, No. 1, 1961, pp. 19–29.
37 Rollie E. Popino, "Imbalance in Brazil," *Current History*, Feb. 1963, p. 100.
38 *Britannica Book of the Year*, 1964, p. 195.
39 Popino, *op. cit.*, p. 103.
40 Johnson, *The Military and Society in Latin America*, see the chapter "The Military in Brazil."
41 Popino, *op. cit.*, p. 104.
42 Cruz Costa, *op. cit.*, p. 12.
43 Johnson, *op. cit.*, p. 239.
44 Gilberto Freyre, "Brazilian Melting Pot," *Brazil Today*, p. 106; Freyre, "Which is the Real Brazil?" *Americas*, April 1964; Freyre, "Ethnic Democracy," *Americas*, Dec. 1963; Crawford, *A Century of Latin American Thought*, pp. 190 *ff*.

CHAPTER IX: *Enigmatic Argentina*

1 Arthur P. Whitaker, *Nationalism in Latin America*, Gainesville, Fla., 1962, p. 26; Scobie, *Argentina, a City and a Nation*, p. 215.
2 Scobie, *op. cit.*, pp. 160 *ff.*; Johnson, *Political Change in Latin America*, pp. 160 *ff*.
3 José Luis Romero, *A History of Argentine Political Thought*, p. 185.
4 George I. Blanksten, *Perón's Argentina*, Chicago, 1953, pp. 33–34; Manuel Gálvez, *Vida de Hipólito Irigoyen*, Buenos Aires, 1939.
5 Blanksten, *op. cit.*, p. 34.
6 Ricardo Rojas, *La restauración nacionalista*, Buenos Aires, 1909; Angel Guido, "Ricardo Rojas, Místico de la Argentinidad," *Boletín de la Academia Nacional de la Historia*, Buenos Aires, 1959, p. 165; Crawford, *A Century of Latin American Thought*, pp. 164 *ff*.

7 Whitaker, *op. cit.*, p. 28.

8 Guido, *op. cit.*, pp. 167, 170.

9 *Ibid.*, pp. 171–172.

10 Whitaker, *op. cit.*, p. 41.

11 Ricardo Rojas, *Eurindia*, Buenos Aires, 1924; Crawford, *op. cit.*, p. 168.

12 Whitaker, *op. cit.*, pp. 44–45.

13 *Ibid.*, p. 46.

14 José Luis Romero, *Argentina: imagenes y perspectivas*, Buenos Aires, n.d. p. 19: "*Nuestra realidad espiritual se caracteriza, en primer lugar, por su bajo indice de coherencia interior, consecuencia, en terminos generales, de la mera yuxtaposición de mentalidades diversas y reciprocamente récias a su fusión.*"

15 Johnson, *op. cit.*, pp. 99–104.

16 Romero, *Argentina*, p. 35.

17 Blanksten, *op. cit.*, pp. 36–37.

18 Harry Bernstein, *Modern and Contemporary Latin America*, Philadelphia, 1952, pp. 262–278; Felix Weil, *The Argentine Riddle*, New York, 1944; Isabel F. Rennie, *The Argentine Republic*, New York, 1945, pp. 230 ff.

19 Herring, *A History of Latin America*, p. 639.

20 Bernstein, *op. cit.*, p. 276.

21 *Ibid.*, p. 277.

22 Blanksten, *op. cit.*, pp. 40–42; Joseph Ray, *Argentine Diary*, New York, 1944.

23 Rennie, *op. cit.*, p. 286.

24 Bernstein, *op. cit.*, pp. 281, 283.

25 *Ibid.*, pp. 284–286.

26 Romero, *A History of Argentine Political Thought*, p. 234; Blanksten, *op. cit.*, p. 47.

27 Blanksten, *op. cit.*, p. 48; see also *Perón Expounds His Doctrine*, Buenos Aires, 1948; *The Voice of Perón*, Buenos Aires, 1950. These are English translations of the master's voice for propaganda purposes.

28 Quoted by Romero, *op. cit.*, pp. 244–245.

29 Robert J. Alexander, *The Perón Era*, New York, 1951, pp. 22–23.

30 Blanksten, *op. cit.*, p. 55.

31 *Ibid.*, p. 56.

32 *Ibid.*, p. 60.

33 *Ibid.*, p. 62.

34 *Interamerican Conference on Problems of War and Peace*, Washington, 1945.

35 Blanksten, *op. cit.*, p. 70; Alexander, *op. cit.*, pp. 48–49.

36 Romero, *op. cit.*, p. 248.

37 *Ibid.*, p. 253.

38 *Ibid.*, pp. 250, 252.

39 Alexander, *op. cit.*, p. 79.

40 Arthur P. Whitaker, *The United States and Argentina*, Cambridge, Mass., 1954, p. 155.

41 Whitaker, *op. cit.*, pp. 175 *ff.*; Blanksten, *op. cit.*, pp. 252 *ff.*; Alexander, *op. cit., passim.*

42 Quoted by Alexander, *op. cit.*, p. 155.

43 For a study of totalitarianism see Sigmund Neuman, *Permanent Revolution*, New York and London, 1942; Hannah Arendt, *The Origins of Totalitarianism*, New York, 1951; Carl J. Friedrich, *Totalitarian Dictatorship and Autocracy*, Cambridge, Mass., 1956; Carl F. Bracher, *Die Nazionalsozialistische Machtergreifung*, Cologne, 1962.

44 Bracher, *op. cit.*, p. 11.

45 Quoted in Whitaker, *op. cit.*, p. 180.

46 *Ibid.*, p. 181.

47 *Ibid.*, p. 117.

48 For an official picture see Jerónimo M. Peralta, *Semblanza Heróica de Eva Perón*, Buenos Aires, 1950; María Flores, *Woman with the Whip*, New York, 1952.

49 Joseph Ray, *op. cit.*, p. 47; Blanksten, *op. cit.*, p. 97.

50 Blanksten, *op. cit.*, p. 95; Eva Perón, *La razón de mi vida*, Buenos Aires, 1951.

51 *Ibid.*, p. 99.

52 *Ibid.*, p. 109.

53 *Time* Magazine, May 12, 1952, p. 38.

54 Quoted by Blanksten, *op. cit.*, p. 290; see also Whitaker, *op. cit.*, pp. 208 *ff.*

55 For the details of the economic crisis see Whitaker, *op. cit.*, pp. 175–208.

56 Alexander, *op. cit.*, p. 211.

57 Whitaker, *op. cit.*, p. 252; New York *Times*, April 10, 1955.

58 *Time* Magazine, June 3, 1957, p. 29; for further literature see Fritz L. Hoffman, "Perón and After," *Hispanic Am. Hist. Rev.*, Vol. XXXVI, No. 4, p. 510.

59 Arthur P. Whitaker, *Argentine Upheaval*, New York, 1956, p. 12.

60 *Ibid.*, p. 35.

61 *Time* Magazine, June 3, 1957; Robert A. Potasch, "Argentine Political Parties," *Journal of Inter-American Studies*, Oct. 1959, pp. 515–524.

62 Whitaker, *Argentine Upheaval*, pp. 76 *ff.*

63 Arturo Frondizi, *La lucha antiimperialista*, Buenos Aires, 1955; Robert A. Potasch, "Argentine's Quest for Stability," *Current History*, Feb. 1962, p. 71; *Hispanic American Report*, Vol. XIV, No. 8, Aug. 1961, p. 732.

64 New York *Times*, April 1, 1961; Potasch, *op. cit.*, pp. 74–75; see also Whitaker, "The Argentinian Paradox," *The Annals*, March 1961, p. 106.

65 Johnson, *The Military and Society in Latin America*, p. 167.

66 Arthur P. Whitaker, "Argentina's Struggle for Recovery," *Current History*, Jan. 1965, pp. 16 *ff.*

67 Johnson, *op. cit.*, p. 140.

CHAPTER X: *The Cuban Revolution*

1 Leland H. Jenks, *Our Cuban Colony*, New York, 1927; Charles B. Chapman, *A History of the Cuban Republic*, New York, 1927; Wyatt MacGaffey and Clifford Barnett, *Cuba, Its People, Its Society*, New Haven, 1962.

2 Jenks, *op. cit.*, p. 7; David D. Burks, *Cuba under Castro*, Headline Series, New York, 1964; Roland T. Ely, *Commerciantes Cubanos del siglo XIX*, Bogotá, 1961; H. E. Freidländer, *Historia Económica de Cuba*, Havana, 1944.

3 Quoted by Herring, *A History of Latin America*, p. 398.

4 For the details see Jenks, *op. cit.*, pp. 281 *ff.*

5 Burks, *op. cit.*, p. 5.

6 *Ibid.*, pp. 5–6; see also Russell H. Fitzgibbon, *Cuba and the United States*, Kenosha, Wis., 1935.

7 Burks, *op. cit.*, p. 9.

8 D. M. Friedensburg, "Notes on the Cuban Revolution," *The New Republic*, Feb. 17, 1958, pp. 11–16.

9 John P. Harrison, "The Confrontation with the Political University," *The Annals*, March 1961, p. 74.

10 Russell H. Fitzgibbon, "The Revolution Next Door: Cuba," *The Annals*, March 1961, p. 114; Alexander, *Prophets of the Revolution*, p. 268.

11 Herbert L. Matthews, *The Cuban Story*, New York, 1961, pp. 140–144.

12 *Pensamiento político, económico y social de Fidel Castro*, Havana, 1959, pp. 29–31; Jules Dubois, *Fidel Castro*, Indianapolis, 1959.

13 The articles are reprinted in Matthews, *op. cit.*, pp. 27–29.

14 Theodore Draper, *Castro's Revolution*, New York, 1962, p. 10. Draper also discusses at some length the copious literature, most of it of legendary character, that has sprung up around the figure of Fidel Castro.

15 *Ibid.*, p. 43.

16 Matthews, *op. cit.*, p. 79.

17 Draper, *op. cit.*, p. 56.

18 *Ibid.*, p. 4.

19 Matthews, *op. cit.*, p. 75; *Time* Magazine, Jan. 26, 1959, pp. 40–47.

20 Burks, *op. cit.*, pp. 9–12.

21 *Time* Magazine, *loc. cit.*

22 Draper, *op. cit.*, p. 18; Fidel Castro, "Why We Fight," *Coronet*, Feb. 1958, pp. 80–86.

23 Draper, *op. cit.*, pp. 48 *ff.*

24 Matthews, *op. cit.*, pp. 89 *ff.*

25 *Ibid.*, p. 127.

26 *Ibid.*, p. 112.

27 Jaime Benítez, chancellor of the University of Puerto Rico, quoted in Matthews, *op. cit.*, p. 105.

28 Burks, *op. cit.*, p. 34. There were several Congressional investigations about communist activities in Cuba, in 1959, in 1963, and the last in 1964: *Communist Infiltration in Latin American Educational Systems,* a report prepared according to the instructions of the Hon. Thomas J. Dodd, Washington, 1965.

29 *Hispanic American Report,* Vol. XIV, April 1961–Jan. 1962; Burks, *op. cit.*, p. 37.

30 James Cameron, "Cuba's Fumbling Marxism," *Atlantic Monthly,* Sept. 1964; *Time* Magazine, April 27, 1962, pp. 33–36.

31 Fitzgibbon, *op. cit.*, p. 114.

32 Karl E. Meyer and Tad Szulic, *The Cuban Invasion,* New York, 1962; Stewart Alsop, "The Lessons of the Cuban Disaster," *Saturday Evening Post,* June 24, 1961.

33 Meyer and Szulic, *op. cit.*, p. 146.

34 It would seem that the ousting of Khrushchev from the Russian government in the fall of 1964 was, at least partially, provoked by his role in the missile crisis of 1962. Richard Loewenthal, "The Kremlin's Difficult Choice," *Atlantic Monthly,* April 1965, pp. 76–83, offers the following explanation: "When the pressure on Berlin (1961) met with unexpectedly determined resistance, Khrushchev sought to make the nuclear blackmail more effective by sending missiles to Cuba. Never before had Soviet hopes of a decisive international victory been so high."

35 Burks, *op. cit.*, p. 56; Burks, "The Future of Castroism," *Current History,* Feb. 1963, p. 78.

36 Ernst Halperin, *Castro and Latin American Communism,* Cambridge, Mass., 1963; Halperin, "The Decline of Communism in Latin America," *Atlantic Monthly,* March 1965, pp. 65, 69; *Time* Magazine, April 27, 1962, pp. 33–36.

37 Burks, *Cuba under Castro,* p. 20.

38 Cameron, *op. cit.*; Carl Migdail, "What Is Castro Doing to Cuba," *U.S. News and World Report,* March 1, 1965, pp. 70–72; *Britannica Book of the Year 1965,* p. 280.

39 Migdail, *op. cit.*, p. 72.

40 *Ibid.*, p. 70; New York *Times,* Jan. 3, 1965, "Castro's Cuba after Six Years."

41 Bernard L. Collier, "Seven Days with Castro," New York *Herald Tribune,* Aug. 18, 1964.

42 Associated Press release, Jan. 5, 1965; Tad Szulc, *The Winds of Revolution,* New York, 1964, pp. 154–172.

CHAPTER XI: *Conclusion*

1 John J. Johnson, "The New Nationalism in Latin America," *Yale Review,* Winter 1965, p. 187; John J. Johnson, Ed., *Continuity and Change in Latin America,* Stanford, Cal., 1964, pp. 14–16.

[2] Germán Arciniegas, *The State of Latin America*, New York, 1952, pp. 153–186; John D. Martz, *Colombia*, Chapel Hill, 1962; Vernon Lee Fluharty, *Dance of the Millions*, Pittsburgh, 1957.

[3] Martz, *op. cit.*, p. 306.

[4] Pat M. Holt, *Colombia Today and Tomorrow*, New York, 1964, p. 191.

[5] New York *Times*, June 20, 1965.

[6] *Time* Magazine, March 12, 1965; R. J. Owens, *Peru*, New York, 1963.

[7] Luis Alberto Monge, *No hay revolución sin libertad*, San José de Costa Rica, 1961, p. 7.

[8] Robert J. Alexander, *The Venezuelan Democratic Revolution*, New Brunswick, 1964, p. 19.

[9] Alexander, *Prophets of the Revolution*, p. 111.

[10] Rómulo Betancourt, *Venezuela: politica y petroleo*, Mexico, 1956; Alexander, *The Venezuelan Democratic Revolution*, pp. 219–232; E. Lieuwen, *Petroleum in Venezuela*, Berkeley, Cal., 1954; *The Economic Development of Venezuela*, Baltimore, 1961.

[11] Alexander, *op. cit.*, p. 80.

[12] *Hispanic American Report*, Feb. 1964, p. 1166.

[13] J. Lloyd Mecham, *Church and State in Latin America*, Chapel Hill, 1954; *Center of Inter-Cultural Formation, Report*, March 1963.

[14] Sánchez Barba, *Las tensiones históricas hispano-americanas en el siglo XX*, Madrid, 1961; Tad Szulic, *New Trends in Latin America*, Headline Series, New York, 1960; W. S. Rycroft and M. M. Clemmer, *A Study of Urbanization in Latin America*, New York, 1962.

[15] Rafael Caldera, "El Crecimiento de la democracia Cristiana y su influencia sobre la realidad social de America Latina," mimeographed copy of lecture given in Chicago, Jan. 1965.

[16] *Ibid.*, pp. 12–13.

[17] *Dece* (*Al servivio de la democracia Cristiana de America Latina*), Santiago, Sept. 1964, Nos. 3, 5, 8.

[18] Eduardo Frei, "The Aims of Christian Democracy," *The Commonweal*, Oct. 9, 1964.

[19] *Ibid.*

[20] *Ibid.*

[21] *Dece*, Santiago, February–March 1965, No. 8.

[22] *Dece*, Santiago, June 1964, No. 1.

[23] Samuel Shapiro, *Invisible Latin America*, Boston, 1963, p. 167; William S. Stokes, *Honduras*, Madison, Wis., 1950; see also the report of the Bank for Reconstruction and Development, *The Economic Development of Nicaragua*, Baltimore, 1953.

[24] Herring, *A History of Latin America*, p. 454.

[25] Department of State, *Intervention of International Communism in Guatemala*, Washington, 1954; Gerhard Masur, "Foreign Ideologies in the Caribbean," Gainesville, Fla., 1956, pp. 21–23.

[26] Juan José Arevalo, *Carta Política al Pueblo de Guatemala*, Mexico, 1963, pp. 36–37.

[27] Alexander, *Prophets of the Revolution,* pp. 144–172; James L. Busey, *Notes on Costa Rican Democracy,* Boulder, Colo., 1962, John D. Martz, *Central America,* Chapel Hill, 1959.

[28] José Figueres, *"No se puede escupir a una política exterior,"* *Combate,* San José de Costa Rica, July–August 1958. The idea of stabilization of prices is one of the pet ideas of Figueres; see his article *"Estabilisación del café,"* *Combate,* July–August 1961.

[29] To mention only a few: William Benton, *The Voice of Latin America,* New York, 1961; Shapiro, *op. cit.;* Lincoln Gordon, *A New Deal for Latin America,* Cambridge, Mass., 1963; Adolf A. Berle, *Latin America, Diplomacy and Reality,* New York, 1962.

[30] Shapiro, *op. cit.,* p. 138 *ff.*

[31] Ernst Halperin, "The Decline of Communism in Latin America," *Atlantic Monthly,* May 1965, p. 65.

[32] The latest events in Santo Domingo must have convinced even the most optimistic fellow traveler that the United States will not tolerate another Cuba close to the American mainland. What would happen if another country—say Brazil or Chile—went communist, remains everybody's guess.

[33] Shapiro, *op. cit.,* p. 144.

[34] Edwin Lieuwen, *Arms and Politics in Latin America,* New York, 1960; Johnson, *The Military and Society in Latin America,* p. 260.

[35] Johnson, *op. cit.,* p. 261.

[36] George Whyte, *The United States and Inter-American Relations,* Gainesville, Fla., 1964, see also *National Development and the University,* Council on Higher Education in the American Republics, New York, 1965 (of special interest are the statements made by the representatives of Colombia and Argentina, pp. 43, 45).

[37] See the forthright discussion of these problems in Berle, *op. cit.,* p. 44; D. H. Shelton, "The Economic Growth of Latin America," *Journal of Inter-American Studies,* April 1959, pp. 153–172.

[38] Berle, *op. cit.,* p. 35.

[39] Berle, *op. cit.,* p. 46.

[40] Shapiro, *op. cit.,* p. 167. Latest reports from the United Nations Economic Commission for Latin America are encouraging: The nascent Central American Common Market countries averaged a 7% increase in domestic production in 1964. See also *Americas,* April 1964, pp. 31 *ff.*

[41] Johnson, "The New Latin American Nationalism," pp. 202–204; Whitaker, *Nationalism in Latin America,* comes to the same conclusion (see p. 76). Latin American writers and statesmen profess a strong belief in nationalism as a necessary stage of the hemispheric development, but the political fragmentation of the continent is reflected in their writings. See Jorge Basadre, "Why Nationalism?" *Americas,* Vol. I, No. 7, 1949, pp. 12–14; Joaquín Edwards Bello, *Nacionalismo continental,* Santiago, 1935; Arturo Frondizi, *Petroleo y política,* Buenos Aires, 1954; Cosio Villegas, *Change in Latin America,* Lincoln, Neb., 1961.

Index

Adams, John Quincy, 199
Agriculture, 63
  in Argentina, 158, 173, 178
  in Bolivia, 111, 114–15
  in Brazil
    coffee, 47, 124–26, 129, 133
    slavery and, 45–46
  in colonial Latin America, 9–11,
    19–20
  in Cuba, 214, 220–23; *see also*
    Sugar
  in Ecuador, 122
  in Mexico, 92
  monocultura system, 64–65, 94,
    111, 114, 200
  in Peru, 122
  in Venezuela, 231
  See also Landownership
Aguirre Cerda, Pedro, 103, 104
Alberdi, Juan Bautista, 36, 157
  political philosophy of, 47, 48
Alegría, Ciro, 99
Alemán, Miguel, 91
Alembert, Jean d', 16
Alessandri Palma, Arturo
  election of, 54–55
  welfare-state policy of, 94, 103
Allende, Salvador, 236
Alliance for Progress, 216, 233, 242
  245–46
Alvarez, Augustín, 157
Alvarez, Juan, 39
Alvear, Marcelo de, 162
Aprista movement, 94–100, 121–22
Aramburu, Pedro, 190, 191
Aranha, Oswaldo, 129
Arbenz Guzmán, Jacobo, 239
Arévalo, Juan José, 239–40
Argentina, 26, 36, 64, 93, 152–97,
  236, 238
  anti-Americanism in, 66, 154, 160,
    171

Britain and, 21, 37, 159, 160, 161
Buenos Aires vs. provinces, 48, 49,
  155
centralism vs. federalism in, 34
coup of 1930 and Concordancia
  in, 159–65
France and, 37
foreign investments in, 65, 66,
  161–62, 175–76, 186, 187,
  192, 194
immigration into, 48–51, 161
Irigoyan as president, 52, 55, 154,
  158–59
Nazism and fascism in, 160, 162,
  163, 166
nineteenth-century stability of,
  47–52, 152–53
Perón's rule in, 166–89
  economic crisis and inflation,
    178–79, 185–86
  evaluation, 195–97
  Roman Catholic Church, 186–
    87
reconstruction after Perón, 188–94
romantic nationalism in, 154–57
urbanization of, 71, 153
War of the Triple Alliance, 32,
  108
Arguedas, Alcides, 99
Army, 245
  in Argentina, 159, 164–66, 187,
    188, 190, 192–93, 196
  in Bolivia, 109, 112, 113, 118
  in Brazil, 126, 137–38, 142, 143,
    148, 149–50
  caudillismo and, 30
  eliminated in
    Costa Rica, 58
    Cuba, 223
    Uruguay, 58
  in Mexico, 40, 83–84, 91
  in Peru, 121

Artigas, José Gervasio, 30, 55
Atacama, Desert of, 52, 65
Avellaneda, Nicolás, 48, 155
Ávila Camacho, Manuel, 87–89
Aztec culture, 7, 80
Azuela, Mariano, *Los de abajo*, 81

Basadre, Jorge, 95
Batista, Fulgencio, 202–3, 206, 208, 209
Batlle y Ordóñez, José, 56–57
Bauer, Otto, 3
Bay of Pigs invasion, 147, 216–17
Belaúnde Terry, Fernando, 122, 228–29
Belgrano, Manuel, 21
Bello, Andrés, 54
Benalcázar, Sebastián de, 8
Betancourt, Rómulo, 102, 230–34, 240
Beveridge, Albert J., 69
Bogotá, 15, 33, 204
Bolívar, Simón, 27, 30, 188
    continentalism of, 25–26, 68, 249
    patriotism of, 24
    pessimism of, 25
Bolivia, 35, 94, 106–22, 164, 166
    boundaries of, 24
    Chaco War, 106–9
    geography of, 110–11
    Indians in, 64, 97, 107, 110, 111, 116–17, 120
    instability of, 44, 61, 108
    national socialism in, 109, 112, 113
    Revolution, 112–22
    War of the Pacific, 32, 52, 107
Braden, Spruille, 171
Branco, Humberto Castelo, 149
Brasília, 144–46
Brazil, 44–47, 71, 93, 104, 123–51, 166, 194, 236
    army in, 126, 137–38, 142, 143, 148, 149–50, 245
    Braganza family flee to, 23
    colonial, 19–21
    Goulart as president, 148–49
    immigration into, 47
    impact of nationalism in, 150–51
    inflation in, 141, 144, 146, 149
    Kubitschek as president, 143–46
    parties in, 137–38, 141, 144
    Pedro II in, 35, 44–46
    Quadros as president, 146–48
    race in, 12, 36, 47
    regionalism in, 124, 139, 145
    Vargas as president, 126–31, 133–43

War of the Triple Alliance, 32, 108
Brenner, Anita, 76
Britain, 16, 55, 102
    Argentina and, 21, 37, 159, 160, 161
    investments of, 57, 65, 66, 133
        in Argentina, 161–62
        in Mexico, 78, 85, 87
    loans from, 26
Brizola, Leonel, 149
Buenos Aires, 15, 18, 21, 34, 50, 71, 169, 172, 188
    vs. provinces, 48, 49, 155
Busch, Germán, 109
Bustamante Rivero, José, 121

Cabildos abiertos, 15, 21
Caldera, Rafael, 234
Calles, Plutarco, 83
Capitalism, 64–66
    lack of understanding of, 70–71
    Latin-American nationalism and, 66–70
    Marxist's problem with, 96
    in Mexico, 43–44
    See also United States
Caracas, 15, 60, 229–30
Cárdenas, Lázaro, 83, 85–87
Carr, H. E., 4
Carranza, Venustiano, 75, 77
Carrión Mora, Benjamin, 99
Castillo, Ramón S., 162–65
Castro, Cipriano, 60
Castro, Fidel, 112, 147, 192, 203–25
    communism and, 206, 209, 211–13, 214–15, 217–18, 219–20, 222
    Latin-American revolutionary activities of, 215–16, 219, 234, 235
    United States and, 206, 209, 213–19
Castro, Raúl, 220
Caudillismo, 105, 227
    ancestry of, 30
    in Brazil, 126
    in Cuba, 216, 224
    ended in Uruguay, 56–57
    in Mexico, 38, 39, 42–43
    in Revolution, 75, 83–84, 88
    personalismo and, 35
Central America, 35, 37, 239–41
Central American Common Market, 249
Chaco War, 106–9
Chile, 26, 36, 166, 194, 235–38
    Alessandri in, 54–55, 94, 103

Christian-Democratic movement in, 236–38
criollo rule in, 35, 53–54
geography of, 52
urbanization of, 71
War of the Pacific, 32, 52, 107
as welfare state, 94, 103–4
China, Red
Brazil and, 147, 148
Cuba and, 214, 221, 223–24
Chocano, José, 98
Christian-Democratic movement, 235–38
CIA (Central Intelligence Agency), 216
Cities, *see* Urbanization; *specific cities*
Cline, Howard, 87, 90
Coffee, 47, 124–26, 129, 133, 228
Colombia, 26, 35, 96, 235
El Bogotazo, 204
Indians in, 99
instability of, 44, 60
liberal-conservative truce in, 227–28
liberal reforms in, 94, 103
Panama servered from, 60, 68, 69
Roman Catholic Church in, 60
as "university," 59
Colonial Latin America, 7–21
Church in, 8–9
compared to English colonies, 10, 13, 16, 18
economics of, 9–11, 14–15
Enlightenment in, 16–18
revolutionary situation in, 18–19, 21; *see also* Independence movement
social organization of, 11–13
Columbus, Christopher, 7, 10
Communism (Marxism), 102, 230, 242
in Argentina, 165, 170
in Bolivia, 111–12, 117–18
in Brazil, 126, 127, 130, 134, 137, 138, 141, 143, 146
in Chile, 236–37
in Colombia, 235
in Cuba, 202, 206, 209, 211–13, 214–15, 219–20, 222
in Mexico, 89
in Peru, 95–96, 235
in Venezuela, 234–35
Comte, Auguste, 43, 46
Concordancia, 161–65
Cortés, Hernán, 8, 15, 41, 42
Costa, Lúcio, 145

Costa Rica, 36, 240
democratic progress in, 58
Cuba, 66, 198–225
as base for Latin-American revolutions, 215–16, 219, 234, 235
Batista's rule in, 202–3, 206, 208
Brazil and, 147, 149
Castro comes to power, 205–10
changes produced by Castro revolution, 219–25
OAS and, 119, 215
United States and, 198–201
Batista, 202
Bay of Pigs invasion, 147, 216–17
early support for Castro, 206, 209
economic domination, 200–1
missile crisis, 217–18
opposition to Castro, 213–19
Platt Amendment, 199, 201
Cunha, Euclydes da, 124, 127

Darío, Rubén, 69–70, 82, 97
Descamisados, 173, 182–83, 186, 187, 188
Democracy, *see* Popular democracy
Deutsch, Karl W., 4
Díaz, Porfirio, 43, 64, 65, 90
overthrow of, 73–74
Drago, Luis Maria, 69
Draper, Theodore, 206, 211
Dulles, John Foster, 240, 242
Dutra, Enrico, 138, 141

Echeverría, Esteban, 47
Economics, 62–72
of colonial Latin America, 9–11, 14–15, 19–20
international cooperation, 248–49
of new republics, 26–27
price stabilization proposed, 244
See also Agriculture; Foreign investments; Foreign trade; Landownership; Nationalization, economic
Ecuador, 35, 94, 96, 100, 104, 122
Indians in, 94, 99
literature in, 99
as "monastery," 59
Eisenhower, Dwight D., 142, 213
Eisenhower, Milton, 244
England, *see* Britain
Enlightenment in Latin America, 16–18

Farrell, Edelmiro J., 166
Fascism
  in Argentina, 160, 162, 163, 167,
    172–73, 182–85, 195
  in Brazil, 130, 134–35
  See also Nazism
Fierro, Martín, 155
Figueres, José, 240–41
Filho, Café, 143
Foreign investment, 26, 65–66, 247–
  48
  in Argentina, 161–62, 175–76,
    186, 187, 192, 194
  in Brazil, 132–34
  in Chile, 237–38
  in Cuba, 200–1, 213, 215
  hostility to, 66–70
  in Mexico, 43, 65
  under 1917 constitution, 78
  in Venezuela, 65, 86, 229–30,
    232–33
Foreign relations, 37
  Chapultepec conference, 170
  Christian democracy and, 238–39
  Drago doctrine, 69
  feeling of solidarity among Latin-
    American states, 25
  idea for American league of na-
    tions, 25–26, 68
  Quadros' policy, 147–48
  See also OAS; *specific countries*
Foreign trade, 62–63
  of Argentina, 159, 161, 175, 178,
    191–92
  free-trade policy of new repub-
    lics, 26
  of Mexico, 92
  Nazi, 105
  Spain's mercantilistic policy, 14–
    15
France, 16, 20, 37, 65, 85, 102
  mexican intervention by, 41–42
  nationalism in, 28–29
Francia, Dr. José G. R., 106, 117
Francovich, Guillermo, 108
Free Trade Area, 249
Frei, Eduardo, 236–38
Freyre, Gilberto, 20, 124
Frondizi, Arturo, 187, 191–94

Gaitán, Jorge Eliécer, 99, 204
Gallegos, Rómulo, 99, 230
Gálvez, Manuel, 157
Germany, 54, 87, 119, 132
  capital from, 65
  influence of national socialism,
    see Nazism
  nationalism in, 28–29
Gilbert, Gil, 99

Gómez, Juan Vicente, 60, 65, 86,
  229, 230
González, Joaquín, 157
Goulart, João, 142, 144, 148–49
Grau San Martin, Ramón, 202
Great Depression, 71, 85, 102, 105,
  108, 125, 128, 158, 160, 165
Guatemala, 96, 239–40
Guevara, Ernesto "Che," 208, 213,
  221
Guicciardini, Francesco, 9
Guzmán Blanco, Antonio, 60–61

Havana, 200, 201, 208, 209, 214,
  217, 221
Haya de la Torre, Raúl, 94–96, 100,
  109, 121–22
Hayes, Carlton J. H., 2
Hayes, Rutherford B., 107
Hernández, José, *Martín Fierro*, 49
Herzog, Silva, 79
Hidalgo y Costilla, Miguel, 24, 30,
  39, 42
Huerta, Victoriano, 77
Hull, Cordell, 101

Ibarguren, Carlos, 157
Icaza, Jorge, 99
Illia, Arturo, 193–94
Immigration, 70–72
  to Argentina, 48–51, 161
  to Brazil, 47
  to Chile, 54
  to colonial Latin America, 13
  to Venezuela, 231–32
Inca culture, 7, 96, 97, 99
Independence movement, 22–31
  influence of foreign revolutions
    on, 19, 21
  intellectual origins of, 17–19
  nationalism in, 23–26, 28–31
  Napoleonic occupation of Spain
    and, 23
Indians, 30
  in Andean countries, 93, 94
    Bolivia, 64, 97, 107, 110, 111,
      116–17, 120
    Peru, 95–100, 122
  in Brazil, 20
  civilizations of, 7
  defended by Church, 12–13
  under *encomienda*, 10–11
  independence movement and, 26–
    27
  land alienated from, 64, 115
  literature and, 99
  in Mexico, 39, 43–44, 64, 98
    education after Revolution, 80,
      91

nationalism and, 36
in Paraguay, 107–117
psychology of, 97–98, 110
Industry
in Argentina, 158, 164, 165, 176–78
in Brazil, 132–35, 139–40, 144, 150
in Cuba, 210, 220–21
in Mexico, 89–90, 92
oil nationalization, 85–87
See also Foreign investment; Nationalization
Ingenieros, José, 157
International Monetary Fund, 118–19
Irigoyen, Hipolito, 52, 55, 154, 158–59, 162

Jews, 9, 12, 13, 160, 182
Jiménez de Quesada, Gonzalo, 8
Johnson, J. J., 44, 226
Juárez, Benito, 39, 41–43
Justo, Agustín P., 161
Justo, Juan Bautista, 66

Kennedy, John F., 216, 233, 240
Khrushchev, Nikita, 214, 217, 218
Kohn, Hans, 2
Korn, Alejandro, 157
Kubitschek, Juscelino, 143–46

Labor movement
in Argentina, 154, 165
Perón and, 168, 171–72, 186
after Perón, 192, 193
in Bolivia, 114, 117–18
in Brazil, 132, 134, 137, 142
in Chile, 103
in Cuba, 209, 219
in Mexico, 77
Landownership
in Argentina, 49, 51, 153
in Bolivia, 111, 114–15
in Cuba, 203, 220
in Chile, 53, 237
impact of capitalism and, 63–64
in Mexico
Nineteenth-century "reform," 40, 43
Revolutionary reform, 77, 79, 85, 90, 92
of Roman Catholic Church, 40, 43, 64
in Venezuela, 231
La Prensa (Buenos Aires), 174, 190
Las Casas, Bartolomé de, 12
Latin America
background of culture of, 11–12
defined, 6
feeling of solidarity in, 25
isolation of, 33–34
nationalism in, see Nationalism—in Latin America
as spiritually superior, 67–70
See also specific topics
Leoni, Raúl, 234
Literature
in Andean countries, 98, 99
in Argentina, 154–57
in Mexico, 40, 81–83
Lleras Camargo, Alberto, 228
López, Alfonso, 103
López, Francisco, 107
López Mateos, Adolfo, 91
López Michelsen, Alfonso, 228
Lugones, Leopoldo, 157
Luiz Pereira de Souza, Washington, 126

McBride, George McCutcheon, 53
Machado, Gerardo, 201
Madero, Francisco, 74, 77
Mariátegui, José Carlos, 95
Martí José, 200, 201
Martínez Estrada, 157
Marxism, see Communism
Matos, Huber, 219
Matthews, Herbert, 206
Maximilian, Archduke, 41–42
Meinecke, Friedrich, 3
Melgarejo, Mariano, 107
Mercantilism, 14–15, 26, 102
Mexico, 37–44, 71, 73–92
archaeology of, 80
art in, 80–81
Castro and, 219, 243
centralism vs. federalism in, 34–35
Díaz as president, 43, 64, 65, 73–74, 90
French intervention in, 41–42
foreign investments in, 43, 65, 92
nationalization of oil, 85–87
return of U.S. capital, 90
subsoil rights under constitution of 1917, 78, 84–85
industry in, 89–90, 92
as inspiration for other nations, 94, 112, 116, 132, 174, 239
La Reforma in, 39–43
Revolution, 73–92
constitution of 1917, 77–79
"routinization" of, 87–92
Roman Catholic Church in, 40, 43, 79, 84, 86–87, 89
United States and, 37–39, 91
Mexican War, 32, 38–39
oil dispute, 87

Mexico City, 15, 18, 33, 42, 84, 91
Middle class (middle sector), 237
  in Argentina, 154, 165, 179
  in Bolivia, 120–21
  in Brazil, 139
  in Cuba, 203, 206–7, 212, 219, 223
  in Mexico, 83, 88–89, 90
  in Peru, 122
  rise of, 71, 72
Military forces, *see* Army
Mill, John Stuart, 3, 13
Minas Gerais, 20, 124, 126, 133, 144
Miranda, Francisco de, 19, 21
Mitre, Bartolomé, 22–23, 48, 155
Molina, Gerardo, 102
Monocultura system, 64–65, 94, 111, 114, 200
Monroe Doctrine, 39, 41
  Roosevelt corollary, 69
Montesquieu, Baron de, 17
Montevideo, 55, 58, 71
Morelos, José María, 24, 39
Moreno, Garcia, 59
Moscoso, Theodore, 251
Muñoz Marin, Luis, 240
Mussolini, Benito, 104, 130, 167, 172, 196

Napoleon III, Emperor of the French, 41–42
Nariño, Antonio, 19
Nationalism
  as ideology in Europe, 28–29
  "integral," 76
  in Latin America, 226–27
    Aprismo influence, 95
    centralism and, 34–35
    culture and, 11–12
    foreign capitalism and, 66–70, 86
    future of, 249–51
    in independence movement, 23–26, 28–31
    isolation and, 33–34
    literary influences, 81–83, 98, 99, 154–57
    middle class and, 72
    races and, 36, 80, 82–83
    regionalism and, 14, 238–39
    wars and, 32
    problems of definition of, 1–5
    totalitarianism and, 177–78
Nationalization, economic, 247
  in Argentina, 171, 175, 176, 192
  in Bolivia, 113–14
  in Brazil, 132, 140, 142, 149
  in Chile, 55, 213, 237–38
  in Cuba, 176, 210, 213, 215, 220
  in Mexico, 85–87
  in Peru, 95
  in Uruguay, 57
  in Venezuela, 213
Nazism (national socialism), 102–3, 104–5, 130–31, 135
  in Argentina, 160, 163, 166
  in Bolivia, 109, 112, 113
  in Brazil, 136
  See also Fascism
Negroes, 30
  emancipation of, 27, 28
  as slaves in colonial Latin America, 10, 11, 20
Neruda, Pablo, 99
New Deal, 94, 102–4, 162
Niemeyer, Oscar, 145
Nitrates, 52, 54, 55, 65
Nixon, Richard, 240
Núñez, Rafael, 60

OAS (Organization of American States, 119, 149, 215
Obregón, Álvaro, 78, 83, 84
Odría, Manuel, 121
O'Gorman, Juan, 80
Oil
  in Argentina, 176, 186, 187, 192, 194
  in Brazil, 142
  in Chaco, 108
  in Colombia, 229
  in Mexico, 78, 84–87
  in Venezuela, 86, 229–30, 232–33
Orozco, José, 80, 81, 88
Ortega y Gasset, José, 50
Ortiz, Roberto, 161–63
O'Sullivan, John L., 37

Padilla, Jorge, 60
Páez, José Antonio, 60
Panama, 60, 68, 69, 96, 100–2
Panama Canal, 100–2
  internationalization of, 95, 100
Paraguay, 59, 164, 166, 188, 190
  boundaries of, 24
  Chaco War, 106–9
  Indians of, 107, 117
  War of the Triple Alliance, 32, 108
Paz Estenssoro, Victor, 109–10, 112–19
Peace Corps, 246
Pedro II, Emperor of Brazil, 35, 44–46

Pérez Jiménez, Marcos, 230
Perón, Evita, 179–82, 183–84, 189
Perón, Juan Domingo, 66, 162, 166–89, 243
  evaluation of, 195–97
  in exile, 190, 191, 194
Personalismo, see: Caudillismo
Peru, 26, 61, 65, 235, 238
  Aprista movement in, 94–100, 121–22
  early rebellions in, 18–19
  recent reforms in, 121–22, 228–29
  War of the Pacific, 32, 52
Pizarro, Francisco, 8, 99
Platt Amendment, 199, 201
Popular democracy, 239
  in Argentina, 51–52, 153–54, 160
  in Chile, 55
  in Costa Rica, 58
  independence movement and, 18
  nationalism and, 2
  representative institutions forbidden by Spanish, 16
  United States policy toward, 244–45
  in Uruguay, 56
  in Venezuela, 234
Portugal, 13, 19–21
  in conquest of Latin America, 7, 8
  racial policy of, 12
Positivism, 43, 46
Prado, Manuel, 121
Prestes, Luis Carlos, 102, 126, 137
Price stabilization, 244
Prío Socarrás, Carlos, 202

Quadros, Jânio, 146–48, 243
Quito, 15, 33

Race
  in Brazil, 47
  in colonial Latin America, 12, 21
  nationalism and, 36, 82–83
  See also Indians
Railroads, 45, 64, 140, 201
Ramírez, Pedro, 165, 166
Ranke, Leopold von, 5
Renan, Ernest, 3
Reyes, Alfonso, 82
Rio de Janeiro, 23, 71, 136, 138, 194
Rivadavía, Bernardino, 180
Rivera, Diego, 80, 88
Rivera, José Eustasio, 99
Roca-Runciman treaty, 161
Rodó, José Enrique, 56, 82, 97
  Ariel, 67–68

Rojas, Ricardo, 154–57
Rojas Pinilla, Gustavo, 227, 228
Roman Catholic Church
  Christian-Democratic movement, 235–38
  in Colombia, 60
  in colonial Latin America, 8–9, 12–13
  in Ecuador, 59
  landownership of, 40, 43, 64
  in Mexico, 40, 43, 79, 84, 86–87, 89
  Perón and, 186–87
  in Venezuela, 61
Romero, José Luis, 49, 172
Roosevelt, Franklin D., 87, 101, 240
Roosevelt, Theodore, 68–69
Rosas, Juan Manuel de, 30, 35, 47, 48
Ruiz Cortines, Adolfo, 91

Sáenz Peña, Rogue, 154
San Martin, José de, 24–26, 30
Sánchez, Luis Alberto, 97
Santa Anna, Antonio López de, 35, 38
Santander, Francisco de Paula, 24, 30
Sarmiento, Domingo, 54, 155
  political philosophy of, 47–48, 49, 51
Sartre, Jean-Paul, 212
Schacht, Hjalmar, 105
Seeley, Sir John, 33
Sigueiros, David, 80
Social organization
  in Bolivia, 120–21
  in Chile, 53–54
  of colonial Latin America, 11–13
  impact of capitalism and, 63–64
  independence movement and, 26–28
  in Mexico, 83, 88–89, 90
  Perón's policy, 182–84
  See also Immigration; Indians; Middle class
Socialism, 72, 74
  in Argentina, 66, 163, 165, 171, 180
  in Bolivia, 117–18
  in Mexico, 85, 93
  national, *see* Nazism
  in Peru, 95–100
  in Uruguay, 56–58
  See also Communism; Welfare state
Solano, Armando, 99

Soviet Union, 94, 119, 147, 222
  Cuba and, 202, 214–15, 217–18, 220, 224
Spain
  Church and, 8–9
  conquest of Latin America by, 7–8
  national character of, 8, 9
  occupied by Napoleon, 23
  refugees from (1936–39), 103
Spanish-American War, 66, 68, 199
Standard Oil of California, 186
Standard Oil of New Jersey, 108, 229
Steel, 135, 140
Sucre, Antonio José de, 24, 30
Sugar
  Brazilian, 19, 46
  Cuban, 65, 200, 201, 213, 214, 218, 221

Tamayo, Rufino, 80
Teixeira, M. A., 128
Tin in Bolivia, 108, 110, 111, 113–14
Tito, 119, 148
Titoism, 113, 119
Toranzo Montero, Carlos Severo, 192
Torres Bodet, Jaime, 82
Totalitarianism, 183
  nationalism and, 177–78
Trujillo, Rafael, 233, 234, 241
Tupac Amaru, 19
Turbay, Gabriel, 103

Unamuno, Miguel de, 68, 156
United Fruit Company, 65, 99
United States
  aid to Latin America by
    Argentina, 185–86
    Alliance for Progress, 216, 233, 242, 245–46
    Bolivia, 118–20
    Brazil, 125, 142
    education, 246–47
  Civil War, 39, 41–42
  colonial Latin America compared to, 10, 13, 16, 18
  Cuba and, *see* Cuba
  fear of and protest against, 39, 66–70, 99, 217
    in Argentina, 66, 154, 160, 171
  future relationship between Latin America and, 241–48
  intervention in Latin America by, 68–69, 199, 216–17

investments in Latin America by, 39, 65, 90
  Argentina, 161, 175, 186, 194
  Chile, 237–38
  Cuba, 200–1, 213, 215
  Mexican oil, 78, 84–87
  Venezuela, 86, 229–30, 232–33
New Deal, 94, 102–4, 162
Mexican War, 32, 37–39
Panama Canal, 69, 95, 100–2
Urbanization
  in Brazil, 133
  in colonial Latin America, 15
  early rapid increase in, 71–72
  nationalism and, 33
  as policy in Argentina, 47–48, 153
Ureña, Pedro Henríquez, 40
Uriburu, José, 159–60
Uruguay, 35, 36, 78, 93, 164, 166, 194
  becomes buffer state, 55
  boundaries of, 24
  urbanization of, 71
  War of the Triple Alliance, 32, 108
  as welfare state, 56–58

Valencia, Guillermo León, 228
Vargas, Getúlio, 126–43
Vasconcelos, José, 78, 80, 88, 156–57
  philosophy of history of, 82–83
Venezuela, 21, 96, 100, 104, 190, 229–35, 236
  as "barracks," 59
  Betancourt as president of, 230–34
  Gómez as dictator of, 60, 65, 86, 229
  instability of, 44, 60–61
Villa, Pancho, 74, 81
Volta Redonda, 135, 140

Weber, Max, 9, 87
Welfare state
  in Argentina, 168, 174, 181–82, 185
  in Brazil, 131, 134, 135
  in Chile, 94, 103–4
  in Colombia, 94, 103
  in Uruguay, 56–58
Whitaker, Arthur P., 25, 186

Xenophobia, 13, 66–70, 117

Zapata, Emiliano, 74, 75, 79, 81